HOW PROPAGANDA WORKS

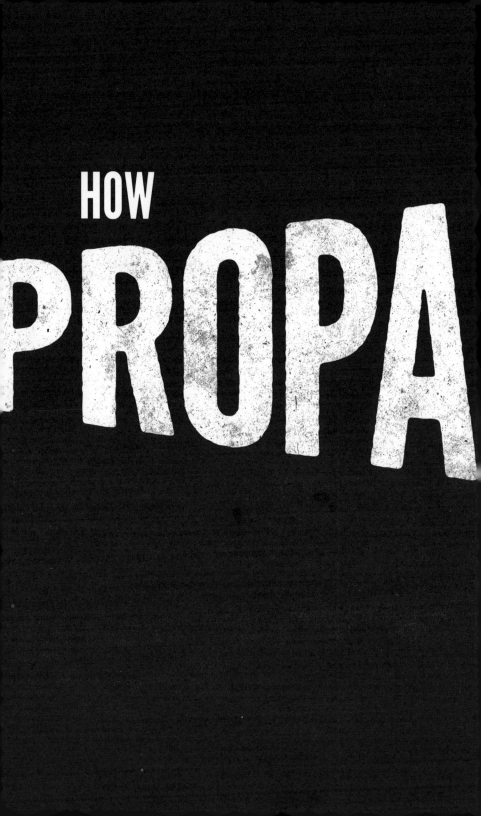

HOW

PROPA

GANDA

WORKS

JASON STANLEY

PRINCETON UNIVERSITY PRESS
Princeton & Oxford

press.princeton.edu

Jacket design by Chris Ferrante

Excerpts from Victor Kemperer, *The Language of the Third
Reich: LTI, Lingua Tertii Imperii*, translated by Martin Brady
© Reclam Verlag Leipzig, 1975. Used by permission of
Bloomsbury Academic, an imprint of Bloomsbury
Publishing PLC.

ISBN 978-0-691-16442-7

Library of Congress Control Number: 2014955002

British Library Cataloging-in-Publication Data is available

This book has been composed in Sabon Next LT Pro and League Gothic

Printed on acid-free paper. ∞

Printed in the United States of America

10 9 8 7 6 5 4 3 2 1

This will always remain one of the best jokes of democracy, that it gave its deadly enemies the means by which it was destroyed.

—JOSEPH GOEBBELS, REICH MINISTER OF PROPAGANDA, 1933–45

CONTENTS

PREFACE

In August 2013, after almost a decade of teaching at Rutgers University and living in apartments in New York City, my wife Njeri Thande and I moved to a large house in New Haven, Connecticut, to take up positions at Yale University. Along with the move in academic affiliations came space. Soon thereafter, my stepmother, Mary Stanley, called me with a request. Could she send me some boxes of books from my father's library? The request filled me with fear as well as anticipation. I spent half my childhood in the house she shared with my father. The walls of every room were filled with books. The shelves were double stacked; behind each row of books was another. Only my father knew the complex code that unlocked the mystery of its organizational system, and he had passed away in 2004. Mary told me that she would be sending me the contents of a room or two, to clear out a little bit of space in the house. Who knew what we would receive? With trepidation, we agreed.

My father Manfred Stanley was a sociology professor at Syracuse University, where he was for many years the director of the Center for the Study of Citizenship at the Maxwell School for Citizenship and Public Affairs; Mary Stanley was also a professor at Syracuse, and his colleague and coconspirator in the Center. He began his career as an Africanist, with a dissertation in anthropology. Sometime during his early career as a professor, in the 1960s, he moved from East African Studies to Sociology, where he regularly taught the theory courses. During his career, he published one book.[1]

My father, like my mother Sara Stanley, was a survivor of the Holocaust. No doubt as a consequence, he devoted his academic career to a theoretical repudiation of authoritarianism in all of its various guises. He argues in his work that no system that usurps the autonomy of persons can be acceptable, even if it is in the name of greater social efficiency or the common good. The lessons of history show that humans are too prone to confuse the furtherance of their own interests with the common good, and their subjective explanatory framework with objective fact.

I owe a substantive intellectual debt to my father and my stepmother Mary. Their project on democratic citizenship has shaped and molded my own. One way of seeing my father's work is as devoted to explaining how sincere, well-meaning people can be deceived by self-interest into unwittingly producing propaganda. My goal in this book is to explain how sincere, well-meaning people, under the grips of flawed ideology, can unknowingly produce and consume propaganda. In the service of acknowledging my debt, I will explain the central themes of his written work, and their joint project, as a preface to my project in this book.

My father's dissertation concerns the destructive effects of British colonialism on the Gikuyu. Its focus is on the Gikuyu land tenure system, a manner of managing land so central to Gikuyu identity that, as Jomo Kenyatta writes, "[i]n studying the Gikuyu tribal organization it is necessary to take into consideration land tenure as the most important factor in the social, political, religious, and economic life of the tribe." The Gikuyu land tenure system was radically different from the system of private property at the basis of British society; "it was a man's pride to own a property and his enjoyment to allow collective use of such property."[2] The dissertation explains how the British belief that their particular system of private property was universal led to unbridgeable misunderstandings between even well-intentioned British colonialists and the Gikuyu people. The moral of colonialism is that it is much harder to make "objective" decisions on behalf of others even for the sake of their own good. Even those British colonialists who were sincere and well meaning found it impossible to distinguish between genuinely liberal values, their own local cultural practices, and naked self-interest.

My father's view of autonomy was richer than mere nondomination by others. His worldview required every citizen to be provided with a liberal education, the goal of which would be to foster the capacity for autonomous decision making about one's life plans, where this involved the kind of reflection that, for him, allowed for genuine autonomy. The description of the contours of an education that could play this democratic role takes up another portion of his academic writings.

The target of my father's book is what he often called "technicism," the view that scientific expertise and technological advancements are the solution to the problems of the human condition. My father saw two chief dangers in the technicist worldview. First, it seeks to replace a liberal education with vocational technical skills. The technicist educational system therefore seeks to rob us of the capacity for autonomy. Secondly, a technicist culture encourages a tendency to defer one's practical decisions to the epistemic authority of experts. As he writes,

Some societies are organized so as to restrict the distribution of important forms of authoritative agency to particular ruling elites. In other societies all normal members of society are considered "responsible free agents." Even in most of these, however, certain people are designated as more equal than others. Why? Because their mastery of a particular cognitive area of discourse or practice seems to make it socially desirable that they be granted the right, under certain circumstances, to intervene in the freedom of other agents. Such privileged people are normally called "professionals."[3]

Of course, modernity demands trusting professionals; we must, after all, see the doctor. There are also salient cases in which distrust of experts is *key* to propaganda; the case of climate change denial is the salient example (though, even here, the form of the distrust has taken the shape of the mobilization of an alternative domain of pseudoexperts, such as the "junk science" commentators discussed in this book). Nevertheless, history shows that even the well meaning are likely to conflate the products of genuine scientific expertise with the imposition of their own subjective values. The British imposed their own conception of private property onto the Gikuyu inhabitants of the land they had occupied, under the misguided belief that their system of property rights was part of universally valid economic theory. The British mistakenly saw their system of private property as part of the universal values liberalism should spread. He saw similar forces at work in the United States, in the education system and the mass media.

My father does not solve the difficult problem of distinguishing legitimate versus illegitimate deference to experts, of drawing on knowledge without being subordinate to it. But he is clear about the dangers of technicist culture.[4] Technicism was a central mechanism liberal democracies employed when the illegitimate subordination of others took place. For example, it is the mechanism so ably described by Khalil Muhammad in his work on the role social science played in the first half of the twentieth century in the subordination of American citizens of African descent.[5] Muhammad there shows how social scientists convinced of their own objectivity used statistical methods to give an objective covering to racial bias. Patricia Hill Collins has drawn our attention to the way that "knowledge validation processes" that privilege quantitative methods also obstruct our access to social reality: "[i]individual African-American women's narratives about being single mothers are often rendered invisible in quantitative research methodologies that erase individuality in favor of proving patterns of welfare abuse."[6] Even if statistics are accurate, they nevertheless can serve a propagandistic role in domination and oppression, by obscuring the narratives that would explain them. This is a use of the ideals of scientific objectivity and the common good in pursuit of social control.

In this book, I define political propaganda as *the employment of a political ideal against itself.* Someone who presents subjective values, or self-interested goals, as the embodiment of objective scientific ideals is therefore producing paradigm examples of propaganda. My father's academic work is thus clearly a large influence on my own.

In sociology and democratic theory, the mid-1980s included the great German political theorist Jürgen Habermas's universal pragmatics turn. Habermas sought to describe the ideal speech conditions for democratic deliberation, and turned to analytic philosophy of language for help. Heading to my freshman year at the State University of New York at Binghamton in the fall of 1986, I knew that I was going to study philosophy, and had the vague sense that the democratic project centrally involved the philosophy of language and Kant. Via a circuitous route, I was led to the intensive study of philosophy of language, logic, and linguistics at the Massachusetts Institute of Technology, where I earned my PhD in 1995.

During the decade I was immersed in the arcane details of formal semantics and pragmatics, the United States was in the throes of a mad experiment in mass incarceration, falling largely on the heads of the minority who were the descendants of slaves. Sylvia Wynter published an article that begins with the information that "public officials of the judicial system of Los Angeles routinely use the acronym 'N.H.I.' to refer to any case that involved a breach of the rights of young Black males who belonged to the jobless category of the inner city ghettos.

N.H.I. means 'no humans involved.'"[7] Wynter's article links the method of dehumanization of American citizens of African descent to the dehumanization of Armenians by Turkish pan-nationalists in the First World War period, and Jews by German nationalists during the Second World War period. In these latter cases, the dehumanization was a preparation for mass slaughter.

It would be one thing if only Black philosophers and intellectuals were calling attention to the crisis of racially driven mass incarceration. But it wasn't just Angela Davis, Sylvia Wynter, and others within ivy-covered walls calling attention to the drastic and worsening situation facing poor Black Americans. In an interview with the artist Tupac Shakur in the early 1990s, he says, "When I sing, 'I'm living the thug life, baby, it's hopeless,' one person might hear that and just like the way it sounds, you know what I'm sayin'? But *I'm* doing it for the kid that really lives the thug life, and feels like it's *hopeless*. So when I say *hopeless*, when I say it like that, like, I *reach* him. You understand? And even if when I reach him it makes it glorious to the guy that doesn't live that life, I can't help it, it's a fact he'll drop the thug life soon enough. But for the person I *was* trying to reach, he'll pick it up and I'll be able to talk to him again."[8] It's hard to think of someone who is describing a lifestyle as *hopeless* as *glorifying* it. Yet Tupac and artists like Ice Cube, who were attempting to communicate the grimness and inhumanity facing inhabitants of the ghetto by representing, in the first person, characters experiencing it, were nevertheless described as "gangsta rappers" who were "glorifying" a situation they were in fact representing as hopeless.

Throughout the 1990s the state and federal prison system was massively expanded, an expansion motivated in the political sphere by racist fear mongering in the guise of objective science. The decade featured notorious examples of the kind of technicist discourse that presents racist ideology in the guise of objective science. The neuroscientist Carl Hart explains how scientists colluded in a racially biased drive to exaggerate the risks of certain illegal drugs to justify draconian sentencing policies, including wildly distorted sentencing policies for cheap versions of cocaine used in poor Black communities, versus versions of the same drug used in wealthy white communities.[9] Hart also shows how the arguments that motivated differential sentencing for crack cocaine and the purer version favored by wealthy whites were part of a racist scientific narrative about drugs and Black pathology dating back to the early parts of the twentieth century.

During my entire adult life in the United States, scientific "experts," from medical doctors to "expert" police interrogators, have packaged racial bias as objective fact. The examples are too numerous to mention, but they include the fictitious "crack baby" syndrome, the Central Park jogger case, and another example I explore in this book, the "super-predator theory," introduced in 1995 by the then Princeton political science professor John Dilulio in a successful attempt to motivate the adoption of adult prison sentences for young Black offenders. Dilulio predicted a fivefold increase in violent crime in the United States from 1995 to 2000 (violent crime in the United States began dropping in 1991, and continued to drop continuously between 1995 and 2000). By the end of the 1990s, it was apparent that somehow, despite the rhetoric of and indeed sincere belief in a recently achieved democratic equality, there was drastic racial and economic injustice, evident to those suffering it, but somehow invisible to most of the rest of us. Around that time I started reflecting upon how to address systematically the topics of this book, though it was far from clear to me then that I would eventually write a book on the topic.

The lead-up in 2003 to the Iraq War again raised the philosophical mystery of the power of propaganda. A *Washington Post* poll in September 2003 found that almost *70 percent* of Americans believed that Saddam Hussein was personally involved in the 9/11 attacks on New York City. Yet a decade later, Donald Rumsfeld claimed that the administration in no way suggested that Iraq was involved in the terrifying terrorist attacks on my country. How is it that propaganda can thoroughly convince the majority of the country of something that later appears to have been obviously false at the time? The questions of the effectiveness of ideology and propaganda bear the characteristic hallmarks of philosophical problems.

Perhaps most disturbingly for me, when I look upon my own discipline, the discipline of philosophy, I find egregious effects of ideology and propaganda. Philosophy is self-consciously devoted to the ideal of objective truth. Yet philosophers from Aristotle to the present day have justified slavery and racism. And the philosopher whose works most drew me into the field, Gottlob Frege, was a virulent anti-Semite and devoted ideologue of Aryan supremacy.

It is to state the obvious to say that philosophy has, throughout its history, demonstrated undeniable sexism and misogyny. However, throughout my own career as a philosopher, I was insensitive to the fact that only a small fraction of my fellow philosophers were female. Women philosophers have produced much of the most significant work in philosophy in the last quarter century. Indeed, the work of feminist philosophers has laid the theoretical basis for this very book. Yet research has showed that there is systematic structural sexism that silences the voices of contemporary female philosophers. For example, the sociologist Kieran Healy has showed that only a tiny fraction of the most cited philosophical work over the last two decades is by female authors. The empirical data makes it beyond serious doubt that philosophy, despite its sincere commitment to objectivity and truth, has been a systematically sexist enterprise my entire career. For much of that time, I did not notice. My theoretical arguments in this book suggest that the reason that I was oblivious to philosophy's misogyny is because I am a beneficiary of it.[10]

Why are we so inclined to confuse, quite sincerely, objective claims of reason with what turns out to be, in retrospect, biased and self-serving opinion? Why does seemingly objective discourse seem nevertheless to tap into bias and stereotype?

And most pressingly, why, across continents and centuries, are the claims of oppressed and exploited groups routinely dismissed at the time, when history has subsequently revealed that the claims should have appeared to be clearly correct? These are the questions at the heart of this book.

Here are two mysterious facts about political contestation. First, the political claims of members of dispossessed groups are routinely dismissed, even by sincerely *well-meaning* elites. Secondly, dispossessed and resource-poor groups are hindered in political action. The obstacles to political action do not merely consistent in a lack of required resources; it is very often the case that members of dispossessed groups seem to lack the required knowledge, or the required confidence, to act to alleviate their own oppression. Fortunately, Timothy Williamson argued that knowledge was the norm of both assertion and action.[11] This was the link I needed. If one could show that *a lack of resources undermined knowledge*, then, via the kinds of links between knowledge, assertion, and action that Williamson described, one could explain some of the distinctively epistemic obstacles facing oppressed groups, and why they were simultaneously *practical* ones as well.

I then turned to epistemology and in 2005 published my first work of epistemology, which was also my first book.[12] In it, I tried to connect practical notions with epistemic ones. I argued that having more at stake in decisions made knowledge harder to acquire. So, for example, poor citizens who would benefit greatly from the extra spending derived from modest tax increases on wealthy citizens, as well as their advocates, would have a considerably higher bar for knowledge. If so, their claims would be taken less seriously. Since knowledge was required for action, poor citizens would also have a higher epistemic bar for political action.

The thesis was greeted with some perplexity. Epistemologists didn't know why I was so strenuously arguing for the interest-relativity of knowledge. Though my desire to make some sense out of the connection between the practical and the epistemic in the political interests motivated the work in the book, I was not very explicit about that fact.[13] But there were clear nonpolitical examples, which had also been noticed by Jeremy Fantl, Matthew McGrath, and John Hawthorne in work around the same time. No doubt one could have different routes to the same destination.

The interest-relativity of knowledge, as I will argue in chapter 6, raises a challenge for democratic practice, as it entails that those with different levels of stakes in a decision will have correspondingly different epistemic resources upon which to draw. But it seems that there are certain kinds of epistemic harm that have their source in *prejudice*, rather than (for example) lack of resources. Miranda Fricker, in her pathbreaking work from 2007, described a notion she called *epistemic injustice*. The two forms of epistemic injustice she describes are crucial for explaining why negatively privileged groups seem at an epistemological disadvantage, or at the very least a presumed epistemological disadvantage, in political debate. Tamar Gendler, in her work on Alief, draws attention to the "cognitive consequences" of living in a society that violates one's normative ideals.[14] This work overlaps with already extant bodies of research in feminist philosophy and philosophy of race. I draw heavily on this work and work drawing upon it, which interacts and overlaps with the large body of work in analytic epistemology evaluating and addressing the interest-relativity of knowledge.

If we judge from history, the desire to relegate one group of society to the task of manual labor is a powerful feature of human social psychology. The justification for such a division of labor is typically based on differential attributions of the human capacity for theoretical reflection. Some groups, it is said, are best equipped for practical tasks and others for theoretical tasks, a view that has traditionally been at the basis of the justification of slavery. But almost every society, whether or not it has a practice of slavery, endorses some version of it. The second project that has occupied me over the last fifteen years, including in my book *Know How*, published in 2011, has been a thoroughgoing repudiation of the scientific and philosophical basis of this ideology. I bring the significance of this work to bear in the final chapter, on the United States educational system.

My anger at the waste of human potentiality involved in mass incarceration has led me to donate my royalties from the sale of this book, except for a small advance, to the Prison Policy Initiative, a Massachusetts-based advocacy group led by Peter Wagner. I relied on their research at various points in the book, which is freely available on their website. I applaud the extraordinary role they have played in the prison abolition movement, manifested by their successful lobbying against usurious prison telephone charges, as well as prison gerrymandering.

The central questions of this book are familiar ones in social and political theory and "continental" philosophy. But the resources I use are largely those of the analytic philosopher. For much of its history, analytic philosophy has appeared to endorse the artificial German split between "theoretical" philosophy and "practical," or normative, philosophy. But analytic philosophers working within feminist philosophy and philosophy of race have showed the value of the tools of so-called theoretical philosophy in the analysis of the central political concepts of power and oppression, suggesting that to divide philosophy in that way is incorrect. Philosophers such as Rae Langton, Jennifer Hornsby, Sally Haslanger, Tamar Gendler, Jennifer Saul, Kristie Dotson, Ishani Maitra, Lynne Tirrell, Rebecca Kukla, José Medina, David Livingstone Smith, and many others employ the tools of apparently nonnormative areas of analytic philosophy to understand the dynamics of injustice. These philosophers have been using the precise tools of analytic philosophy to address the traditional philosophical questions, centrally among which of course are the questions of social and political philosophy. As will become apparent from the book, I owe an enormous debt to this work, accomplished mostly by analytic feminist philosophers and philosophers of race. They created the path upon which this book travels, which was already well traveled by the time I began it.[15]

Yet I could not have written this book working only within the paradigm of analytic philosophy. During the writing of this book, I began to realize that the books Mary Stanley had sent me were not a random sampling, merely the result of emptying one room. There was the full supply of classical social theory, works I was familiar with in my youth, but needed to revisit. There were several boxes of books on perversions of liberalism. There were many boxes of books on the US educational system. Over time, the collection started to make sense. Mary had sent me the tools of social theory, as well as material for several different case studies, for the book on propaganda that she knew I was writing. The year was spent reabsorbing myself in classical social theory, books from the grandest moments of sociology, from Weber, Durkheim, and Du Bois, to Mills and Mannheim. I have come to profoundly regret philosophy's abdication of many of its central questions to sociology and social theory. My aspiration for this work is that it can serve as some evidence of how much richer both philosophy and social theory can be when they are, as they were for so many centuries, combined.

HOW PROPAGANDA WORKS

INTRODUCTION:
THE PROBLEM OF PROPAGANDA

Victor Klemperer was a professor of romance studies in Dresden, Germany. More notably, he was a German citizen of the Jewish faith who had the remarkable good fortune to survive in his hometown throughout the entire period of National Socialist rule. Klemperer managed to survive because he was a World War I veteran with a distinguished record of service. He was also married to another German citizen, not of the Jewish faith, who refused to leave him. As a result, he had a special status. He has the distinction of being one of the few people whose lives were saved by the firebombing of Dresden, which destroyed the Gestapo records that assuredly were about to order his deportation.

Klemperer wrote a lengthy diary of the Nazi years. In 1947, he published one of the great twentieth-century case studies of propaganda, *The Language of the Third Reich*.[1] The concept that Klemperer seeks to elucidate in his examples is my focus in this book. Here is Klemperer's description of the characteristic effects of the Language of the Third Reich, which he called *Lingua Tertii Imperii*, or LTI:

> The LTI only serves the cause of invocation. . . . The sole purpose of the LTI is to strip everyone of their individuality, to paralyze them as personalities, to make them into unthinking and docile cattle in a herd driven and hounded in a particular direction, to turn them into atoms in a huge rolling block of stone.

The first chapter of Klemperer's book, "Heroism: Instead of an Introduction," is devoted to describing the symbols associated with the term "heroism," what he describes as the "uniform," in fact the "three different uniforms," of the word. The first uniform was that of the "blood soaked conqueror of the mighty enemy," the image of the original Storm Troopers of the 1920s. The second uniform was that of "the masked figure of the racing driver," representing German success at the beloved sport of auto racing. The third uniform was that of the wartime tank driver. These are the "symbols which assemble emotions" that the term "heroism" evoked. In all three cases, the symbols were "closely tied up with the exaltation of the Teutons as a chosen race: all heroism was the sole prerogative of the Teutonic race." Specifically, Jews were at the time stereotypically neither race-car drivers, Storm Troopers, nor tank drivers. Finally, here is how Klemperer describes the *effect* of the term "heroism" on those raised under National Socialism:

> What a huge number of concepts and feelings it has corrupted and poisoned! At the so-called evening grammar school organized by the Dresden adult education center, and in the discussions organized by the Kulturbund and the Freie deutsche Jugend, I have observed again and again how the young people in all innocence, and despite a sincere effort to fill the gaps and eliminate the errors in their neglected education, cling to Nazi thought processes. They don't realize they are doing it; the remnants of linguistic usage from the preceding epoch confuse and seduce them. We spoke about the meaning of culture, or humanitarianism, of democracy and I had the impression that they were

beginning to see the light, and that certain things were being straightened out in their willing minds—and then, it was always just round the corner, someone spoke of some heroic behavior or other, or of some heroic resistance, or simply heroism per se. As soon as this concept was even touched upon, everything became blurred, and we were adrift once again in the fog of Nazism. And it wasn't only the young men who had just returned from the field or from captivity, and felt they were not receiving sufficient attention, let alone acclaim, no even young women who had not seen any military service were thoroughly infatuated with the most dubious notion of heroism. The only thing that was beyond dispute, was that it was impossible to have a proper grasp of the true nature of humanitarianism, culture, and democracy if one endorsed this kind of conception, or to be more precise misconception, of heroism.[2]

Klemperer notes that the effect of "heroism" on those raised during the Third Reich is to make everything "blurred." Rational deliberation was impossible. And somehow, because of associations between the words and symbols, the political ideals of liberal democracy became incomprehensible. My hope is by the end of the book to have provided a complete explanation of the effects Klemperer here describes.

National Socialist ideology involves a hierarchy of race, an explicit elite group, and the dehumanization of other groups. It is an example of what I will call a *flawed ideology*. When societies are unjust, for example, in the distribution of wealth, we can expect the emergence of flawed ideologies. The flawed ideologies allow for effective propaganda. In a society that is unjust, due to unjust distinctions between persons, ways of rationalizing undeserved privilege become ossified into rigid and unchangeable belief. These beliefs are the barriers to rational thought and empathy that propaganda exploits.

Group identities are the coral reefs of cognition; much of the beauty of the production of human intellect is due to their existence. But certain group identities are democratically problematic; the Teutonic identity constructed by National Socialism is an obvious example. Such identities channel rational and affective streams in specific ways, creating obstacles to self-knowledge, as well as to the free flow of deliberation required in a healthy democracy.

My focus in this book is political rhetoric; "propaganda" is my name for it. Rhetoric is among the earliest topics of philosophical reflection. If philosophy has "core" topics, rhetoric is among them. Both Plato and Aristotle wrote treatises on political rhetoric, the subject of this book. It is one of the basic topics of philosophy, traditionally conceived. On the surface of things, it is a topic that has lain fallow in twentieth- and twenty-first-century philosophy. However, appearances here are deceiving; I will argue, for example, that much of analytic epistemology involves struggling with the central topics of political rhetoric, albeit with fictional, depoliticized examples.

Political rhetoric is the subject of Plato's dialogue the *Gorgias*. Socrates there argues that rhetoric is not a science; it is a "knack" based on "guess work." Socrates is suggesting that there are no general principles that one can convey to others which predict what one should do to successfully sway others nonrationally. One cannot therefore teach how to manipulate others. The manipulation of others depends upon particular facts about societies that are not part of a science of rhetoric. For example, successful creators of advertisements do not learn their craft via attending schools and acquiring a body of general principles. Success at advertising involves knowing a great deal of particular facts about popular culture. This part of advertising at least isn't something one learns scientifically, as a body of general principles.

I do not here provide a manual of propaganda. Instead, I explain what it is, why it matters, and the mechanism by which it is effective. I argue that harmful propaganda relies upon the existence of flawed ideologies present in a given society. Different flawed ideologies exist in different societies. Propaganda exploits and strengthens them. This book therefore does not aim at providing a manual for instilling flawed ideologies in others. In contrast, I will suggest that it is a multidecade process that involves seizing power and therefore control of the information flow, in the form of media and schools. A book on propaganda that neglects to lay the groundwork for a craft of manipulating others, or to provide a set of instructions guiding the art of total deception for political gain, is not empty of content. Understanding what propaganda is and the mechanism that makes it effective is an essential task for understanding political reality.

My account of the effectiveness of harmful propaganda, the subject of most of this book, rests on a theory of flawed ideology. This material involves extensive use of recent work in analytic epistemology and cognitive and social psychology. I begin with an analysis of propaganda, which I then employ in the explanation of its effectiveness. Essentially, the analysis explains how effective propaganda exploits and strengthens flawed ideology. In the latter half of the book, I argue that flawed ideologies rob groups of knowledge of their own mental states by systematically concealing their interests from them. Flawed ideologies are also severe impediments to democratic deliberation. One kind of propaganda, demagogic speech, both exploits and spreads flawed ideologies. Hence demagogic speech threatens democratic deliberation. A different kind of propaganda, *civic rhetoric*, can repair flawed ideologies, potentially restoring the possibility of self-knowledge and democratic deliberation.

Each stage in this explanation poses distinctive challenges. The challenge facing a theory of propaganda is explaining its nature and effectiveness. The challenge facing a theory of ideology is to explain what Etienne de la Boétie, in his 1548 discourse on the subject, called *voluntary servitude*: the (alleged) tendency of the negatively privileged masses to accept the flawed ideology of the elites.

Demagogic speech does not just occur under the Nazis. Even those of us who live in states guided by liberal democratic ideals are all familiar with the confusing effects of propaganda. In a recent article in the popular press, Jonathan Chait writes about the phenomenon with respect to political discourse in the United States of America. Chait explains the recent history of Republican Party propagandists, who explicitly set out to connect conservative vocabulary and ideals with implicitly racist messages, so-called dog whistles. As a result of this effort, when conservatives assert their beliefs in ordinary discussion they are invariably accused of racism by liberals. Chait betrays understandable perplexity when he writes:

> Yet here is the point where, for all its breadth and analytic power, the liberal racial analysis collapses onto itself. It may be true that, at the level of electoral campaign messaging, conservatism and white racial resentment are functionally identical. It would follow that any conservative argument is an appeal to white racism.... Impressive though the historical, sociological, and psychological evidence undergirding this analysis may be, it also happens to be completely insane ... advocating tax cuts is not in any meaningful sense racist.

Chait rightly points out the efforts of propagandists to tie the language of poverty and aid to the supposed inferiority of American citizens of African descent have made democratic deliberation about how to handle poverty impossible. He expresses befuddlement about how that happened, and cannot explain the rationality of the charges of racism that inevitably emerge from attempts at deliberation of this sort. Chait is drawing our attention to the effects of propaganda on democratic deliberation. But Chait lacks the theoretical apparatus to explain it. The challenge facing the task of explaining how propaganda undermines democratic deliberation is to provide the relevant theoretical apparatus that lets us understand individual cases, such as this example.

In his paper "The Diversity of Objections to Inequality," the philosopher T. M. Scanlon characterizes five "reasons for pursuing greater equality."³ But none of the reasons involves the tendency inequality has to cause *flawed ideologies*. I will argue that there is a powerful democratic objection to inequality: inequality tends to lead to epistemic barriers to the acquisition of knowledge, ones that imperil democracy. This is not one of the objections to inequality considered by Scanlon, at least not obviously so. But I will argue that it is a traditional democratic objection to inequality, dating back to the Ancient Greeks. It is this objection to inequality that I wish to develop, using the various tools of philosophy and the human sciences.⁴

Both the view that flawed ideologies is one of the most serious problems for democracy and the view that conditions of inequality engender them are familiar in democratic political philosophy. In Federalist No. 10, James Madison recognizes the problem that inequalities raise for democratic governance. Madison is even clear that material inequality is a central source of flawed ideologies.⁵ The point of Federalist No. 10 is to argue that, given the existence and inevitability of what are (in my terminology) flawed ideologies, what Madison calls "pure democracy" is impossible. Madison believes a *representative* democracy will provide the requisite safeguards against the illiberal effects of flawed ideologies.

Representatives are supposed to solve the illiberal effects of flawed ideologies, because they are supposed to be impartial. However, it is safe to say that representative democracies have not invariably been composed of impartial representatives. On the level of examples, many of the cases I discuss suggest that the problems flawed ideology raises for a "pure democracy," problems that Madison astutely worried about, do arise in the case of representative democracies; representatives are not immune from flawed ideological belief, or from using it to propagate propaganda. More generally, in the United States, the undermining of campaign finance reform laws has led to clear partiality on the side of representatives. Given the need to raise immense funds for reelection in campaigns that now feature open avenues to corporate donations, representatives are beholden to the clearly partial motives of big business and high-wealth individuals. So, while a great deal of this work is devoted to vindicating Madison's concerns about the illiberal and antidemocratic effects of flawed ideology, I do not share his optimism that the solution is to be found in replacing a pure democracy with a representative one, especially in a context in which the safeguards have been removed.

Flawed ideology is an obstacle to realizing one's goals. On the one hand, those benefiting from large material inequalities will tend to adopt flawed ideologies in the form of false legitimation narratives. These false legitimation narratives will blind them to injustice, and hence from realizing their ethical goals. On the other hand, those suffering materially from large inequalities, via lack of land, access to high-status positions, or other obstacles to equality of opportunity and attainment, will be led to adopt a flawed ideology of their own inferiority. This will prevent them from realizing their *material* interests.

In *The Republic*, Plato sought to describe the ideal polity, which was for him an aristocracy of philosophers. Yet Plato engages deeply in the methodology of evaluating political systems in terms of their potential stability, given actual social and psychological facts about humans. A central part of his discussion is devoted to why certain political systems have an illusory appeal. The central discussion of democracy occurs in book 8 of *The Republic*. In book 8, as in *The Republic* as a whole, Plato moves back and forth between his critiques of cities with particular political systems and men with the characters of that political system.[6]

In the case of democracy, a city is democratic in virtue of having a certain *character*, personified by the democratic man. What is democratic in a city for Plato, in the first instance, is the *culture* of a society, not the particular voting procedures employed. Plato's critique of democracy is a good place to begin with the topic of the nature of a democratic culture.

Plato distinguishes between five forms of government: an aristocracy, a timocracy, an oligarchy, a democracy, and a tyranny.

An aristocracy, Plato's favored form of government, is "government of the best."[7] A timocracy, Plato's second-favored form, is a form of government whose central virtue is honor and victory (Sparta serves as Plato's example of a timocracy). In a timocracy, the great military general is the most admired figure. An oligarchy has a "constitution based on a property assessment, in which the rich rule, and the poor man has no share in ruling" (550c). The greatest good of an oligarchy is wealth. Plato introduces democracy as the adversary of oligarchy (557a).

Plato is a fierce critic of democracy. Plato is quite aware that the chief features of the democratic city appear to be virtues, but he holds their apparent virtuous nature to be illusory.

In a democracy, the greatest good is *freedom*. Plato writes, "Freedom: Surely you'd hear a democratic city say that this is the finest thing it has, so that as a result it is the only city worth living in for someone who is by nature free" (562b, c). A democratic city is "full of freedom and freedom of speech" (557b); "everyone in it [has] the license to do what he wants" (557b). Plato has many trenchant criticisms of democracy. One of the chief criticisms is that democracy will lead to *equality*, equality between slaves and freemen, and between men and women:

A resident alien or a foreign visitor is made equal to a citizen, and he is their equal. . . . The utmost freedom for the majority is reached in such a city when bought slaves, both male and female, are no less free than those who bought them. And I almost forgot to mention the extent of the legal equality of men and women and of the freedom in the relations between them. (563b)

It is clear here that Plato at least means by "equality" something we can call *political equality*, equal share in deciding the policy for the city. A problem with the democratic city, for Plato, is that slaves have political equality with nonslaves, and women have political equality with men.

We can take from Plato's classic discussion of the ills of democracy a characterization of the character of a democratic society. A democratic society is one that values liberty and a distinctive kind of equality, which I have been calling political equality. It is suffused with tolerance of difference. Since Plato's time, some of the central questions of democratic political theory have concerned the nature of these goods: that is, the nature of liberty as it pertains to democracy, and the nature of political equality as it pertains to democracy.

Plato's discussion pertains to the nature of a democratic culture. But, as Elizabeth Anderson reminds us, democracy can be understood in two other ways:

> Democracy can be understood at three levels of analysis: as a membership organization, a cultural formation of civil society, and as a mode of governance. As a membership organization, it requires (actual or easy access to) universal and equal citizenship of all permanent denizens of a state. As a culture, it involves free interaction and cooperation of members from all walks of life. As a mode of governance, it involves institutions such as periodic competitive elections of individuals to major public offices, a universal franchise, transparency of state operations, the rule of law, and equality under the law.[8]

I will use the expression "liberal democracy" to refer to a society that exemplifies the traits of Plato's democratic city and has a democratic mode of governance and membership criteria.[9] This is compatible with distinct understandings of liberty and distinct understandings of political equality. So a system is only a democratic system if it places some conception of liberty as its highest value and allows for political equality.

There are many distinct notions of liberty. But we do not need to decide between them for the purposes of this book. As we shall see, there is universal agreement that certain ideals are not forms of liberty. This is enough for us for our purposes. The problem raised by propaganda for democracy is perfectly general across different conceptions of liberty and different conceptions of proper democratic methods. What is this problem?

The most basic problem for democracy raided by propaganda is the possibility that the vocabulary of liberal democracy is used to mask an undemocratic reality. If so, there could be a state that *appeared* to be a liberal democracy. It would be a state the citizens of which *believed* was a liberal democracy. But the appearance of liberal democracy would be merely the outer trappings of an illiberal, undemocratic reality. There is no corresponding existential threat for authoritarian regimes. It is utterly standard to mask the nature of an authoritarian regime with the use, for example, of revolutionary or socialist vocabulary. This is not a threat to the authoritarian nature of the regime. In contrast, masking the undemocratic nature of a state with democratic vocabulary is an existential threat to a democratic regime. But propaganda poses more specific threats to all varieties of democracies.

There are distinct conceptions of liberal democracy, which correspond to distinct conceptions of liberty. If liberty is the freedom to pursue one's self-interest, then political equality leads to a system in which each person is free to pursue her self-interest through the political process. This conception of democracy is captured by the *economic theory of democracy*. Other conceptions of democracy reflect richer and more demanding conceptions of liberty.

According to the economic theory of democracy, a policy is genuinely democratic if it is voted on by majority vote by fully rational agents who are wholly self-interested.[10] This is supposed to be the realistic conception of democratic legitimacy. This model presupposes that people have reliable access to their interests. But, we shall see, propaganda is characteristically part of the mechanism by which people become deceived about how best to realize their goals, and hence deceived from seeing what is in their own best interests.[11] Propaganda short-circuits "economic" rationality.

There are more plausible cousins of the economic theory of democracy. The economic theory involves the assumption that people know what is in their interests. One might agree that the pursuit of self-interest is at the heart of liberal democracy, but hold that "nobody can know who knows best and that the only way by which we can find out is through a social process in which everybody is allowed to try and see what he can do."[12] But even this more plausible version of a self-interest-based view of democracy is imperiled by propaganda. A society that is deeply affected by propaganda will be one in which certain legitimate routes that an individual's life path can take will be closed off. So even an individualist conception of liberal democracy that does not require people to know their own interests is threatened by the presence of ideology and propaganda.

Propaganda poses an equally obvious threat to the *epistemic conception* of democracy, championed by the philosopher David Estlund and the political scientist Hélène Landemore.[13] Epistemic democrats hold that democracy should be given an *epistemic* justification (perhaps in addition to its autonomy-related justification), one that rests upon the superiority of collective reasoning for deciding outcomes. On this view, democracy is the best form of government, because collective deliberation followed by majority rule is the most reliable way to make decisions. Propaganda poses an obvious problem for the epistemic conception of democracy, because propaganda bypasses rational deliberation.

I began this introduction by posing the central tasks of this book using the expression "democratic deliberation." But what is democratic deliberation? Democratic deliberation is a kind of joint deliberation, the kind that is at the heart of another conception of a proper democratic method in political philosophy. According to the *deliberative conception* of democracy, policies are democratic only if they emerge from joint deliberation of this kind.[14] Deliberative democracy embodies a conception of liberty grounded in the notion that genuine liberty is having one's interests decided by the result of deliberation with peers about the common good. Another challenge propaganda poses for liberal democracy is that it undermines or shortcuts joint deliberation of this sort.

Plato speaks of the democratic city as one that values liberty and equality. Here, Plato is not referring to a specific means of voting. He is referring rather to a certain kind of character of a culture, properties that are true of a society. A democratic society is one that values freedom and equality.

How likely is it that there are actual states that are liberal democracies in name only? Let's consider, as a representative example, the United States of America, the world's oldest liberal democracy. It is a representative democracy, and not a direct democracy. But the representatives, by being accountable to the people in the form of elections, are supposed to represent their collective will. Is the United States a kind of democracy, as its citizens believe it to be? Does it have a democratic culture, one that values freedom and political equality? Or is the language of democracy and self-rule merely used to conceal a thoroughly undemocratic reality? I am going to explore, without endorsing, some suggestive reasons for thinking the latter is the case.

The American political philosopher Martin Delany draws attention to a deep hypocrisy of the rhetoric of democracy in the American body politic, a hypocrisy that we will come to recognize as characteristic of the propagandistic use of the language of liberal democracy:

> The United States, untrue to her trust and unfaithful to her professed principles of republican equality, has also pursued a policy of political degradation to a large portion of her native born countrymen, and that class is the Colored People. Denied an equality not only of political, but of natural rights, in common with the rest of our fellow citizens, there is no species of degradation to which we are not subject.

The publication date of this work is 1852, eight years before the outbreak of the Civil War. There was a robust Anti-Slavery movement in the North. Delany is thoroughly convinced that there are many sincere, honestly committed white members of the Anti-Slavery movement. He also imputes to them the very best of (at least conscious) intentions.[15] Delany maintains nevertheless that even in a civil society solely with members of the Anti-Slavery movement, the treatment of American citizens of African descent is manifestly untrue to the liberal democratic principles of the United States, which guarantee equality of opportunity. What is his argument?

Delany draws our attention to a curious phenomenon. The cause of dissatisfaction among American citizens of African descent was the fact that they were "proscribed, debarred, and shut out from every respectable position, occupying the places of inferiors and menials"[16] It is reasonably expected that the cause was explicit racism, in the form of the explicit failure to sincerely and honestly take oneself to be respecting the principles of political equality between fellow citizens. If so, then living among members of the Anti-Slavery movement would alleviate the cause of their dissatisfaction. But American citizens of African descent "are nevertheless still occupying a miserable position in the community, wherever we live"[17] Even among well-meaning whites who sincerely believe in principles of equality between races, American citizens of African descent still are "coachmen, cookmen, waiting-men," or "nurse-woman, scrub-woman, maid-woman."[18] Therefore, explicit racism is not the sole cause of the degradation of American citizens of African descent. Remove explicit racism, and little changes.

Perhaps it might be thought that there was then political equality between races in nonslave states, despite Black failure to attain societal position of equal rank. But Delany argues that "[b]y the regulations of society, there is no equality of persons, where this is not an equality of attainments."[19] Delany provides a lengthy argument in the book that the only plausible explanation of failures of Black achievement is a lack of equal respect between races.[20] Failures of Black attainment show that whites fail to have equal respect for Blacks. And perhaps most powerfully, what emerges from Delany's pen is that white obstacles to Black achievement lead to a systematic loss of *self-worth*, a loss that Delany takes upon himself to counter at length with accounts of heroic Black attainment in the face of large structural obstacles. Delany's book is an argument for equality of attainment; its failure reveals lack of equal respect, and leads to loss of self-worth, the social basis of self-respect.

One might of course maintain that there is political equality between persons, and the degradation of American citizens of African descent is due to their inferiority. But this is explicit racism, straightforwardly inconsistent with other aspects of the liberal belief in the equality of persons, and, as Delany argues, with the fact of "the general equality of men"[21] It is therefore in the end racism that is the cause of the degradation of American citizens of African descent. Delany's point is that sincere professions of antiracism on the part of white abolitionists in the North coexisted with a practice that was clearly racist. The racist reality was somehow masked by the antiracist ideals. The point of Delany's discussion of white abolitionists is that even among sincere, good faith adherents to liberal democratic ideals, those ideals function to disguise an illiberal reality.

In 2014, there remains a significant gap in resources, life possibilities, and protections of the law between American citizens of African descent and American citizens of European descent. The economic disparities between these two groups are extreme. A national survey in 2009 found that the net worth of the median white household was $113,149 compared to $5,677 for the median Black household.[22] Moreover, since the 1970s, the United States has also witnessed a drastic increase in the rate of imprisonment in the population of American citizens of African descent, both absolutely and relative to American citizens of European descent.[23] Black Americans also continue to face the stigma of school segregation, more than fifty years after the Supreme Court in *Brown v. Board of Education* declared "separate but equal" to be discrimination.

In a Gallup poll in March 1963 in the United States, a time of now universally acknowledged racial inequality, 46 percent of white Americans agreed that "blacks have as good a chance as whites in your community to get any kind of job for which they are qualified."[24] Public opinion in the United States still remains disconnected from the conditions of inequality between races. In a poll of eighteen- to twenty-four-year-old Americans taken on April 19, 2012, by the Public Religion Research Institute, 58 percent of whites agreed with the claim that "discrimination against whites has become as big a problem as discrimination against blacks."[25] The failure of fit between white belief and Black reality appears inconsistent with the possibility of democratic deliberation.

There are other reasons, aside from what might appear to be a systematic, persisting racist culture, to think that the United States is a democracy in name only. A *democratic culture* is one in which everyone has a say in the policies and laws that apply to them. A corporate or *managerial culture* is quite distinct from a democratic culture. Yet public culture in the United States, since the industrial revolution, has been dominated by a managerial ethos. The educational historian Raymond E. Callahan writes that by 1900, "the acceptance of the business philosophy was so general that it has to be considered one of the basic characteristics of American society in this period."[26] During the industrial revolution, the idea of success as material success and the "business ideology" of management were a heavy emphasis in popular journalism. It was during this time that politicians also started to speak of themselves as businessmen running corporations, something that survives today not only in the United States, but in the European Union.

In 1941, James Burnham published a book, *The Managerial Revolution*, predicting the end of an era in which communism faced off against capitalism, and Stalinism against democracy.[27] Burnham argued that the future would be "a managerial society" in which heads of multinational corporations would have de facto policy control over individual states.

Burnham argues that in a managerial society "managers can maintain their ruling position only ... through assuring for themselves control of the state," a task that is "not so simple" in a democracy, which guarantees "freedom for minority political expression." Burnham writes, "[T]he economic structure of managerial society seems to raise obstacles for democracy. There is no democracy without opposition groups. Opposition groups cannot, however, depend for their existence merely on the good will of those who are in power."[28] But since in the managerial society of the future "[a]ll major parts of the economy will be planned and controlled by the single integrated set of institutions which will be the managerial state," there is "no independent foundation for genuine opposition political groups."[29]

Burnham raises the possibility that in the future, the United States, as well as other alleged liberal democracies, will be managerial states instead of democracies, yet ones that use the vocabulary of liberal democracy to conceal their true nature. Yet there are some obvious problems with Burnham's prediction. Burnham predicts that in the future, there will be essentially only single-party rule, as a consequence of the managerial state. Yet there are two parties in the United States, the Democratic Party and the Republican Party, a reality mirrored in other liberal democracies. Has Burnham's prediction been therefore refuted? And if not, how is propaganda implicated in masking our recognition of Burnham's prediction?

Democracies are supposed to have policies that reflect the views of their citizens. The Harvard Law School professor Lawrence Lessig reports that polling by his organization reveals that over 90 percent of Americans "believe it's important to reduce the influence of money in politics. And that's true for Republicans as much as Democrats and Independents. This is just a universal view."[30] Yet the Supreme Court, in two decisions, in 2010 and 2014, essentially eliminated campaign finance reform. Even before this, Lessig reports, politicians in Congress spent 70 percent of their time not on legislation, but on raising campaign funds. In order to run in elections, politicians first must be selected by members of a sliver of Americans (Lessig reports that this group is the wealthiest 1 percent of the wealthiest 1 percent). Public opinion across a range of issues is often radically misaligned with national policy.

One might argue that whatever the problems of democracy in the United States are, propaganda is not one of them. After all, despite intensive and successful efforts by the wealthiest Americans to dismantle campaign finance laws, polling reveals that Americans continue to support campaign finance reform. Furthermore, one might think that there is no significant problem for democracy, because Americans do not rank campaign finance reform high on their list of priorities. But both of these arguments result from a failure to understand the strategy taken by sophisticated propagandists.

Americans do think that there is a serious problem about campaign financing, and they do think that there is a serious problem about climate change. The propaganda that has been employed against them has been in the service of convincing them that the kind of laws that they want passed are invariably in the service of agendas most of them oppose. For example, 80 percent of Americans think that actual campaign finance reform laws are or would be corrupt, having the purpose of "helping current congress members get reelected" rather than of improving the system.[31] Similarly, in a statement on May 7, 2001, from the Bush White House spokesperson Ari Fleisher, "in response to a question about whether the president would urge Americans to change their world-leading energy-consumption habits," he replied:

> That's a big "no." The president believes that it's an American way of life, that it should be the goal of policy-makers to protect the American way of life. The American way of life is a blessed one.... The president considers Americans' heavy use of energy a reflection of the strength of our economy, of the way of life that the American people have come to enjoy.[32]

In the case of climate change, the function of corporate propaganda has been to push the idea that climate change legislation is not in the service of doing anything about the climate, but rather in the service of changing lifestyles to accommodate a socially progressive agenda: climate change policy as gay marriage.

Propaganda is of course not the only obstacle to the realization of liberal democratic ideals. The influence of money on politics means that voters are presented with a narrow choice of options at the voter's booth. The choices are all between candidates who were able to raise the titanic sums required to run for national office from corporate and special interests and wealthy oligarchs. The candidates do not differ from one another in their representation of the interests of wealth and power, though they often represent different corporate interests: lawyers versus doctors, for example. Given the frequent career movement between private industry and government, it is no wonder that when public opinion at large is divorced from what is in the interest of corporations and high-wealth individuals, it is not reflected in policy. This would appear to be an obstacle to the realization of democratic ideals that is independent of the mechanisms of propaganda.

However, the mechanisms that underlie effective propaganda are implicated even in barriers to liberal democracy that seem not to involve them. I will show that underlying effective propaganda are certain kinds of *group identities*. Some group identities lead to the formation of beliefs that are difficult to rationally abandon, since abandoning them would lead them to challenge our self-worth. When our own identity is tied up with that of a particular group, we may become irrational in these ways. When this occurs, when our group affiliates are such as to lead us to these kinds of rigidly held beliefs, we become especially susceptible to propaganda.

In the United States, the two-party system works as a way to manufacture an artificial group identity, akin to an ethnic or national one or an allegiance to a sports team. Part of the identity seems to consist in allegiance to certain conclusions on a range of "hot button" political issues. On those issues, political party affiliation does seem to result in rigidly held belief and loyalty in the voting booth. Allegiance to the group identity forged by political party affiliation renders Americans blind to the essential similarities between the agendas of the two parties, similarities that can be expected to be exactly the ones that run counter to public interest, in other words, those interests of the deep-pocketed backers of elections to which any politician must be subservient in order to raise the kind of money necessary to run for national office. Satisfaction at having one's group "win" seems to override the clearly present fundamental dissatisfaction with the lack of genuine policy options.[33] If the function of the two parties is to hide the fact that the basic agenda of both is shared, and irrational adherence to one of the two parties is used propagandistically to mask their fundamental overlap, then we can see how Burnham's prediction may have come to pass, despite the existence of two distinct political parties.

In a managerial society, the greatest good is *efficiency*. In a democratic society, by contrast, the greatest good is *liberty*, or autonomy. There are many different senses of "liberty" and "autonomy." But in none of these senses does it mean the same thing as "efficiency."

In *The Republic*, Plato defends his vision of the ideal state, and argues against alternatives. In Plato's ideal state, each man is given an occupation at which he is judged most beneficial to society. As Plato writes, "[W]e prevented a cobbler from trying to be a farmer, weaver, or builder at the same time and said that he must remain a cobbler in order to produce fine work. And each of the others, too, was to work all his life at a single trade for which he had a natural aptitude and keep away from all the others, so as not to miss the right moment to practice his own work well" (374c). There is no free choice of profession. Plato's ideal state is not a democracy. It is rule by experts, city planners guided by the principles of justice, who rule over skilled craftsmen and mere physical laborers. Whether someone is fit to be a philosopher, skilled craftsmen, or mere physical laborer is determined by their nature. The philosophers who know the Platonic Forms decide which pursuits are suited for which members of society and educate them accordingly.[34]

Plato gives several reasons for rejecting democracy, chief among them, as we shall see, that it is most likely of all systems to lead to tyranny. But one reason Plato gives for rejecting democracy is what we have just seen, that it leaves life-decisions, such as the pursuit of a career, in the hands of those whom he regarded as unfit to make the decision, unfit because it would reduce social efficiency. The philosopher Terence Irwin writes the following about this antidemocratic argument of Plato:

> His argument assumes that democratic participation in government has only instrumental value, determined by its efficiency in promoting interests that are quite distinct from it. Against Plato, however, we might value control over what happens to us, and shared responsibility for it, even at some cost in efficiency. Each of us values himself as an agent who to some extent plans his life; and each of us shows respect for others as agents of the same sort, in so far as we decide collectively about our lives.[35]

Plato rejected democracy as a system, because by concentrating on liberty, it failed to maximize efficiency. A managerial society is a society ruled by technocrats who make decisions on behalf of the masses. It is, since Plato's time, regarded as a system that is *opposed* to democracy, rather than one *exemplifying* it.

Plato's ideal state is one in which philosopher "guardians" make decisions on behalf of society. Plato chooses those with a "philosophical nature" (Republic 375e) to play this role, because, he argues, only "a lover of learning and wisdom" can be "gentle toward his own and those he knows" (Republic 376b, c); that is, only philosophers are capable of caring first and foremost about the common good. Philosophers will be able to make sure the state is efficient for all. In a managerial state, by contrast, one can expect that what "efficiency" means is efficiency for *those who control the resources,* or efficiency for the *managers,* or those who own the companies, rather than the *managed.* But even if there were a state controlled by Plato's ideal philosophers, who somehow manage it to be more efficient for all, such a state is not a democracy.

As Plato's discussion assumes, the political culture of a society is determined by what it values. As Plato makes clear in his critique of democracy, in a democratic city, freedom and equality are the primary values. In contrast, one would expect, in a managerial culture, even Plato's "ideal" one, that hard work would be a central value, and respect would be accorded on the basis of one's ability to work hard. One would expect, in a managerial culture, that accusations of laziness would be particularly stinging. A democratic culture is different. Efficiency may be a value, but it is not a *democratic* value. In a democratic culture, someone who is a bad worker, or lazy, still deserves equal respect.

Are alleged liberal democracies now exploiting confusion between democratic values and managerial values to advance antidemocratic policies? Let's look at some examples, the first in the United States, and the second in Europe.

In the US state of Michigan, on March 16, 2011, the Republican state legislature, with the backing of the Republican governor of Michigan, Rick Snyder, passed Public Act 4. The bill provides "for the appointment of an emergency manager" who will replace democratically elected local officials in making decisions about "expenditures, investments, and the provision of services by units of local government," including "modification or termination of contracts," in cases of supposed financial emergency. In November 2012, the citizens of the state of Michigan voted to repeal Public Act 4. The Michigan legislature responded to the rejection of Public Act 4 by passing Public Act 436, essentially reinstating it, and the governor signed it into law in December 2012.

In March 2013, Governor Snyder appointed Kevyn Orr as emergency manager of Detroit. Orr claims that Detroit has over $18 billion in long-term debt. However, extensive independent analysis by the think tank Demos has raised troubling questions about the accuracy of the claims of financial exigency; the Demos report calls the figure of $18 billion "irrelevant to analysis of Detroit's insolvency and bankruptcy filing, highly inflated and, in large part, simply inaccurate."[36] In any case, speculative assumptions about long-term debt are irrelevant to the question of bankruptcy, which is a matter not of eventual long-term debt, but of cash-flow shortfall, currently pegged at $198 million. The Demos report argues that "[t]he biggest contributing factor to the increase in Detroit's legacy expenses is a series of complex deals it entered into in 2005 and 2006" with banks. The deals made with Detroit are widely regarded as suspicious.

The Michigan emergency manager has not vigorously challenged the legality of the contracts that have led Detroit and the utilities that serve it to transfer huge sums to the banks. He has also not attacked the state's decision to invest over $250 million in a new hockey arena in Detroit. Orr has chosen instead to make the citizens of Detroit bear the brunt of the financial pain. In the name of financial efficiency, city services have been slashed. Detroit is a city that sits atop the world's greatest reserve of fresh water, the Great Lakes. Yet Detroit is shutting off water to customers who are more than two months late on their bills and who owe $150 or more. As of July 2014, about 2 percent of Detroit's citizens had their water cut off; nearly half are under threat. During this time, the debts of golf clubs and hockey arenas have largely been ignored.

Shutting off water for nonpayment is technically legal. As a matter of public administration, however, rapidly cutting off water to such a large percentage of a city is extraordinary. Writing for the *Guardian*, Martin Lukacs argues that Orr's focus on privatizing the water utility, "a prized resource worth billions," turns the shutoffs into "a way to make the balance-sheet more attractive in the lead up to its privatization."[37] But privatizing the water utility is a further step in removing public accountability. The discretion inherent in executive power is being exercised to maximize financial efficiency. But there is no obvious connection between financial efficiency and the public good. It is true that handing off debt to future generations is a kind of restriction on their freedom. But so is cutting off their access to water, even though that step may be financially efficient. In general, one can expect that the most draconian possible interpretation and execution of the legal code will be carried out if the goal is to maximize profit and the mechanism for public accountability is lifted.

In Plato's view, most people are not capable of employing their autonomy to make the right choices, that is, choices that maximize overall efficiency. Michigan is following Plato's recommendation to handle the problems raised by elections. Though there are many different senses of "liberty" and "autonomy," none means the same thing as "efficiency." Singapore is a state that values efficiency above all. But by no stretch of the imagination is Singapore a democratic state. A society ruled by technocrats who make decisions on behalf of the masses is, since Plato's time, regarded as a system that is opposed to democracy, rather than one exemplifying it.

Plato was aware of the need, in his ideal state, for the rulers to be selfless. There is good reason to believe that in actual cases the rulers who are supposed to ensure "efficiency" are not like Plato's philosophers. We can see this in the case of Detroit. After all, for whom are the policies of the emergency manager efficient? Surely not for the Detroit residents whose children cannot drink water, bathe, or flush toilets in the midst of summer. Or for those who suffer from the drastic cutbacks in all city services. This is not to deny that the Detroit emergency manager's policies are efficient for some people. For example, they are efficient for the banks that are being paid back for what look to be ethically dubious loans, as well as for those who stand to benefit from the potentially huge profits of privatizing one of the world's great freshwater supplies at a time of increasing global water scarcity.

But let us suppose for the sake of argument that the emergency manager, like Plato's philosopher rulers, made decisions that were efficient for all. For example, suppose the benefits of privatizing southeastern Michigan's freshwater utility were to flow not to private investors in the company, but to the nearly four million Michigan residents it serves. It matters not. The actions of Michigan's governor and legislature would be no less antidemocratic. In a democracy, one cannot replace democratically elected officials in the interest of efficiency. It is not that Public Act 4 and Public Act 436 are morally wrong. Rather, they have no place in a democracy. It is simply no surprise at all that a democratic state can be less efficient than some nondemocratic states. In a democracy, someone who would be a good doctor is allowed to be a bad lawyer. Autonomy cannot be subsumed under efficiency in a democracy. The fact that politicians can so easily claim that efficiency usurps autonomy in US politics testifies to the confusion of democratic values with managerial ones in the United States.

A more internationally salient example of the confusion of democratic values with managerial ones is the case of the European Union. The sociologist Wolfgang Streeck argues that the massive state bailout of financial institutions, leading to immense public debt, was followed by a demand by those very same financial institutions that were bailed out by those states for the states to pay down their debt.[38] As a result, elections in member states of the European Union have had less and less significance; the decision to pay back debt is not left to individual states.[39] Policy is geared toward "market efficiency," which means austerity policies to pay back the banks for the debt incurred by bailing out the banks.

The use of democratic language to mask an antidemocratic worldview that places market efficiency at its center, rather than liberty, is so pervasive and important a misuse of democratic vocabulary that it deserves its own case study, which is the subject of the final chapter. There, we shall see that the usurpation of liberal democratic language to disguise an antidemocratic managerial society is at the basis of the American public school system as it was restructured between 1910 and 1920.

Here is one final reason to think that the United States may be a state that uses the language of democracy to mask an undemocratic reality. An oligarchy is a system in which only those with a certain amount of money or land have access to the political process. An oligarchy is not a majoritarian electoral democracy. For years, the political scientist Martin Gilens has been trying to test empirically the claim that the United States is, as we learn it to be in schools, a "majoritarian electoral democracy." Gilens and his coauthor Benjamin Page conclude that the empirical evidence between 1981 and 2002 entails that the hypothesis that the United States is a pure majoritarian electoral democracy "can be decisively rejected."[40] Wealthy individuals and powerful interest groups (such as the gun lobby) have significant impact on policy. In contrast, "[n]ot only do ordinary citizens not have uniquely substantial power over policy decisions; they have little or no independent influence on policy at all."

Gilens's work is the subject of continuing debate.[41] But it seems nevertheless widely agreed that the available empirical evidence makes it at the very least worthy of serious consideration that the language of liberal democracy does not accurately explain the cause of most US policy. One must worry about even apparently robustly liberal democratic states that the language of democracy is simply used to mask an undemocratic reality.

1

PROPAGANDA IN THE HISTORY OF POLITICAL THOUGHT

There is a simple and compelling argument, known since Plato, which would lead us to expect that even apparently robust liberal democracies are such in name only. The argument is as follows. A certain form of propaganda, associated with demagogues, poses an existential threat to liberal democracy. The nature of liberal democracy prevents propagandistic statements from being banned, since among the liberties it permits is the freedom of speech. But since humans have characteristic rational weaknesses and are susceptible to flattery and manipulation, allowing propaganda has a high likelihood of leading to tyranny, and hence to the end of liberal democracy.

The argument is central to the lengthy history of political philosophy, from antiquity to the twentieth century. Jean-Jacques Rousseau is correct when, in *The Social Contract*, published in 1762, he declares the problem to be political philosophy's central reason for skepticism about democracy:

> The reason our political theorists go astray is the following: All the states they see were badly constituted to begin with, and they are struck by the fact that no polity of the kind I

have described could possibly be kept going within those states. They tell over to themselves, with vast amusement, all the absurdities that a crafty scoundrel or spell-binder could pass off on the people of Paris or London.[1]

It is not accidental that the problem propaganda poses for democracy is so central in the long history of political philosophy. Philosophers have historically taken the *stability* of a political system to be a way of evaluating it against other political systems. It is for this reason that Aristotle chooses democracy as the least bad of the various forms of government in his *Politics*. But even Aristotle recognized (in *Politics*, book 5, chapter 5) that democracy's flaw, the particular instability it faces, came from "demagogues" who alternately "stir up" and "curry favor" with the people. Aristotle clearly recognized that a chief danger to democracy was flawed ideology and demagogic propaganda.[2]

The argument has been at the center of philosophical discussions about the stability of the system of any form of democracy from antiquity to the twentieth century, and has been accordingly central to the evaluation of liberal democracy as a political system. Curiously, however, the problem has completely dropped out of discussion in philosophy. Why so? Here is a suggestion. On one conception of normative political philosophy, the goal is to describe the normatively ideal components of an ideal liberal democratic state. But in an ideal liberal democratic state there is no propaganda. So propaganda as a topic is no longer visible.

In *ideal political theory*, the problem of how to move from an actually flawed state guided incompletely by liberal democratic ideals to an ideal liberal democratic state is known as the *transition problem*. It is usually posed in terms of how to change from an unjust distribution of goods to a just distribution of goods. The tension between two liberal values, rights to private property and equality, is at the center. Given the self-conception of political philosophy as the study of properties of the ideal liberal democratic state, the transition problem counts as "applied" political philosophy. To label something as "applied" in philosophy is to marginalize its study. Ethics is "pure" philosophy; applied ethics is "impure" philosophy, fit for those who cannot absorb the discipline in its pure form.

It is possible to frame the problem of propaganda in terms of the transition problem. The question would be how to transition from a kind of deliberation that is not democratic to genuine democratic deliberation without violating the freedom of speech.[3] Ideal political theory does therefore allow for a space to address what one may arguably regard as the most central question of democratic political theory. It is a question, yet to be addressed in the discipline, of *applied political philosophy*. It is to be addressed at some point after the issue of how to move from an unjust distribution of goods to a just distribution of goods is solved.

The problem raised for liberal democracy by propaganda is whether the most central expression of its value, liberty (realized as the freedom of speech), makes liberal democracy fundamentally unstable. The conception of normative political philosophy I have sketched allows a space, though a marginalized one, to address the question. But it hinders insight into the historical centrality of the problem. Rousseau very clearly attributes to all political philosophers of his time the view that "no polity of the kind I have described [a democracy] could possibly be kept going within those states." But the idea that it could pose some kind of fundamental conceptual problem to liberal democracy is now difficult to understand.

Charles Mills has developed this point into an objection to the very methodology of ideal theory:

> [I]deal theory either tacitly represents the actual as a simple deviation from the ideal, not worth theorizing in its own right, or claims that starting from the ideal is at least the best way of realizing it. . . . Almost by definition, it follows from the focus of ideal theory that little or nothing will

be said on actual historic oppression and its legacy in the present, or current ongoing oppression, though these may be gestured at in a vague or promissory way (as something to be dealt with later).[4]

In the same paper, Mills argues that ideal theory presupposes an "idealized cognitive sphere," in which "[a] general social transparency will be presumed, with cognitive obstacles minimized as limited to biases of self-interest or the intrinsic difficulties of understanding the world, and little or no attention paid to the distinctive role of hegemonic ideologies and group-specific experience in distorting our perceptions and conceptions of the social order." In other words, topics such as flawed ideology and propaganda clearly fall outside the scope of the ideal theoretic project.

In previous work, Mills calls our attention to the nonideal character of the classic texts in political philosophy:

> The classic texts of the central thinkers of the Western political tradition—for example, Plato, Hobbes, Locke, Burke, Marx—typically provide not merely normative judgments but mappings of social ontologies and political epistemologies which explain why the normative judgments of others have gone astray. These theorists recognized that to bring about the ideal polity, one needs to understand how the structure and workings of the actual polity may interfere with our perception of the social truth.[5]

Political philosophy concerns itself with normative judgments, how things ought to be. One view of normativity holds that it is only reasonable to hold someone to what they ought to do if it is within the bounds of her capacity to do it. If one ought to obey a law, it must be possible to obey that law. Otherwise, that law sets an impossible demand. On this view, the normative judgments of political philosophy are bounded by what is within the reasonable capacity to expect of human societies. On another view of normativity, ideals can guide even if they cannot be completely realized. But even this view is bounded by the possibility of being guided by those ideals; it may be that sufficiently remote ideals cannot function to guide in human societies. The study of what is within the reasonable capacity of human societies is social theory.

The view that political philosophy can be done without social theory presupposes that social theory will not place significant and unexpected restrictions on political possibility. Therefore, political philosophy without social theory involves extreme idealization in the construction of its models. As the philosopher Kwame Anthony Appiah has argued, the idealizations involved in ideal theoretic political philosophy are akin to the ideals involved in the decision theoretic axioms governing rationality. My view of the decision theoretic ideals is that they provide a false and distorting view of the ordinary picture of rationality when they are considered as ideals for agents with bounded rationality like us. I hold a similar view for ideal conceptions of the state, when such ideas are theorized without simultaneous attention to social theory.[6]

This book is clearly influenced by Mills. However, it is easy to misunderstand Mills in ways in which it may also be easy to misunderstand the project here. There is a commonly held view that politics is simply about power and interests, and the political vocabulary is only ever used strategically. The rhetoric of political and moral ideals is just one more weapon in a game whose object is to seize power and, along with it, the goods of society. One might worry that Mills's objections to ideal theory come from this dark perspective.

In a book published in 1901, Vilfredo Pareto begins the twentieth century with an articulation of the view that politics is simply about power and interests:

> Buddhism, which proclaimed the equality of all men, has generated the theocracy of Tibet; and the religion of Christ, which seemed especially made for the poor and humble, has generated the Roman theocracy.... The decline of the

old elite and its increasing arrogance at the time of the Reformation can be clearly seen in the emergence of the robber barons: Sickingen and Hutten are two types of such a revolutionary knighthood. As usual, the new elite leaned on the poor and humble; as usual, these believed in the promises made to them; as usual they were deceived, and the yoke weighed even heavier on their shoulders than before. Similarly, the revolution of 1789 produced the Jacobin oligarchy and ended with the imperial despotism. This is what has always happened and there is no reason to believe that the usual course of events should change now.[7]

The view is also clearly articulated in the works of Carl Schmitt, who writes, "[A]ll political concepts, images, and terms have a polemical meaning. They are focused on a specific conflict and are bound to a concrete situation; the result (which manifests itself in war or revolution) is a friend-enemy grouping, and they turn into empty and ghost-like abstractions when this situation disappears."[8]

Because of the enduring controversy of Schmitt's National Socialist political affiliations, he is not the official mid-twentieth-century spokesperson for the view that politics is only about power and interests. But it is a not uncommon view in political and social science that the complexities of administration make democratic accountability too difficult to be realistically managed by a society substantively guided by democratic norms. On this view, the democratic vocabulary has no application, and should instead be employed by those versed in economics and policy—what we now call "experts"—to mask from the masses an illiberal and undemocratic reality. The wide contemporary acceptance of the antidemocratic position is due to the fact that what could be regarded as an authoritarian conclusion has been presented in the economic language of efficiency.

It is one thing to dismiss descriptions of the regular misuse of democratic political ideals when they are presented alongside National Socialist ideology or the Orwellian ideology of certain branches of contemporary social science. It is much more difficult to dismiss such descriptions when they issue from the pens of philosophers suffering under the yoke of oppression. The former eschew normative vocabulary in their description of what they take to be the inevitable political reality. The latter are clearly engaged in a normative project of critique. There is no possibility, in reading Delany, W.E.B. Du Bois, C.L.R. James, or Charles Mills, of construing them as endorsing the elites' use of the concepts of liberal democracy to seize power. It is clearly a demand for oppression to be philosophically addressed, rather than a philosophical endorsement of the mechanism of oppression. It is not inconsistent with ideal theory. It is a demand for the reformulation of the task of normative political philosophy to place social theory on equal footing. It is why many political philosophers who are members of oppressed groups self-describe as working in "social and political philosophy," whereas members of privileged groups often self-describe as working in "political philosophy."

Philosophy, classically understood, has as its task *both* the presentation of reality and the explanation of the illusions that deceive us from recognizing it. Normative political philosophy so conceived should have among its most central tasks not just a defense of the political ideal that is so often masked by political illusion, but also an explanation of political illusion itself. Normative political philosophy that fails to place political illusion at the same level of importance as political ideal faces the legitimate objection that the practice of normative political philosophy is itself part of the machinery that produces illusion: in this case, the illusion that there is no illusion.

In *The Republic*, Plato is clear that one task of philosophy is to cast off illusions. His worry with the democratic city is that most of its members are not philosophers and suffer under the illusions that philosophers have dispelled. The liberty granted by democracy gives tyrants the power of illusion over the masses. Democracy suffers from "an excess of liberty" that "seems destined to end up in slavery" (564a).

Plato and Joseph Goebbels, the Reich minister of propaganda, were both enemies of democracy, Plato because he thought it was too likely to be exploited by people such as Goebbels. There are differences between Plato's conception of democracy and the Weimar Republic, the democracy whose freedoms gave rise to National Socialism. It is nevertheless plausible to take Plato as drawing our attention to the point Joseph Goebbels is making in the epigraph to this book. The liberties allowed by democracy too easily allow demagogues to seize power and thereby end democracy. The risk is too great that someone who is in fact a "towering despot" (566d) will represent himself as a protector of the people and seize power. This is the classic statement of the problem propaganda poses for democracy. Democracy is a system of self-rule that is supposed to maximize liberty. Freedom of speech, especially public political speech, cannot be restricted in a democracy. But the unrestricted use of propaganda is a serious threat to democracy.

In book 1 of *The Social Contract*, Jean-Jacques Rousseau poses a question: "Is a method of associating discoverable, which will defend and protect, with all the collective might, the person and property of each associate, and in virtue of which each associate, though he becomes a member of the group, nevertheless obeys himself, and remains as free as before?" Rousseau's solution is the *social contract*. There is a tacit agreement between members of a civil society to place themselves under the same laws, which "place the same burden on everybody." What results is a "collective moral body," which Rousseau calls a *Sovereign Power*. The sovereign is a state that "consists exclusively of the individuals who are its members" and hence "has no interest that goes against theirs, and cannot possibly have such an interest."[9]

Rousseau calls the freedom humans have in the state of nature *natural liberty*. Natural liberty, for Rousseau, is a person's "unlimited right to anything that [she] is tempted by and can get." The problem Rousseau seeks to answer is how, in civil society, humans can remain free, despite losing their natural liberty.[10] Rousseau's solution is to motivate a distinct kind of liberty. Natural liberty, for Rousseau, is more often than not mere "motivation by sheer apatite." Genuine liberty is, for Rousseau, different than this; it is what he calls *civil liberty*. By being a citizen in a sovereign power, one gains civil liberty. It is "obedience to self-imposed law," of the sort formed by deliberation in citizens' assemblies, which is genuine freedom. True freedom, for Rousseau, is accepting the decisions that are arrived at by a majority under conditions of full civil liberty, that is, political equality.

The purpose of the assemblies is for each citizen to vote about possible policies for the Sovereign Power. The citizens have a "rudimentary right to vote on every act of the sovereign. This nothing can take away from them, any more than their right to express opinions, offer proposals, disagree, and discuss—the latter being a right that the government is always at great pains to reserve for its members."[11] About the method of deliberation, Rousseau writes, "Men who are simple and upright are hard to deceive."[12] But Rousseau is clear about the risks to a Sovereign Power: "If . . . debates drag themselves out, if counsels are divided, if voices are raised, this heralds the ascendancy of private interests and the decline of the state."[13] A mark of the declining state is when "the people, swayed by intimidation or flattery, now acts by acclamation rather than by casting votes; it has ceased to deliberate, and either worships or damns."[14]

For the people to be the rulers, there must be genuine individual deliberation. Having one's vote be the result of forcible coercion is not deliberation. But when Rousseau speaks of being "swayed by intimidation or flattery," he does not mean compelling others via forcible coercion. He means something that results in the appearance of an autonomous vote but is not. He uses the word "deception" to describe what is occurring in such cases, cases that are instances of "acclamation" rather than "casting votes." Demagogic propaganda, in the form of "intimidation or flattery," leads to acclamation rather than "casting votes." This is a classic statement of the problem propaganda poses for democracy.[15]

The philosopher Stephen Darwall singles out a notion of respect he calls *recognition respect*. He distinguishes between two kinds of recognition respect. The first is the kind of respect one has between equals, with those one regards as having the right "to claim and demand" equal treatment. This is respecting the dignity of someone as a fellow human being, a person whose perspective must be given equal weight.[16] The second kind of recognition respect is that derived from "recognizing or honoring" someone as having "some specific social role, status, or place that, in principle, not everyone can have." Darwall calls this *honor respect*.[17] Honor respect is the appropriate governing principle of a monarchy, as it is the appropriate set of attitudes to underlie obedience to authority. Respect of the first kind, treating "people equally without regard to their status or social place," underlies the possibility of genuine democratic deliberation.[18] This is what I have called *political equality*. Rousseau's point is that when casting votes descends into "acting by acclamation," it transforms into monarchy or authoritarian rule. This is Rousseau's way of describing the descent from democracy to tyranny described in book 8 of *The Republic*.

Rousseau's conception of liberty is "obedience to self-imposed law." A common complaint is that Rousseau does not make room for the preservation of individual liberty, and hence he has been criticized as defending a system that allows for despotism. As the French Enlightenment political philosopher Benjamin Constant wrote, what Rousseau omits is that "[t]he citizens possess individual rights independently of all social and political authority, and any authority which violates these rights becomes illegitimate. The rights of the citizens are individual freedom, religious freedom, freedom of opinion, which includes the freedom to express oneself openly, the enjoyment of property, a guarantee against all arbitrary power."[19]

The general conception of liberty emerging from Rousseau is one that may allow for laws against propaganda. After all, it does not obviously place unrestricted free speech at its center. If we replace Rousseau's conception of liberty with *prevention from arbitrary domination*, we obtain a different basis for exploring the restriction of the problematic use of propaganda.[20] The way to argue for restrictions on speech with a so-called negative conception of liberty is to show that certain kinds of speech are *silencing*, as the philosophers Jennifer Hornsby and Rae Langton have argued. If so, restricting silencing speech is a demand from negative liberty, since the liberty to *say what one likes* is an individual liberty. Speech that is silencing has the effect of restricting our free speech rights; this is why states that seem closer to embodying liberal democratic ideals, such as Canada and United States, have considerably less hate speech in the public domain than states further away from such ideals, such as Hungary. Since silencing speech is propagandistic (as we shall see), this sort of defense of restrictions awaits a thorough discussion of the nature of propaganda, which it is my aim to provide.

Rev. Martin Luther King begins his sermon "Propagandizing Christianity," delivered at the Dexter Avenue Church on September 12, 1954, as follows:

> For the average person, the word "propaganda" has evil and malicious overtones. Propaganda is considered something used by the demagogue to spread evil ideologies. Because of the high state of development that propaganda has reached in totalitarian nations, it is readily dismissed as something to be condemned and avoided. But propaganda does not have to be evil. There is a noble sense in which propaganda can be used. Remember that the term originated in the Catholic Church.[21]

Here, King follows a lengthy tradition in political philosophy in which "propaganda" refers to something acceptable in certain conditions in states that follow liberal democratic ideals.

In W.E.B. Du Bois's paper "Criteria of Negro Art," published in 1926, he calls on the African American artist to use what Du Bois calls "propaganda." By "propaganda," Du Bois means emotional appeals to win the respect, empathy, and understanding of whites. Du Bois clearly uses "propaganda" in a neutral sense, rather than a pejorative sense, and calls for propaganda to be used as a weapon for Black liberation. Libratory propaganda of this kind does not aim at the truth. But it nevertheless seems acceptable, and even at certain moments necessary, as a method of realizing those ideals in states that follow liberal democratic ideals. The difficulty of the topic of propaganda lies not just in describing its nature and efficacy. An account of propaganda must also explain when it undermines liberal democratic ideals and when it supports them.

In English, the word "propaganda" has acquired a pejorative connation. It lacks that pejorative connotation in the writings of American authors in the early twentieth century. There are no doubt historical reasons for this. One can imagine that the English word "propaganda" and some of its translations could have acquired a pejorative connotation from the undemocratic effects of the latter. As I will discuss, there might be something prima facie wrong about employing propaganda in a liberal democracy, no matter the goal. But certain kinds of propaganda are particularly problematic morally and politically. I will use the word "demagoguery" as a label for propaganda in this all-things-considered bad sense.

Normative political philosophy takes the form of an inquiry into ideal democratic practices. Given the centrality of public debate about policy to some versions of democracy, it is clear to all who share those conceptions that a task of such inquiry is to describe ideal public discussion. However, describing the various features of propaganda that threaten ideal democratic practice is not part of the task of describing liberal democratic ideals. It is a topic that therefore falls outside the confines of this task.

PROPAGANDA DEFINED

The Report on the Governability of Democracies to the Trilateral Commission, published in 1975, was titled (of course) "The Crisis of Democracy."[1] It was coauthored by Michel Crozier, Samuel P. Huntington, and Joji Watunuki, described as "experts" on the topic. Crozier was a sociology professor and research director at CNRS in Paris, Huntington was a professor of government at Harvard University, and Watunuki was a professor of sociology at Sophia University in Tokyo. In his report on Europe, Crozier writes that teachers, "even more than other intellectuals, [are] directly confronted with the revolution in human relations that perturbs their traditional mode of social control." Crozier warns that "with its cultural drift society has lost the stimulating moral guidance it requires," with the consequence that "the transmission of social, political and cultural norms has been very deeply perturbed."[2]

Samuel Huntington's contribution to the report contrasted the "vitality of democracy" with "the governability of democracy," and raised the question of whether the "democratic surge of the 60s" had "swung the pendulum too far in one direction."[3] Huntington worries about the potential of the "democratic surge" to "weaken authority," and noted that it had resulted in, for example, university students "who lacked expertise" becoming involved in decision making in their institutions.[4] Huntington argues that effective leadership in a democracy requires a people who have the proper obedience to authority, and worries about the undermining of such obedience caused by an excess of democratic expression.[5] Huntington worries about the increasing power of the national media and its role in challenging political authority.[6] Huntington argues that the problems of the United States in the 1970s result from "an excess of democracy," and recommends "claims of expertise, seniority, experience, and special talents" in order to "override the claims of democracy as a way of constituting authority."[7]

Huntington's recommendation for the United States was to try to reinstall some measure of obedience to authority by making various central domains in life, ones that should be governed democratically, the domain of experts, who are employed to make the masses feel unqualified to weigh in on central decisions about their lives. Huntington is recommending installing obedience to authority in negatively privileged groups, by making them feel unqualified to make autonomous democratic decisions in the face of self-proclaimed "experts" of various sorts. Huntington is recommending *epistemic authority*, in the form of "experts," as a means to instill *practical authority* over the masses. Huntington's suggestion for handling the "excess of democracy" in the 1960s is to employ the vocabulary of scientific expertise in a political way, in effect using epistemic ideals as forms of coercion. Such mixtures of epistemic and practical authority, where epistemic authority is used to gain practical authority over the domain of democratically autonomous decision, tend to undermine the epistemic ideals. It leads to distrust of those who self-present as "scientific experts," even when they want to warn us about the importance of vaccines or climate change. My purpose in this chapter is to explain what it is for a contribution to be propagandistic in this and similar ways.

In this chapter, I provide my characterization of propaganda. Since political propaganda can occur in all political systems, my characterization is perfectly general, intended to capture instances of propaganda regardless of political system. The chapter is structured around arguments against two claims about the nature of propaganda, which one might be tempted initially to adopt. The first claim about propaganda is that a propagandistic claim must be false. The second claim about propaganda is that a propagandistic claim must be made insincerely

I will argue against both of these conditions on propaganda in this book. In fact, I argue that even the species of propaganda I call *demagoguery* can consist in claims that are true and made sincerely. I provide a preliminary argument against the first claim here, that propagandistic claims must be false; the argument is completed in chapter 4. I give a complete argument in this chapter against the second claim, by showing that propaganda can be delivered perfectly sincerely. The reason why propaganda, and even demagoguery, can be delivered sincerely is because of the relation between propaganda and flawed ideological belief. This is a relation that can only be adequately explained by rejecting the condition that propaganda must be insincerely delivered. It will turn out that, given the relation between *ideology* and *propaganda*, it will often not be clear at the time when a particular contribution to public debate is propaganda. Charges of propaganda, and even demagoguery, will therefore invariably be political. I conclude the chapter with a defense of this consequence.

It is useful to distinguish the object of the account that follows from related targets. A certain kind of propaganda is employed characteristically by demagogues; this is demagoguery. A demagogue is the tyrant Plato describes in the last part of book 8 of *The Republic*, one who sows fear among the people and then presents himself as "the people's protector" (565e), all the while intending to exploit them. Perhaps the concept of a demagogue, as Plato intends it, brings insincerity with it; perhaps, that is, a demagogue is someone who engages in insincere propaganda. I am not here interested in this question.

The threat that a *demagogue* poses to liberal democracy does not require a book-length treatise. The threat I discuss is rather *demagogic propaganda*, which is the *method* characteristically used by demagogues to seize and retain power in a liberal democratic state.

Here are two initially plausible assumptions to make about propaganda. The first is that propaganda is false. I call this *the falsity condition* on propaganda. The second is that propaganda must be delivered *insincerely*. I call this *the insincerity condition* on propaganda. Before presenting and defending my own characterization, I will reject both the falsity condition and the insincerity condition on propaganda. A true claim, uttered with sincerity, can be propaganda, and even demagoguery.

I begin with a sketch of an argument against the falsity condition on propaganda; the necessary details to complete the case against the falsity condition are given in chapter 4. There are obvious cases of demagogic speech that involve the expression of truths. Imagine, for example, a non-Muslim politician in the United States saying, "There are Muslims among us." The assertion is true; there are many Muslims in the United States. But the claim is clearly some kind of warning. The speaker is raising the presence of Muslims to the attention of his audience to sow fear about Muslims. Therefore, even demagogic claims can be true.

It is natural to think that this argument is too quick. One might reply that "there are Muslims among us" *expresses* a truth. But the reason it is propaganda is that it communicates something false. The claim is propaganda because it communicates that Muslims are inherently dangerous to others, which is false. The falsity condition, properly understood, is the claim that something is propaganda because it *communicates* something false, either by expressing it directly or by communicating it indirectly.

Here are two points to make in reply, which will be developed at length at various points in the book. First, I will give examples of propaganda in which someone is being *misleading*, rather than stating something false, or even implicating something false. One expresses a truth, and relies on the audience's false beliefs to communicate goals that are worthwhile.[8] Falsity is implicated in such cases, but not by means of the expression or communication of a falsehood. I argue that propaganda depends for its effectiveness on the presence of flawed ideological belief. But it simply does not follow that the flawed ideological belief that makes some claim effective as propaganda is expressed or communicated in that claim.[9] Secondly, as I will explain in subsequent chapters, there is a perfectly natural way of thinking of the effects of propaganda according to which it can involve the *expression* of truths and the *communication* of emotions. If emotions are not true or false, then propaganda need not be false. In fact, the case of "there are Muslims among us," used to elicit a fear of Muslims, is a case of exactly this structure.[10] Fourth, as will also emerge, too many utterances at least indirectly convey something false. So the falsity condition does not really explain what is distinctive about propaganda.

I now move to the argument against the insincerity condition on propaganda. Understanding that propaganda can be sincere is necessary to understand the relation between propaganda and ideology.

Klemperer reports that ordinary Germans often construed Hitler's appeal to the Jewish people as enemy as a *harmless* employment of propaganda. For example, here he writes of a young student who had lived in his home for several years, and whom he had befriended, who became enamored of the National Socialists:

> I began to have serious doubts about the extent and strength of his common sense. I tried a different tack in my attempt to make him more skeptical. "You have lived in my house for a number of years, you know the way I think, and you have often said yourself that you have learned something from us and that your moral values accord with ours—how,

in the light of all this, can you possibly support a party which, on account of my origin, denies me any right to be a German or even a human being?—"You're taking it all much too seriously, Babba. . . . The fuss and bother about the Jews is only there for propaganda purposes. You wait, when Hitler is at the helm he'll be far too busy to insult the Jews."[11]

The young student who had lived with Klemperer defended his support of the National Socialists by claiming that Hitler's various horrific representations of Jews were "only there for propaganda purposes." Klemperer notes that Hitler only ever speaks of Jews in one of two styles, "scornful derision" or "panic stricken fear."[12] In the first style, Hitler represents Jews as less than human (for example, when he compares them to "maggots in a rotting corpse"). In the second style, Hitler represents them as being a fundamental threat to safety and stability. By being "only there for propaganda purposes," Klemperer's young student acquaintance meant that Hitler's negative portrayal of the Jews was only intended to rally political support. This may appear to motivate a sense of "propaganda," or the species of it that interests us here, according to which it means something like "the product of conscious intentions to deceive by interested parties."[13] In this sense of "propaganda" (and perhaps with propaganda generally), propaganda is by definition insincere. If Hitler's analogy between Jews and "maggots in a rotting corpse" is propaganda in this sense, then by definition Hitler didn't believe that the analogy was a good one (since, by definition, he would have been engaged in deceit, that is, making an analogy he believed to be poor).

It is straightforward to show that there are some paradigm instances of propaganda that are inconsistent with the insincerity condition. But it is a matter of no small import to our understanding of propaganda to explain what is wrong with the insincerity condition. Explaining what is wrong with the insincerity condition on propaganda will reveal the important connection between ideology and propaganda, which any account of propaganda must explain. The superficial connection is that someone in the grip of a flawed ideology will often express it in propaganda. Since many paradigm cases of demagogic speech or imagery are of this sort, any view that endorses the insincerity condition will be inconsistent with many paradigm cases. What this reveals is that the insincerity condition fails to respect the deep connection between ideology and propaganda.

Let's begin by seeing that the insincerity condition does not fit paradigm cases. Klemperer points out that it does not fit Hitler's demagogic use of anti-Semitism:

> But whilst Hitler's anti-Semitism is a correspondingly basic feeling, rooted in the man's intellectual primitiveness, the Fuehrer also possesses, seemingly from the outset, a large measure of that calculating guile which doesn't seem to accord with an unsound mind, but so often seems to go hand in hand with it. He knows perfectly well that he can only expect loyalty from those who inhabit a similarly primitive world; and the simplest and most effective means of keeping them there is to nurture, legitimize and as it were glorify the instinctive hatred of the Jews. In the process he plays on what is the weakest spot in the cultural thinking of the nation.[14]

In short, Hitler was in fact an anti-Semite who sincerely believed that everything he said about the Jews was accurate. Of course, Hitler did not literally believe that Jews were "maggots in a rotting corpse." This is a metaphor, meant to convey that Jews are a deadly public health menace. The question of sincerity, given a metaphorical utterance involving an analogy, is whether or not Hitler believed that the analogy was apt. Hitler was utterly sincere in his belief that Jews were a deadly public health menace, and clearly did believe the analogy was apt. Simultaneously, even he knew that his appeal to anti-Semitism was meant strategically. It is one thing if Hitler did not intend many of his anti-Semitic pronouncements to be strategic political claims. But he clearly did so intend. These are paradigm cases of propaganda. So we should want the account of propaganda to classify them as such. On the reasonable assumption that propaganda is the intended subject of his book, Klemperer rejects the restriction of the notion of propaganda to insincere claims. Hitler's analogies were sincere, and yet also intended to attract political support.

There are paradigm cases of propaganda that are delivered sincerely. There is also a theoretical explanation why many paradigm cases of propaganda are ones in which the claims are made sincerely. The theoretical explanation involves the connection between propaganda and *ideology*. The genuine problem with the insincerity condition is that it fails to respect the connection between propaganda and ideology. Flawed ideologies characteristically lead one to sincerely hold a belief that is false and that, because of its falsity, disrupts the rational evaluation of a policy proposal; as Rosen notes about Hume's notion of irrational belief, a flawed ideological belief leads to "an unwillingness to amend immediate judgment in light of reflection."[15] Many paradigm demagogic claims are statements sincerely asserted by someone in the grip of a false belief caused by a flawed ideology. Presumably, much Nazi propaganda was of this sort. I assume here, as throughout this work, that any account of propaganda must explain the connection between propaganda and ideology.

Many and perhaps most propagandistic claims are made by those in the grip of a flawed ideology. The insincerity condition cannot explain this. So the insincerity condition is false. Any account of propaganda must explain how possession of a flawed ideology can lead to the tendency to engage in propaganda. An account of propaganda that incorporates the insincerity condition cannot do this. So we must reject it.[16]

Klemperer's description of life under the Third Reich reveals the distinctive dangers of propaganda in totalitarian societies. In totalitarian societies, there is an official ministry of propaganda. Because of that, it is easy in such societies not to take propaganda seriously. But because propaganda can be sincere, the danger propaganda poses in totalitarian societies is that *it is not taken seriously*. The danger propaganda poses in democratic societies is entirely different. Part of the propaganda of states that consider themselves liberal democracies is that they do not allow propaganda. So the distinctive danger propaganda poses in liberal democracies is that it is *not recognized as propaganda*. When effective propaganda is demagogic, it undermines the democratic legitimacy of the goal it is used to motivate.[17]

There is no problem in totalitarian societies recognizing something as propaganda. Claims that are propaganda are those that emerge from the ministry of propaganda. The problem in totalitarian societies lies in figuring out which pieces of propaganda are to be taken seriously.[18] It is only natural in liberal democratic societies to take at least the news media seriously. The problem in democratic societies lies in figuring out which apparently nonpropagandistic claims are in fact propaganda.

I have given some examples of propaganda, together with some impressionistic characterizations. What emerges is the idea that demagogic contributions employ, whether intentionally or unintentionally, flawed ideologies to cut off rational deliberation and discussion. In characteristic cases, they do so by using the flawed ideologies to overwhelm affective states. But more can be said about the properties of a claim in virtue of which it is an instance of propaganda, and more can be said about what makes a particular instance of propaganda an effective instance. And that is my aim in the rest of this chapter.

It is natural to think of representations themselves as propaganda. But my focus is rather on *claims*, or *arguments*, and representations only insofar as they play a role in these claims or arguments. An image showing Saddam Hussein as a little boy who needs to be punished plays a role in a propagandistic argument that America should invade Iraq. The image functions propagandistically in the argument. My task is to explain when arguments for certain goals or certain theories are propagandistic ones. This will involve talking about representations, but only as they play a propagandistic role in certain arguments.

In his book *The Phantom Public*, Walter Lippmann writes,

> Since the general opinions of large numbers of persons are almost certain to be a vague and confusing medley, action cannot be taken until these opinions have been factored down, canalized, compressed and made uniform. The making of one general will out of multitude of general wishes is not an Hegelian mystery, as so many social philosophers have imagined, but an art well known to leaders, politicians and steering committees. It consists essentially in the use of symbols which assemble emotions after they have been detached from their ideas.[19]

Klemperer writes of the Language of the Third Reich (LTI), "Its entire vocabulary is dominated by the will to movement and to action."[20] Indeed, "all the rhetoric of the LTI can be traced back to the principle of movement."[21] The goal of LTI was encourage citizens to rush over deliberation and into direct action.

Propaganda is not simply closing off rational debate by appeal to emotion; often, emotions are rational and track reasons. It rather involves closing off debate by "emotions detached from their ideas." According to these classical characterizations of propaganda, formed in reflecting upon the two great wars of the twentieth century, propaganda closes off debate by bypassing the *rational will*. It makes the state move as one, stirred by emotions that far surpass the evidence for their intensity. It is in this way that all propaganda unites citizens as one. Propaganda is *manipulation of the rational will to close off debate*.[22] This is what I will call *the classical sense of propaganda*.

Lying too is a betrayal of the rational will. But it is a different kind of betrayal of the rational will than propaganda. At least with lying, one purports to provide evidence. Propaganda is worse than that. It attempts to unify opinion without attempting to appeal to our rational will at all. It bypasses any sense of autonomous decision.

There is a more nuanced version of the classical sense of propaganda. It is a notion that animates, for example, Noam Chomsky's work on propaganda.[23] This is propaganda as *biased speech*. Propaganda is speech that irrationally closes off certain options that should be considered. This is related to the classical sense of propaganda, but does not require as a goal immediate action. Action could be reached by several steps of propaganda, in the sense of biased speech. I shall call this *propaganda as biased speech*.

I am not opposed to these models of propaganda. Perhaps the notions I discuss are versions thereof. But these two models of propaganda don't help us explain the attractions of propaganda, nor its relation to ideology. In what follows, I distinguish two types of propaganda. I leave open the nature of their relation both to the classical conception of propaganda and to propaganda as biased speech.

My concern in this book is with liberal democracy, rather than with either the extreme authoritarian state discussed by Klemperer or the still quite undemocratic moment during World War I that motivates Lippmann's characterization. Authoritarian states clearly have propaganda and use it unabashedly, as Klemperer testifies. But liberal democratic cultures seem on the surface free from propaganda: politicians and television hosts shy away from the claim that they are delivering overt propaganda. In liberal democracy, propaganda standardly occurs masked.

Suppose we are in a state that putatively follows liberal democratic ideals. But the reality diverges deeply from those ideals. For example, perhaps the citizens do not treat one another with equal respect, of the sort governing conversation or free market exchange between equals. What will be needed to keep the state stable, to keep the citizens from fomenting dissent, is some way to hide the gap between illiberal reality and professed liberal ideals. For example, perhaps the liberal democratic ideals are used to refer to a political system that tolerates massive political inequality (as some think when "liberalism" is used to refer to neoliberalism). Propaganda in this context is more complicated. The liberal ideals themselves are propagandistically used.

The German political theorist Carl Schmitt argued in 1927 that "all political concepts, images, and terms have a polemical meaning. They are focused on a specific conflict and are bound to a concrete situation; the result (which manifests itself in war or revolution) is a friend-enemy grouping, and they turn into empty and ghostlike abstractions when this situation disappears." Schmitt thinks that political concepts like "constitutional state" and "economic planning" only have a polemical meaning. In short, Schmitt thinks they are only ever used to motivate people to action, in a characteristically propagandistic way (for example, calling the Iraq War in 2003 "Operation Iraqi Freedom"). On Schmitt's view, the liberal democratic vocabulary, as with other political vocabulary, works like propaganda.

Schmitt's view is that the only use of political vocabulary is as propaganda, to bypass the rational will to "war or revolution." This view does not need to be accepted. We can still recognize that he is right that the liberal democratic vocabulary is *often* used propagandistically, in states whose practices fall too short of its ideals. It is not atypical to redefine "democracy" so that it does not include equal respect, but rather market efficiency. It is not atypical to call something that is not a war for freedom at all a "war for freedom." This is the kind of propaganda I want to focus on in this book. To say that the democratic concepts can be propagandistically used is not to say that they cannot also be used straightforwardly. But I speculate that it is the propagandistic use of the liberal democratic vocabulary that is responsible for many cases in which we do not notice gaps between ideals and reality.

The classical conception of propaganda and the conception of propaganda as biased speech are too rough to help us understand the distinctive nature of the propagandistic use of political concepts. We began this chapter with a discussion of Samuel P. Huntington's call for claims of "expertise, seniority, and experience" as a way to override democratic claims. This is not something we can explain with Lippmann's characterization. Huntington is calling for the language of objective science to be strategically used. In particular, he is calling for people to claim expertise over matters of value, with the result that citizens defer their autonomous judgment to these so-called experts. This is to use an attractive and admirable ideal, the ideal of objectivity, in a nonobjective way, a way that tends to undermine trust in objectivity. We need a narrower characterization of propaganda that comes closer to this.

How could one grow up naively into adulthood in a state that professes to follow liberal democratic ideals, but in which there is overwhelmingly illiberal practice? To maintain stability, the propagandistic use of the liberal democratic ideals will be required to cover up the significant gap between ideals and reality. This is the species of propaganda that centrally concerns me in this book, the kind that characteristically masks the gap between the given ideal and reality by the propagandistic use of that very ideal. Failures of democracy could be hidden by the propagandistic use of the very vocabulary of liberalism.

This kind of propaganda is what one may think of as masking propaganda. But there are forms of propaganda that are not masking. Propaganda that extols the virtue of Aryanism is, for example, not of the form that centrally interests me. But we can obtain a general conception of propaganda, of the kind that is most interesting and important and of the more obvious kind, by reflecting on the notion of an ideal. Propaganda in the sense of this book essentially exploits an *ideal*. The ideal can be aesthetic, health-related, economic, or political. *Advertising* is a kind of propaganda that typically exploits an aesthetic ideal or an ideal of health. Given my focus in this book, I will concentrate on political ideals. I will characterize propaganda using political ideals, bearing in mind that the characterization is meant to be general across different domains.

Different political systems are characterized by distinct political ideals. For example, a monarchy involves a political ideal of obedience to authority, in the typical example, a monarch, such as a king or a queen or a pharaoh. Liberal democracy, as we have seen, centrally involves the political ideals of liberty and equality.

The home of the study of political propaganda generally is in its application to *public political discourse*. The nature of public political discourse depends upon the political system. In a monarchy, public political discourse is, for example, pronouncements by a king, queen, or pharaoh. In a democracy, public political discourse is either in political debate in elections, between representatives in the chambers of government seeking to pass policy (such as Congress and the Senate), and in media discussions of either. Public political discourse is best thought of in contrast to the discourse of private citizens in their homes. It is discourse that is in some sense official, and that takes place in the contexts that are official contexts of public political claims, which depend on the political system in question.

I am now ready to introduce my proposed characterizations of the various species of propaganda. The two basic kinds of propaganda that I initially distinguish are structurally distinct, and together exhaust the category of propaganda as I characterize it. I am interested in this book in political propaganda, so I will restrict my attention to that category.

The essence of political propaganda on my approach is that it is a kind of speech that fundamentally involves political, economic, aesthetic, or rational ideals, mobilized for a political purpose. Propaganda is in the service of either *supporting* or *eroding* ideals. The first distinction between kinds of propaganda has to do with whether or not it erodes or supports the ideals it appears to embody. This is the distinction between *supporting* and *undermining* propaganda.

Supporting Propaganda: A contribution to public discourse that is presented as an embodiment of certain ideals, yet is of a kind that tends to increase the realization of those very ideals by either emotional or other nonrational means.

Undermining Propaganda: A contribution to public discourse that is presented as an embodiment of certain ideals, yet is of a kind that tends to erode those very ideals.[24]

Undermining propaganda involves a kind of contradiction between ideal and goal. It's an argument that appeals to an ideal to draw support, in the service of a goal that tends to erode the realization of that ideal.

I will restrict attention for the moment to propaganda that supports or undermines a *political* ideal (where this is broadly construed). Supporting propaganda can be used in the service of worthy goals, neutral goals, or unworthy goals. The goal of supporting propaganda is to increase the realization of a political ideal. It does so not by directly providing a reason that increases the probability of the truth or virtue of the political ideal. It does so indirectly by seeking to overload various affective capacities, such as nostalgia, sentiment, or fear. These emotional effects can lead to the discovery of reasons, reasons that in turn will support the political ideal in a characteristically rational way. But supporting propaganda does not support the goal that helps to realize the ideal via beliefs that appeal solely to what Immanuel Kant calls *the rational will*: the faculty rational beings have of acting in accordance with rational law.[25] Supporting propaganda is intended to close off possibilities and move emotion behind a goal that furthers an explicitly provided ideal.

The definition I have given of undermining propaganda is very specific. It requires the call to action to be one that runs counter to the very political ideal it is explicitly represented as embodying. Daniel Putnam (in personal correspondence) suggested to me a more expansive characterization of propaganda, according to which one political ideal is being deployed to wear down another political ideal held within the same political system. Consider, for example, the political ideal of *liberty*. This is a political ideal of the United States. Another political ideal of the United States is *opportunity*. This is also a political ideal of the United States. One might characterize as an instance of propaganda an appeal to liberty in the service of wearing down the political ideal of opportunity (say, an appeal to cut taxes because of economic liberties, the consequence of which is to reduce opportunity for impoverished citizens). This would not be an instance of supporting propaganda according to the characterization I have given. Here is a more inclusive characterization of undermining propaganda according to which it does count as undermining propaganda:

> *Undermining Propaganda$_2$*: A contribution to public discourse that is presented as an embodiment of certain political ideals, but is of a kind that tends to erode a political ideal that belongs in the same family.

My worry with this more inclusive characterization is that it threatens to overgeneralize. Sometimes political ideals simply *do* conflict; in fact, many hold that there is such a conflict between liberty and equality. My concern with Putnam's proposed definition is that it will entail that what are, in fact, examples of genuine conflict between political ideals are misclassified as undermining propaganda.

The characterizations of propaganda I have given are characterizations of what it is for contributions, paradigmatically utterances or images, to be propaganda. But we also speak of newspapers and schools as being *vehicles of propaganda*. It is tempting to define a vehicle of propaganda as follows:

> *Vehicle for the Production of Propaganda*: A site or mechanism for the production of propaganda.

A media source or a school can be a vehicle of propaganda, even though it never produces actual instances of propaganda. It can, for example, be a vehicle of propaganda in virtue of *withholding* crucial information that, by its nature, it is supposed to provide. A news station that represents itself as providing all the relevant news for political decision making is, intuitively, a vehicle of propaganda if it regularly withholds highly relevant news for political decision making. A school is a vehicle for propaganda if it represents itself as providing all the relevant information for being an informed citizen, yet regularly withholds information for being an informed citizen. These are the kinds of vehicles of propaganda we should expect to find in liberal democracies. Characterizing vehicles of propaganda in this sense is therefore of crucial importance to the aims of this book.

Here is the characterization of a sense of a vehicle of propaganda that is perhaps more useful for theorizing about propaganda in liberal democracy:

> *Vehicle of Propaganda*: An institution that represents itself as defined by a certain political ideal, yet whose practice tends to undermine the realization of that ideal.

A school in a liberal democracy is intended to make its students into informed citizens who have the information necessary for informed participation in political deliberation. Suppose the school intentionally leaves out certain information, for example, about the country's systematic injustice toward certain groups. The students it produces therefore have incomplete information, but believe the information to be complete. The school therefore undermines the ideal of having fully informed citizens. A school that produces partially informed citizens who believe they are fully informed is a vehicle of propaganda, *even if it never produces any actual propagandistic claims*. Similarly, if a television news station or newspaper presents itself as reporting all relevant news for political decision making in a country, yet withholds crucial information for decision making, it too is a vehicle of propaganda, even if it never produces any actual propagandistic utterances. It is a vehicle of propaganda in virtue of undermining the political ideal it represents itself as embodying, that of fully informing its audience.[26]

I have now characterized two different types of propaganda, as well as two ways in which institutions can serve as mechanisms for the production of propaganda. My topic in this book is political propaganda, propaganda that exploits political ideals, rather than other kinds of ideals. But many forms of *advertising* are obviously cases of propaganda and count as such according to the characterization I have given. An advertisement that uses, for example, the ideal of good health in the service of selling a product that undermines health is propaganda and counts as such according to my characterization. For example, an advertisement that uses pictures of healthy rock climbers to sell an unhealthy beverage or food item uses the ideal of good health in the service of a goal that can be easily seen to undermine it. So many advertisements simply are instances of propaganda.

However, another class of advertisements seeks to associate a goal with an ideal that is simply *irrelevant* to that ideal. For example, advertisements standardly use aesthetic ideals to promote a product, possession of which is irrelevant to the further realization of that aesthetic ideal. An advertisement that suggests that purchasing a certain kind of car will make one more attractive is an example of this. If we bear in mind that many things we would call "advertisements" are straightforwardly instances of propaganda, it is still useful to isolate a theoretical category of advertising that captures this class of advertisements:

> *Advertising*: A contribution to public discourse that is presented as an embodiment of certain ideals, but in the service of a goal that is irrelevant to those very ideals.

Commercial advertising is an attempt to attach possession of the product advertised to an attractive ideal, when possessing that product is in the normal case irrelevant to achieving that ideal. Effective advertisement exploits flawed ideology that connects, for example, material possessions to aesthetic worth.

Undermining propaganda by its nature undermines a political ideal. It undermines a political ideal by using it to communicate a message that is inconsistent with it. As I will explain below, it is able to achieve the task by exploiting already existing *flawed ideological belief*, and even contributing to the formation of such belief. *It is flawed ideological belief that masks the contradictions of undermining propaganda.*

Flawed ideological belief masks the contradictions of undermining propaganda by erecting difficult epistemic obstacles to recognizing tendencies of goals to misalign with certain ideals: for example, obstructions to understanding liberal democratic concepts and what they entail. In chapters 5 and 6, the chapters on ideology, we will investigate the nature of these epistemic obstacles, and explain why they are so difficult to surmount.

Undermining propaganda is thus *far more complicated* than supporting propaganda. Judging the moral as well as the political acceptability of an instance of undermining propaganda is correspondingly a vexed and complex matter. But there are many other facts at play in evaluating the acceptability of a use of undermining propaganda. We can, after all, evaluate morally and politically the *means* by which someone seeks to achieve a goal. We must not ignore the possibility that undermining propaganda is a democratically unacceptable *means*, even in cases in which the message or goal is worthy (or the political ideal being undermined is unworthy).

Immanuel Kant famously argued that lying was "the greatest violation of man's duty to himself."[27] Kant rejected even lying for a noble purpose, categorically rejecting the spread of untruthfulness into relationships between persons. I have argued that propaganda can be both sincere and true. Nevertheless, insofar as propaganda of either variety is a method to bypass the rational will of others in the service of some goal, the Kantian would regard propaganda in either sense as a moral violation. In the Kantian sense, propaganda, regardless of goals, is not morally acceptable. The ethical basis of Kantian philosophy has an undeniable purchase on our intuitive moral judgments, and this is no doubt the source of the sense that propaganda, regardless of its goal, is morally problematic. For Kant, the rational will is minimally one that operates independently of alien causes and is subject to rational principles. But propaganda runs counter to rational principles. Insofar as a form of propaganda is a kind of manipulation of rational beings toward an end without engaging their rational will, it is a kind of deception.[28]

I do not here presuppose a Kantian theory of morality. But even prescinding from a moral evaluation of propaganda as such, one must worry that most arguments that employ undermining propaganda are democratically suspect.

Let's now look at some examples of supporting and undermining propaganda. Examples of supporting propaganda are simple to provide. One example of supporting propaganda is the use of a country's flag, or the appeal to a romantic vision of the country's history, to strengthen patriotism. A second example is delivering a very frightening public health warning to raise excessive fears about (for example) smoking, with the goal of increasing public health by the use of exaggerated fear. A third example is appealing to past wrongs against a group to strengthen ethnic pride and self-identification. For example, Slobodan Milosevic, the former president of Serbia, regularly appealed to the defeat of Serbians in the Battle of Kosovo to instill a sense of historical grievance in those of Serbian ethnicity, thereby strengthening their ethnic identification.

I have said that propaganda is invariably democratically problematic. As will emerge in the next chapter, there is a kind of unproblematic and indeed necessary form of propaganda. The reason it is necessary is that it is necessary to employ when there are undemocratic features of a state that need to be addressed. So it is not itself part of democratic deliberation, properly conceived. But there are certain examples of supporting propaganda that are perfectly acceptable in a democracy. For example, cigarette packs in many democratic countries carry stark warnings, such as "cigarettes kill." These are clearly intended to overwhelm affective capacities to further the realization of ideals, in this case, the ideal of health. But propagandistic warning labels on cigarettes seem democratically acceptable, in a way that Milosevic's propaganda is not. What is the difference?

We can think of a ministry of health as tasked to look out for the physical health of a democratic nation when its citizens do not have time to do the relevant research. In a sense, therefore, we task the ministry of health with giving us warnings that will convey a message that will have the effect of doing all the work of informing us about the relevant health issue. In the case of warning labels on cigarette packs, presumably the idea is that we have tacitly granted our permission to the ministry of health to take such steps. If we have not tacitly granted our permission in this manner, then such warning labels are democratically problematic.[29]

Let us now turn to some basic examples of undermining propaganda. Here is the first. Carl Hart discusses stumbling across explicit racist ideology surrounding Blacks and cocaine, in the early part of the twentieth century. He cites the following passage from 1914, by a medical doctor in the *New York Times*, expressing the view that Blacks have an exceptional reaction to that drug:

> Most of the negroes are poor, illiterate, and shiftless . . . Once the negro has formed the habit he is irreclaimable. The only method to keep him away from the drug is by imprisoning him. And this is merely palliative treatment, for he returns to the drug habit when realized.[30]

Crack cocaine is a degraded form of the drug favored by wealthy elite in cities. Yet during the "drug war" in the 1980s and 1990s, politicians successfully argued for 100–1 sentencing disparities between the degraded form that urban Blacks could afford and the purer version favored by wealthy whites. Hart persuasively argues that it is this flawed ideology, so explicit in the early part of the twentieth century, which operated tacitly during the worst days of the "drug war," when politicians convinced citizens that these sentencing disparities were consistent with law and order. The flawed ideology of Black exceptionalism with regard to reactions to drugs masks the contradiction between the attractive ideal of law and order, or justice, and the otherwise obviously unjust sentencing disparities between the degraded version of the substance used by poor Blacks and the purer version favored by wealthy Whites. The goal of establishing the sentencing disparities is not consistent with law and order, but the ideal used in the service of that goal is law and order.

Here is a second example of undermining propaganda. According to James Hoggan, in his book *Climate Cover-Up*, the American Petroleum Institute created a team to assemble a "Global Climate Change Communication Action Plan." According to Hoggan, "The document plainly states that its purpose is to convince the public, through the media, that climate science is awash in uncertainty."[31] Stephen Milloy was a founding member of that team. Hoggan reports that Milloy now appears on Fox News as a "junk science expert." Milloy has "spent his entire career in public relations and lobbying, taking money from companies that include Exxon, Philip Morris, The Edison Electric Institute, the International Food Additives Council, and Monsanto in return for his work declaring environmental concerns to be 'junk science.'"[32] Milloy's assertions are presented as embodying the ideals of scientific objectivity. However, anyone not convinced by the ideology of the corporate-funded anti–climate science movement would recognize that they clearly conflict with the ideals of scientific objectivity.[33]

Here is a third example of undermining propaganda. A poster from the Cultural Revolution in China states: "毛主席的无产阶级革命胜利万岁!" Translated literally, it means "Chairman Mao's proletariat revolution triumphs ten thousand years!" Slightly more loosely, "Let Chairman Mao's proletariat revolution triumph forever!" Here are the literal correspondences between the phrases:

毛主席的	Chairman Mao's
无产阶级	Proletariat
革命	Revolution
胜利	Triumph
万岁	Ten thousand years; metaphorically: forever

The phrase that is problematic is "万岁," or, literally, "ten thousand years." For thousands of years it was used mainly in the sentence "皇帝万岁万岁万万岁!," which citizens would shout toward the emperor. Literally, it says, "Emperor ten thousand years [repetition ignored here]," meaning of course, "Long live the emperor!" The word "万岁" is directly associated with the long rule of an emperor. Here is what is happening. The political ideal of a monarchy is obedience to authority. Revolution is being taken as the embodiment of obedience to authority. But it is effective because of the existence of a flawed ideology connecting revolution to the will of a state that makes decisions on one's behalf. Those who possess this flawed ideology would not see the clear contradiction between revolution and obedience to authority.

Here is a fourth example. In the US Supreme Court decision *Citizens United v. Federal Election Commission*, written in 2010, the US Supreme Court decided that the rights in the US Constitution extended to corporations. The Court presented the decision as if extending free speech and other rights to corporations was like the Civil Rights Act, namely, an extension of rights to hitherto unrecognized persons. It was therefore presented as an embodiment of the principles of democracy. Yet the unlimited corporate donations that Citizens United gave rise to are themselves an existential threat to democracy, promising to hand over the mechanism of government to corporations that do the bulk of funding for political campaigns.[34]

Here is a fifth example. In the United States, some Christian televangelists have promoted what has come to be known as "the Prosperity Gospel." According to this doctrine, Jesus shows his favor by dispensing wealth. Accepting Jesus is the way to acquire prosperity. If one wants prosperity, one should accept the Christian faith. Thus, the goal of prosperity is advanced as an embodiment of Christian faith. Yet Jesus is as clear as possible that this could not be correct. In the Gospel of Matthew, Jesus makes clear that it is the poor and persecuted who are blessed, not the wealthy. Only by accepting a flawed ideology linking the materialist values of capitalism to the doctrines of Christianity could one fail to see the obvious inconsistency between the doctrines espoused by Jesus and the goal of prosperity.

Here is a sixth example. In the National Socialist press, the Jews were described as a public health threat, as in Hitler's claim that "Jews are the Black Death." The claim that "Jews are the Black Death" is clearly a public health alert. It makes an assertion that purports to be true and provides a genuine reason that reasonable people must take into account. People in the grip of a flawed anti-Semitic ideology delivered the claim sincerely. However, many Germans at the time in fact were Jewish. The public health threat was inconsistent with the health of a group of citizens of that country. So the content of the claim was clearly inconsistent with the political ideals it represented itself as embodying.[35]

Here is a seventh example. In 1935, W.E.B. Du Bois published the book *Black Reconstruction in America: 1860–1880*. In it, Du Bois challenges the then prevailing view, exemplified by the "Columbia School" of historians, John Burgess and William Dunning, that the end of Reconstruction was brought about by incapacity of freed Black citizens to govern themselves. Du Bois's alternative account of the failure of Reconstruction is that white economic elites exploited the racism of poor whites to prevent poor whites and newly freed Blacks from joining together in a labor movement with unified class interests. Though it took several decades, the accuracy of Du Bois's account of why Reconstruction came to an end has long since been widely acknowledged. At the time, Du Bois's correct reading was disregarded, in favor of a manifestly racist interpretation. In the final chapter of the book, Du Bois argues that Burgess and Dunning's view undermines history, by twisting its ideals of truth and narrative accuracy to the service of dominance and power. The chapter is called in "The Propaganda of History," and in it he writes:

> If history is going to be scientific, if the record of human action is going to be set down with that accuracy and faithfulness of detail which will allow its use as a measuring rod and guidepost for the future of nations, there must be set some standards of ethics in research and interpretation.
>
> If, on the other hand, we are going to use history for our pleasure and amusement, for inflating our national ego, and giving us a false but pleasurable sense of accomplishment, then we must give up the idea of history either as a science or as an art using the results of science, and admit frankly that we are using a version of historical fact in order to influence and educate the new generation along the way we wish.[36]

Du Bois here criticizes Burgess and Dunning, and white history of the Reconstruction more generally, as propaganda. It is propaganda, because it appeals to the ideals of history in the service of goals, power, and interest, which undermine the ideals of truth and science.

The seven examples of undermining propaganda I have given are uniformly negative. It is worthwhile to look at examples of undermining propaganda that targets a problematic ideal. In his paper "Criteria of Negro Art" from 1926, Du Bois calls on the Black artist to engage in propaganda to represent the humanity and value of her people. Yet he argues that the Black artist cannot simply present the case for Black humanity directly:

> Suppose you were to write a story and put in it the kind of people you know and like and imagine. You might get it published and you might not. And the "might not" is still far bigger than the "might." The white publishers catering to white folk would say, "It is not interesting"—to white folk, naturally not. They want Uncle Toms, Topsies, good "darkies" and clowns.[37]

Du Bois recognizes that simply directly appealing to whites by showing them the Black perspective will not work. An indirect method is required to stir white interest, one that appeals "to white folk," yet will somehow call attention to the Black perspective. Du Bois is calling for a certain kind of undermining propaganda.

According to the musicologist Ingrid Monson's analysis of John Coltrane's version of "My Favorite Things," a popular Christmas song from that iconic cinematic celebration of whiteness, *The Sound of Music*, is a way of taking a white aesthetic ideal and using it to represent the Black American voice and experience.[38] If so, it is an example of Du Bois's appeal. Monson writes:

> [Coltrane's] transformation of "My Favorite Things," or what Gates would term signification upon the tune, inverts the piece on nearly every level. It makes the interludes, not the verse, the subject of the performance; it transforms waltz time into a polyrhythmically textured six-feel; and it transforms a sentimental, optimistic lyric into a vehicle for a more brooding improvisational exploration. Since the lyrics would have been on the sheet music the song plugger brought to the quartet, Coltrane would have been well aware of the emphasis on white things in the lyric—girls in white dresses, snowflakes on eyelashes, silver white winters, cream-colored ponies. In 1960—a year of tremendous escalation in the Civil Rights movement and a time of growing politicization of the jazz community—there was certainly the possibility that Coltrane looked upon the lyrics with an ironic eye.[39]

Monson's persuasive analysis of Coltrane's "My Favorite Things" represents it as an exemplar of Du Bois's call. Coltrane takes the song and gives it a powerful subversive twist, presenting a white aesthetic ideal in a fashion that subverts it to reveal Black experience and Black identity.[40]

After the killing of Michael Brown in Ferguson, Missouri, in the summer of 2014, the singer Lauryn Hill released a song she had been playing live called "Black Rage." The song is also a version of "My Favorite Things." "My Favorite Things" contains lines like "cream-colored ponies and crisp apple strudels"; Lauryn Hill's version contains lines like "rapings and beatings and suffering that worsens." Whether or not Coltrane intended his version of "My Favorite Things" to be propaganda in the sense of Du Bois's call in "Criteria of Negro Art," it is undeniable that Lauryn Hill explicitly intended it to be so. A song extolling favorite things that are racially and culturally white but assumed to be universal is used to explain the damaging consequences on Blacks of the racial ideology in which that aesthetic ideal is embedded.

Du Bois does not restrict his call to employ propaganda to impel whites to recognize the perspectives of Black citizens to the aesthetic realm. The rhetorical structure Du Bois describes in "Criteria of Negro Art" has had influence in diverse areas of intellectual production. A good exemplar in the field of philosophy is Tommie Shelby's paper "Justice, Deviance, and the Dark Ghetto," published in 2007. The topic of the paper is the moral criticisms of Black inner-city "ghetto" youth, and it explains what constitutes certain forms of "deviance," namely, "crime, refusing to work in legitimate jobs, and having contempt for authority."[41] In short, the paper concerns the ideal of obedience to authority and the pursuit of legitimate legal work, taken unrestrictedly. The paper focuses on the forms of deviance involved in deviating from these ideals. But in focusing on those forms of deviance, it ends up demonstrating that the unrestricted form of the ideal must be rejected.

The paper is presented as an attempt to justify a white ideology that we are in conditions of justice, and so the ideals of
obedience to authority and pursuit of legitimate work can be
exceptionless. However, what the paper in fact does is *undermine* the exceptionless ideal, by rejecting the presupposition
that we are in a just state; the conditions of the dark ghetto
represent a "failure of reciprocity." So, for example, Black refusal to take menial jobs is not a form of deviant "laziness,"
but a rejection of an unjust social order. This is an example
of the structure urged by Du Bois. Shelby's paper targets the
exceptionless generalization that one should be obedient to
authority and pursue legitimate work. It seems at first to rely
on that generalization, and pursue the question of how it is to
be applied. Shelby's discussion however eventually reveals that
it is false by rejecting the idealizing presupposition, using the
example of the unjust conditions in "the dark ghetto."

Du Bois's call for propaganda is designed to deal with situations in which a dominant group is suffering under a flawed
ideology that leads them to embrace a problematic ideal, or a
problematic conception of an ordinary ideal. It is hard to see
how direct challenges to the ideals will be effective. Du Bois's
proposal is to wrap challenges to the ideal in the tempting vocabulary of the ideal itself. It is a novel and powerful rhetorical
suggestion.[42]

There are hard cases that may not appear to fit the model
I have sketched. Liberalism is a view in political philosophy
that places the ideals of autonomy and equality above all others. There are, however, political views that are represented as
embodying liberalism yet interpret some of these ideals in a
problematically narrow way. For example, what we might call
neoliberalism treats competitive markets as the way all goods
should be allocated (I make no claim to accuracy about the
description of any preexisting view here). One might naturally think, in the absence of a theoretical argument, that an
argument for neoliberalism that, for example, appeals to the
founding fathers' conception of liberalism to justify the view

that markets are the only legitimate way to divide goods that is consistent with liberty is a deformation or undermining of the ideals of liberalism in a way that is characteristic of undermining propaganda. Yet market exchanges *are* included in the scope of liberal autonomy. Markets are a legitimate means of dividing up some goods, and dividing some goods up in this way is allowed by any version of liberalism. So one might worry that arguments for neoliberalism that are framed as defenses of classical liberalism do not count as propaganda, because markets are not inconsistent with the domain of liberal freedom.

Let's assume that there is no persuasive argument that market exchange is central to liberalism. If so, then representing, for example, the liberalism of the founding fathers of the United States as the view that every division of goods must be a market exchange does count as undermining propaganda. It counts as undermining propaganda because it is no part of the liberalism of James Madison, for example, that markets possess this universal domain. So on the assumption that there is no persuasive argument privileging market exchange in this way, arguments for neoliberalism that frame it as the expression of the liberalism of (for example) the founders of the United States are propagandistic.

There are certain traditional views of liberalism that privilege market exchange. But it is nevertheless undermining propaganda to present even these views as the view that what *now* passes for market exchange in the United States is this kind of liberalism, for example, as the kind of view of liberalism espoused by Adam Smith in *The Wealth of Nations*. Smith has a very particular conception of market exchange, one connected to *political equality*.[43] But the system of market exchange prevalent in the United States is one that has systematically barred certain minorities from participation in contracts, for example, Blacks from fair mortgages.[44] It also typically involves unfair exchanges between rich and poor. If so, it is undermining propaganda to represent the liberalism of Adam Smith as connected to market exchange as historically practiced in the United States. Market exchange as historically practiced in the United States does not have the connection to political equality, fair exchange between equals that is at the heart of traditional conceptions of liberalism that emphasize market exchange.

Now that we have drawn the distinction between supporting and undermining propaganda, it is simple to characterize the kind of propaganda that is *most* threatening to liberal democracy. The kind of propaganda that is most threatening to liberal democracy is a species of undermining propaganda we may call *demagoguery*. Demagoguery is propaganda in the service of unworthy political ideals. What counts as demagoguery therefore depends on moral and political facts. Demagoguery can come in the form of strengthening unworthy political ideals. For example, Leni Riefenstahl's depiction of German athletes in her film *Olympia* from 1938 is a glorification of the superiority of the Teutonic race. But a different kind of demagoguery will be of central interest in this book: demagoguery that takes the form of undermining propaganda that is presented as embodying *worthy political ideals*.

Of course, it is a matter of contestation which political ideals are worthy. A fascist does not find the political ideals of liberal democracy worthy. However, our concern in this book is with the problem propaganda raises for liberal democracy. It is therefore safe to assume for the purposes of this book that the liberal democratic ideals of liberty, humanity, equality, and objective reason are worthy ideals. In the case of a liberal democratic state, demagogic speech includes speech that uses liberal democratic ideals in the service of undermining these ideals.

An obvious example of demagoguery in a liberal democratic state is occurring at the present time, during the writing of this book, in the United States. The American Republican Party does not draw votes from Black and Hispanic voters. It has engaged in a multiyear, concerted, and completely successful effort to appeal to the fear of voter impersonation to justify harsh voter registration laws that effectively disenfranchise Black and Hispanic voters. In 2012, a news organization undertook an "exhaustive public records search," involving "thousands of requests to elections officers in all fifty states, asking for every case of fraudulent activity including registration fraud, absentee ballot fraud, vote buying, false election counts, campaign fraud, casting an ineligible vote, voting twice, voter impersonation fraud, and intimidation."[45] The study covered a twelve-year period between 2000 and 2012 and found exactly ten cases of voter impersonation out of 146 million registered voters during that time. (In that twelve-year period, the study uncovered just over two thousand cases of total election fraud.) Yet, thirty-seven states as of 2012 had implemented or were considering implementing tough voter ID laws out of the fear of voter impersonation. In the state of Pennsylvania alone, 758,000 voters lacked proper identification. The clearest possible example of propaganda is therefore the use of ideals like "one man, one vote," together with the appeal to voter fraud, to motivate restrictive voter ID laws.

Undermining demagoguery is a kind of undermining propaganda. The full characterization is therefore:

> *Undermining Demagoguery*: A contribution to public discourse that is presented as an embodiment of a worthy political, economic, or rational ideal, but is in the service of a goal that tends to undermine that very ideal.[46]

Those in the grip of a flawed ideology often *unknowingly* engage in demagoguery. A flawed ideology will lead someone to fail to recognize tension between the goal that an argument she provides serves and the political ideals it employs in that service. Her problematic ideology may in fact prevent her from seeing that she is engaged in demagoguery, even when she is. An audience who shares the speaker's flawed ideology would not recognize that the message is demagogic. But this is of course one reason why undermining demagoguery is so insidious.

Of course, the characterization of demagoguery I have provided is obviously consistent, as any characterization of demagoguery must be, with *insincere* attempts at communication being demagogic as well. The insincere demagogue seeks to exploit flawed ideology that prevents the audience from recognizing the tension between the desired goal of the communicative act and the political ideal it is presented as embodying. Someone who hates Muslims may know perfectly well that American Muslims are not dangerous. They may nonetheless insincerely appeal to the rule of law in advancing a proposal to spy on or imprison American Muslims. One way to do so is to elicit irrational fear about fellow Muslim citizens, by invocation of a flawed ideology that includes the belief that Muslims are terrorists and therefore a public safety menace. The resulting fear may blind citizens to the fact that imprisoning and spying on Muslim citizens in fact violates the rule of law. Alternatively, someone may try to elicit love of country as a way of blinding rationality (propaganda does not obviously correlate with what one may think of as negative emotions).

According to my characterization of undermining demagoguery, its effects are to cut off options that rationally should be considered (for example, that generally Muslims aren't terrorists) to motivate an action that is not consistent with the political ideal that it is advanced as furthering. In this sense, it has similar effects to the model of propaganda as biased speech. But undermining propaganda crucially involves appeal to a cherished ideal, usually a political ideal, which it then in fact tends to undermine. Its deviousness is due to the fact that it is masked as the very political ideal its consequences threaten to erode. The masking need not be, and in fact is often not, intentional; when it is not intentional, what does the masking is a *flawed ideology*, in the sense I will explain in chapters 5 and 6.

In many cases of undermining propaganda, the attempt of the contribution will be to make it the case, by the very act of making the contribution, that the political ideal should be reinterpreted to be consistent with the desired goal. If a political ideal must be reinterpreted to fit the goal that it is being used to advance, what that simply means is that the goal is not consistent with the original meaning of the political ideal. The characterization I have given explains why propaganda of the indirect sort is often in the service of an attempt to *alter* the meaning of the political ideal. That is because the original meaning of the political ideal is rationally inconsistent with the goal it is being invoked to motivate.[47]

Cases in which the producer of undermining propaganda is sincere—that is, does not realize that she is delivering propaganda—will be ones in which the question of whether or not the goal is consistent with the political ideal is itself a contested political issue. Accusations of propaganda will therefore often be sincerely viewed as politically motivated. This has consequences for the *political utility* of a philosophical account of the nature of propaganda of the sort I here provide.

In "Oppressions," the philosopher Sally Haslanger gives a characterization of oppression, in other words, a metaphysical account of what oppression is.[48] The question she is interested in answering is "not just who is oppressed, but what groups are oppressed *as such*." Her focus is on giving an account of the conditions under which an institution oppresses Fs as such, meaning as a consequence of their Fness. So, for example, she discusses the example of whether Chicago's child welfare policy oppresses Blacks *as Blacks*. Her account of the conditions under which an institution oppresses a group as such in a context appeals to the notion of *being F being unjustly disadvantaging in context C*. So we need to know whether being Black in Chicago in the 1990s is unjustly disadvantaging to know whether the child welfare policies in Chicago oppressed Blacks as such. Toward the end of her chapter, Haslanger poses, and then addresses, the following objection to her project in the chapter:

> One might object, however, that the account I've offered is not helpful, for whether group membership is relevant in

explaining an injustice will always be a matter of controversy. In short, the account does not help us resolve the very disagreements that gave us reason to develop an account of group oppression in the first place.[49]

A precisely analogous objection arises to my project in this chapter, to give an account of the conditions under which a contribution to public reason is propagandistic. There will be many cases in which it is a contested political issue whether or not the goal is of a kind that tends to undermine the political ideal. Consider the expression "job creator," used in the American political context as a description of persons with great wealth. The goal of the introduction of the expression "job creator" was to defend cutting the taxes of wealthy Americans. The expression appeals to the economic ideal of a thriving economy for all citizens. The reason it is effective is because of the widely held belief that the wealthy use their money to start small businesses. The politicians, or political operatives, who introduced the expression "job creator" were financially supported by wealthy campaign donors. So there is reason to believe that they are either insincere or suffering from flawed ideological beliefs. But it does seem that some politicians do in fact believe that the wealthy use their money in just this way, rather than, say, investing in private equity or the stock market. It is a contested political issue whether the economic ideal of a thriving economy for all is rationally well served, or in fact undermined, by cutting taxes on the very wealthy. In such cases, my account of propaganda will not help us resolve whether or not the relevant claims or expressions are propagandistic.

The straightforward answer to the objection is that it miscasts the project of giving a metaphysical account of a political kind. As Haslanger writes, "[T]he point of this discussion has not been to offer an *epistemic* method or criterion for distinguishing oppression (or group oppression) from other rights and wrongs."[50] Mutatis mutandis for this chapter's discussion of propaganda. But surely there remains a lingering concern.

What is then the point of producing a metaphysical account of fundamental political kinds, when such accounts cannot play a central role in resolving the relevant political debates? What is the political utility of a metaphysics of the political?

There is political utility to my account of propaganda, because its subject matter is *arguments* of a certain kind. For example, someone who argues that the current economic system in the United States lives up to Adam Smith's ideals is making a factual claim about Adam Smith's political philosophy. Someone who appeals to the liberalism of James Madison or Thomas Jefferson is making a factual claim about an author's intent. There are multiple ways to construe the intents of these authors. We know these authors took themselves to be addressing only citizenship for white men. But it is legitimate to suspect that they saw the eventuality predicted by Plato, that the concepts they discussed would lead to more general equality. Therefore, we now take them to be making more universal claims. Regardless, it is still the case that there were certain political systems they envisaged when they spoke of democracy, freedom, and the kind of equal respect presupposed by contracts in a free market. We can evaluate whether current realities fit the models of these authors, when arguments appeal to their authority (for example, "the wisdom of the Founding Fathers of the United States"). If the authority of these authors is used, in appeals to the ideals they promoted, for purposes that tend to undermine those ideals, the arguments are propagandistic.

This is not to deny that many cases of propaganda may never in fact be recognized as such. Indeed, there may be cases of demagoguery that we cannot ever know are demagoguery. It might be important for reflection and decision making about our life plans to be clear about such possibilities. But we need a sense of what propaganda is, by its nature, to formulate such possibilities. Here we have a need for a metaphysical account of the sort I have provided.

Let us suppose for the sake of argument that it is unknowable whether the central claims of the Catholic Church are true. The Church has a ministry of propaganda; indeed, the term "propaganda" derives from it. The Sacred Congregation *de Propaganda Fide* is tasked with spreading Catholicism, in the name of truth, and its head has come to be known as "the Red Pope." Suppose that the doctrines of Catholicism are true. Then the productions of The Sacred Congregation *de Propaganda Fide* are not demagoguery, but rather supporting propaganda. They embody truth and, by appealing to emotion, lead to the spread of true belief. Setting up Catholic schools in colonized countries, together with economic systems that require going to such schools and social practices that essentially preclude followers of native religions from positions of economic power, is not demagoguery, though it may be wrong for other reasons having to do, for example, with permissible deviations from true belief.

Suppose for the sake of argument, however, that the doctrines of Catholicism are false, but we do not and indeed cannot know that they are false. Suppose that religious belief is (as David Hume argued) a kind of flawed ideology that is resistant in various ways to change. If so, then the productions of The Sacred Congregation *de Propaganda Fide* are demagogic. The massive effort to Christianize conquered colonies was not spreading truth, but was an act, many acts, of brutal cultural suppression of native cultures. Presumably, even Catholics admit that if the doctrines of Catholicism are false, then the productions of The Sacred Congregation *de Propaganda Fide* are demagoguery. We therefore have, in the example of the productions of The Sacred Congregation *de Propaganda Fide*, a clear example of the possibility of sincere claims by well-intentioned people that are nevertheless demagoguery. If the doctrines of Catholicism are false, then even if no one could come to know that they are false, the intuitive view is that the productions of The Sacred Congregation *de Propaganda Fide* are demagoguery, albeit forever to be recognized as such. Suppressing other belief systems in the name of truth, with the goal of instilling false belief systems in their place, is characteristically demagogic. So it is clearly possible for a sincere, well-intentioned person to engage in demagoguery unwittingly, and with no one ever recognizing it as demagoguery.

It is, as we have just seen, possible for there to be a case in which it is widely believed that a certain goal exemplifies a political ideal but is in fact, unbeknown to everyone, propaganda, because everyone is in the grip of a flawed ideology. If a demagogue is someone who is devoted to demagoguery, this means that many people who sincerely do not identify as demagogues, and even have the best intentions, are demagogues. This may seem problematic. A demagogue seems to be someone who has malicious intent.

There are two readings of "someone who is devoted to demagoguery." The first is that a demagogue is someone who is devoted to a practice *they think of as demagoguery*. The second is that a demagogue is someone who is devoted to a practice, and as it happens, that practice is a form of demagoguery (though the person may not be aware of it). The ordinary concept of a demagogue is the first, not the second.[51] Therefore, it is not the case that someone who regularly produces demagoguery, but fails to realize that it is demagoguery, is a demagogue.

Accusations of propaganda will often be contested, because there may be gaps, even excusable ones, between facts and our access to those facts. Structural features of our society might prevent us from accessing the facts that would help us determine whether or not an accusation of propaganda is true. This limits the political usefulness of the characterization of propaganda I provide, but it does not eliminate it. There are facts about what ideals demand, even in cases in which those ideals are not fully determinate.

Insofar as the facts are under dispute, so too will be many claims about what falls under the category of propaganda. Accusations of demagoguery in particular will invariably be political, because many people with flawed ideologies do not accept that their ideologies are flawed. Some charges of demagoguery will be intentionally strategic, and others will be taken to be intentionally strategic, even when they are not. But this book is about the nature of propaganda and propaganda generally, that is, about the *metaphysics* of propaganda. It is no part of my metaphysical claim about the nature of propaganda that every instance is, or even that most instances are, simple to recognize, or even *possible* to recognize. The example of the Catholic Church, under the hypothetical condition of the unknowable falsity of its central doctrines, makes it clear that this is the right result.

What good is a characterization of demagoguery if it does not allow us access to some kind of neutral stance from which to adjudicate claims of demagoguery? It is a fact about life that there is no neutral stance. We all have background beliefs that we bring to any deliberative engagement. One needs to assume many things simply in order to get on in the world, and even to navigate oneself to any supposed neutral stance. A great deal of what one assumes to be true will derive from one's ideology, in the sense I explain in chapters 5 and 6. One's ideology involves beliefs that are tightly connected to one's self-conception. One's ideological beliefs are correspondingly difficult to evaluate rationally. But this of course does not show that the beliefs are *false*, or not instances of knowledge.

The belief that the theory of evolution is a correct description of reality is connected tightly to my self-conception as a certain kind of thinker: a rational, cosmopolitan intellectual who trusts certain sources of evidence over others. I know this. But I also know that the theory of evolution is a correct description of reality. Knowing that I have a personal investment in evolution does not make me think I lack knowledge.[52] Similarly, the belief that Christ is the Savior might be closely connected to someone's identity, and they might know this about themselves. But they still believe that Christ is the Savior, and if Christ is the Savior, then their belief is true. I will argue that we all have ideological beliefs, which are simply beliefs with certain properties. It may be, I will argue, essential for creatures limited by time and memory to have beliefs with these properties. But beliefs with these properties, that is, ideological beliefs, can be true, they can be known, and they can be central to our best theoretical understanding. If a neutral stance means a stance without ideological belief, then the neutral stance is a myth.

It might be thought that my project in this book requires a neutral stance, a nonideological perspective. After all, I am engaged in the theory of ideology. That is, I am engaged in the project of theorizing about ideology, and that theorizing takes place in another theory, the theory of ideology. It might be thought that if ideological belief affects theorizing about ideology, then the theory described cannot be true, or cannot be known. But we have just seen that this thought is incorrect. Ideological beliefs, beliefs that have the properties I discuss in chapter 5, can be true, and they can be instances of knowledge.

It might be thought that the theory of ideology has ideology as its subject matter, and so cannot itself contain its subject matter. But this thought too is incorrect. The logician Alfred Tarski provides a proof of the soundness of the axioms of the calculus of classes in a metatheory.[33] But the reason the soundness proof works is that the meta-theory also has axioms that express those same principles. The meta-theory is not an attempt to provide a justification of the propositions expressed by axioms of the theory to someone who doubts them. Its task is different: it is to deliver important knowledge about the object theory. Similarly, the task of the theory of ideology is to yield important knowledge about ideology. Even if the theory of ideology is ideological, it can issue in knowledge. As in the metatheory for logic or set theory, a neutral stance is neither possible nor required.

The fact that there is no neutral stance cannot lead us to political paralysis, or to skepticism about political and moral reality. It is an error to try to evade the facts of our epistemic limitations by adopting metaphysical antirealism. We must come to terms with the fact of our limited perspective while occupying that very perspective. There is simply no other

option. Some charges of demagoguery will be obviously correct: for example, a European anti-Semitic political party's
charge that Jews are corrupting the social fabric of the nation,
or misplaced appeals to the authority of the work of various
political philosophers. Many charges of demagoguery will not
obviously be correct. The fact that many of the most interesting charges of demagoguery will be contested is due to a
variety of factors, from structural features of our society that
prevent us from acquiring the resources to resolve dispute, to
epistemic limitations that arise in the normal course of even
well-ordered societies. And even if the utility of resolving debates at the moment is maximally limited, we still require an
account of propaganda to understand what did happen or
what could happen politically.

The characterization of demagoguery I have given yields
a rough sense of how it operates. Demagoguery operates by
tending to erode a worthy political ideal it appears to exploit
in the service of a goal. We have explored one way in which it
erodes the political ideal that it appears to embody, namely, by
exploiting false beliefs derived from a flawed ideology. In chapter 4, I will argue that demagoguery can also contribute to the
formation of the very flawed ideological beliefs that mask its
demagogic nature. We can now also see the clear possibility of
various kinds of nondemagogic propaganda. Supporting propaganda in the service of a worthy political ideal is one species
of nondemagogic propaganda. It helps to achieve the political
ideal it appears to embody, either by appeal to emotion or via
the kind of false beliefs derived from a flawed ideology.

An example of nondemagogic propaganda of this latter
sort is explicitly nationalist rhetoric in the service of helping
the physical environment of the country. A representation
of the United States as the most physically beautiful country
in the world is an expression of nationalist political ideals. A
representation that elicits feelings of nostalgia for the land,
with the goal of motivating an audience to protect its natural
resources, is propaganda.

Nondemagogic propaganda can also appeal to flawed ideology. Suppose for the sake of argument that the central doctrines of Christianity are false (if you are a devout Christian, replace "Christian" with "Muslim" in what follows). An argument about social welfare spending that appeals to, for example, the ideal of political equality, but relies on the religious teachings of Christianity to bring about the effect of furthering the ideal of equality, is a case of supporting propaganda that is not demagogic, yet relies on a flawed ideology.

The aim of the explicit demagogue is to disrupt rational evaluation in such a way as to prevent her audience from reflecting about whether the goal of the demagogic claim is consistent with the political ideals it represents itself as embodying. But insincerity is not necessary to engage in propaganda. Someone in the grip of a flawed ideology can nevertheless engage in demagoguery, since the effect of their flawed ideology can be to prevent them from reconsidering the relation between their goal and the political ideals they incorrectly think their goal serves. I may firmly believe the doctrines of my religious cult, which maintain that everyone not in the cult will burn in the lake of fire forever. On this basis, I may kidnap your children, on the grounds that it is the most reasonable thing to do for their overall welfare. But kidnapping your children is not consistent with the ideal of the welfare of children. Only the flawed ideology of my religious cult leads me to believe that it is.

I now turn to the topic of propaganda in a liberal democratic society. A liberal democracy is governed by particular political ideals that have, since Aristotle, made it special among the political systems: the political ideals of liberty and equality. Aristotle furthermore argues that since democracy is likely to lead to a great deal of economic equality, it is also the most stable of the various systems. So democracy has a special role in political philosophy, and its political ideals—*the democratic ideals*—are my focus in the next chapter.

Every political system has stability as an ideal, as well as law and order. Democracy adds to that the ideals of liberty and equality. If all citizens participate equally in deliberation about the policies that will hold for all of them, then any policy that applies to all will be at least one that, during the process of deliberation, will be forced to reckon with the perspectives and interests of all citizens. Because of one's own political participation in the formation of the policy, abiding by that policy is not a genuine sacrifice of liberty. So in a democratic state, it is very important that all citizens can politically participate, and that the resulting political discussion is reasonable and rational, in the senses I will define. In a democracy, *the norms governing political speech*, that is, speech between citizens or representatives about policies and laws, are also political ideals. In fact, they are, together with liberty and freedom, the most important political ideals. In the next chapter, we turn to the nature of propaganda in a political system governed by democratic ideals.

PROPAGANDA IN
LIBERAL DEMOCRACY

Political propaganda presents itself as an embodiment of cherished political ideals. Therefore, in a democracy, propaganda of the demagogic variety will characteristically be presented as an embodiment of democratic ideals. In a democracy, propaganda of a nondemagogic variety, specifically of the positive kind, is contributions that strengthen democratic ideals. A chapter on propaganda in liberal democracy therefore of necessity must be devoted to identifying various candidate democratic ideals of normative political theory. The ideals will be guides in identifying instances of propaganda, and its most nefarious species, demagoguery.

In a democracy, for reasons I will explain, normative political philosophy has it that among the central ideals are normative ideals governing public political speech. I will discuss different candidate ideals, which are typically in the literature presented as rivals. As will emerge, along with many others, I conclude that one is central: the ideal that John Rawls has called "reasonableness." However, I do not have to decide between them for the purposes of identifying cases of propaganda. We should expect propaganda in a liberal democracy to come packaged as a plausible and intuitively attractive democratic political ideal. It does not have to be packaged as the one true ultimately correct political ideal governing democratic deliberation. Nevertheless, we can learn a great deal about what politicians and their handlers think of as the intuitively correct normative political ideals of democracy by inspecting in particular their propaganda.[1] We can use cases of propaganda in this way to shed light on which of the normative ideals governing public political speech tend to guide ordinary politics.

I begin the chapter explaining why propaganda is a special problem for democracy. At the end of the chapter I conclude by trying to characterize in somewhat precise structural terms the distinction between propaganda that is required to mend tears in the fabric of liberal democratic states, on the one hand, and democratically unacceptable undermining propaganda, on the other: the distinction between *civic rhetoric*, on the one hand, and demagoguery, on the other.

According to the economic theory of democracy, if citizens are voting on the basis of rational self-interest, then voting has occurred. This allows voting by "acclamation," if voters' self-interest is in the pleasures of servitude. Nevertheless, even the economic theory of democracy requires an open media and honest politicians; that is, it requires voters to have reliable access to the information that will enable rational decision making on the basis of self-interest. At least some of the norms of richer deliberative conceptions of democratic theory will apply in the economic theory of democracy. So it should not be thought that I am restricting my focus to the deliberative tradition in democracy. The economic theory of democracy requires ideals governing formal public speech as well, though perhaps different ideals than deliberative democracy requires.

In the introduction, we saw that propaganda poses a *special* problem for democratic states. Reflecting on the fact that democratic ideals centrally include ideals governing political speech, we can explain this. Propaganda that is presented as embodying an ideal governing political speech, but in fact runs counter to it, is antidemocratic. It is antidemocratic because it wears down the possibility of democratic deliberation. Such propaganda is demagoguery. In a democracy, even if one's goal is laudable, it is still impermissible to engage in demagoguery. It is impermissible because it is illiberal; though it may serve a goal beneficial in some way to society, it threatens the democratic status of that society. The danger, as we saw in the first chapter, is that deliberation will then be replaced by "acclamation," in which case, as Rousseau warned, citizens should not be considered as voting at all.

Let's take a recent example of propaganda in a liberal democracy that was delivered for a beneficial goal.[2] The example comes from a recent *New York Times* piece I wrote with my brother, the economist Marcus Stanley. US fiscal policy involves the ways in which the US government funds its own debt. The expression "the fiscal cliff" was introduced to the broader public by Ben Bernanke, the chairman of the Federal Reserve of the United States, in February 2012 to describe the threat to the recovering economy posed by the confluence of two events. First, Congress was again facing their repeated promise to restore income taxes to their levels during the Clinton presidency in order to reduce the deficit. Secondly, Congress was simultaneously facing large self-imposed spending cuts (the so-called sequester). Curiously, however, a poll found that 47 percent of the public thought that it was going *over* the "cliff" that would result in higher deficits. Only 14 percent understood that it would reduce deficits. In fact, it would have reduced them drastically, effectively eliminating the deficit problem.

The poll suggests that the public was quite misled. If so, it is not unreasonable to pin the blame on the expression "fiscal cliff." Going over cliffs is clearly a bad thing, possibly resulting in death. Also, the major parties seem to agree that deficits are a terrible thing. The Democrats invoke the awfulness of deficits when discussing additional tax cuts for the wealthy, and the Republicans invoke deficits when confronted with additional entitlement programs or additional spending on existing ones.

A widening government deficit also seems similar to personal borrowing, an excess of which leads to reduced credit scores, calls from bill collectors, and possibly foreclosure. So it was natural to assume that a "fiscal cliff" is simply a metaphorical warning of an especially threatening increase in the deficit.

Let's assume (speculatively but not unreasonably) that Bernanke's introduction of this expression was meant to intentionally steer the debate about this issue. That is, let's assume that Bernanke was well aware that his warning would be misunderstood, and that the misunderstanding would lead to its effectiveness. One reason speaking clearly about deficits is hard is because of the entrenched language that is used to speak about the process by which a government funds its activities, a process that is described as "borrowing." A second reason is that both major parties are invested in using deficit fear strategically.

Describing the process by which the US government funds its activities as involving "borrowing" suggests a false analogy between government borrowing and the borrowing an individual or a family does. The analogy makes some sense for a public entity that does not print its own currency—for example, the state of California or the (Euro-employing) country of Greece. And the analogy also made much more sense during the true gold standard era in this country. For these reasons, and because the government does issue bonds that look like corporate bonds, the vocabulary is entrenched. But a government borrowing in a currency it controls (and can print) has little in common with the borrowing we experience as ordinary citizens. Its benefits—creating jobs and income that prevent a self-perpetuating downward spiral in a slack economy—are not benefits associated with private borrowing. Likewise, its risks—the possibility of inflation, "crowding out" private investment in capital markets, and changing exchange rates—are not factors any individual has experience with through their private borrowing.

Sadly, even many experts do not precisely understand the benefits and risks of government financing through deficits.

The short-term benefits in terms of jobs and income are clear (just ask any lobbyist who wants to maintain spending on their priorities or avoid taxation of their clients). But while there are certainly risks to excessive government debt, controversy continues to rage about when and how these risks occur and what level of debt will create them.

Politicians understand this well, and that's why for decades both parties have subordinated deficit reduction to short-term policy goals. Republicans are willing to put deficit reduction second to tax reduction, and Democrats are willing to prioritize preserving key entitlements and reducing unemployment. Behind the scenes, we have Dick Cheney's famous comment that "Reagan proved deficits don't matter." But in front of the camera, both parties cooperate in generating periodic deficit "crises" to cudgel their opponents and get them to give way on their more central priorities. A great deal of maneuvering on domestic policy can be understood as the strategic deployment of the "deficit" charge against your opponent while working behind the scenes to keep the debt machine going for your own purposes.[3]

Bernanke was correct to worry about the consequences of so much liquidity evaporating from the US markets in one go. He chose to handle the situation by relying on the false beliefs of the public to communicate alarm. It was demagoguery because it was a message that reinforced the public's false beliefs about economics, wrapped in the mantle of the sage advice of the Fed chief. As such, it eroded democratic ideals. The consequence of Bernanke's failure to explain economic reality was that the public remained confused. This allowed politicians to continue to employ the fear of a rising deficit for political purposes, leading to a fiscal crisis surrounding the debt ceiling in October 2013, which was later shown to take nearly 1 percent of US GDP (nearly 150 billion dollars) and resulted in the loss of an estimated 750,000 jobs.[4] This can be regarded as some empirical confirmation of the view evident from democratic political theory that propaganda that exploits democratic ideals, even if wielded for a good purpose, occludes democratic deliberation.

Bernanke's goal in using the phrase "fiscal cliff" was laudable: to move public opinion to avoid a devastating loss of jobs. But in so doing, he relied on false ideological beliefs about the economy, rather than lucid explanation. Bernanke thus set the stage for the subsequent irrational public deliberation that preceded the debt ceiling crisis in 2013. This is a specific illustration of the risks of demagoguery in a democracy, even when wielded for a praiseworthy goal. Flawed ideological beliefs corrode rational debate. In a healthy democracy, the goal of a public official should be to dissolve them, rather than rely on them. Relying upon them only strengthens them and makes them much more problematic barriers in subsequent debate.

I have given one specific example of the dangers of propaganda in a liberal democracy. The example I gave is one in which false beliefs were supported for a good cause. We have seen how this leads inexorably to later problems with democratic deliberation. The political scientist Sarah Sobieraj has devoted a book to documenting problems propaganda raises in liberal democracy, even when wielded in support of worthy causes. For example, Sobieraj persuasively argues that propagandizing by activists tends to "sabotage discourse" in ways that ultimately hinder the kind of social change that that very activism seeks to engender.

I now turn to the overview of democratic political ideals in normative political philosophy. I begin with an explanation of why, in a liberal democracy, the normative ideals governing public political speech are *political* ideals. We then turn to some of the candidate normative ideals governing public political speech. Once we have a good sense of the different candidate normative ideals governing public political speech in a democracy, we will be in a much better position to recognize cases of propaganda in liberal democracies such as the United States. So my goal is to explain some basic details of democratic political theory, which will allow us to see both why the ideals governing political speech are so important in a democracy and which ideals are the most plausible. This will take some work. But it is essential to identifying the structure propaganda takes in a liberal democracy, since propaganda is presented as embodying one or another normative ideal of political speech.

The idea of a "regular assembly" in which citizens gather to deliberate about just policy is a core element of the Western philosophical tradition.[5] In *The Politics* Aristotle also makes it clear that the concept of a state involves the idea of "courts ... who enforce engagements of contracting parties."[6] On Aristotle's view in *The Politics*, man's role as a citizen of the state is to have as chief concerns "the safety of navigation" and "the salvation of a community." According to Aristotle, "[M]an is by nature a political animal."[7] The purpose of speech "is intended to set forth the expedient and inexpedient, and therefore likewise the just and the unjust." Political philosophy since its inception has contained within it the notion that states have certain forums for speech that have a politically central role, arenas for public political discourse. Public political discourse occurs in informal gatherings of citizens, as well as in the houses of Congress and in presidential debates. The role of the media is somewhat more complex, but given its role, discourse about politics in the news media too should count as belonging to public political discourse.

In a liberal democracy, public political discourse occurs in political debate in elections, between representatives seeking to pass policy in the chambers of government (such as Congress and the Senate), and in media discussions of either. In his late essay "The Idea of Public Reason Revisited," John Rawls attempts to characterize this realm by defining the notion of a *public political forum*:

> the discourse of judges in their decisions, and especially of the judges of a supreme court; the discourse of government officials, especially chief executives and legislators;

and finally, the discourse of candidates for public office and their campaign managers, especially in their public oratory, party platforms, and political statements.[8]

Rawls's essay concerns in part *the ideal of public reason*, by which he means the standard that ought to guide debate in public political forums in a liberal democracy. But the ideals of public reason should not just guide formal forums of the sort Rawls discusses. Citizens gather to speak about politics in all sorts of *informal* settings. These informal settings guide us in our political choices. The ideals of public reason therefore should apply equally to these informal settings.

In Senate debate in September 2013, Senator John McCain called on his Republican colleagues to abandon their strategy of trying to shut down the US government to halt the implementation of the Affordable Care Act. McCain said: "We fought as hard as we could in a fair and honest manner and we lost. One of the reasons was because we were in the minority, and in democracies, almost always the majority governs and passes legislation." McCain's point was that democratic citizenship requires taking yourself to be subject to the laws that emerge from a "fair and honest" process of deliberating among one's fellow politicians and the public, even when those laws are not the ones that you yourself support. The ideals of public reason are central to democratic political philosophy, because it is through debate that is "fair and honest" that the democratic legitimacy of a policy emerges.

Democracy is a system of government that, minimally, preserves the liberty of its citizens by ensuring that they are not subject to arbitrary restrictions. If a polity agrees to laws governing all of its citizens, the rules must be fairly decided upon by the entire public, with the full participation of all the citizens, for the rules to not illegitimately restrict the liberty of some of the citizens.

Suppose you are part of a group jointly deliberating about a policy the group intends to adopt. Perhaps it is a town hall meeting about whether to allow fracking in exchange for the building of a school or some jobs. Suppose you are in the group, and the policy runs counter to your own self-interest. For example, perhaps your house has a well fed by a spring that is likely to be poisoned by the fracking. You are initially therefore opposed. However, the main advocate of the policy produces an argument that the policy is best for all, and convinces the majority to adopt the policy. Suppose that you later find out that the main advocate was lying, or otherwise employing deceit. Furthermore, the reason that the main advocate pushed for that policy is that she was paid to do so. In such a situation, you would feel tricked. You would feel that the decision to adopt that policy was not legitimate. You would feel that the group's demand that you adhere to the policy was also not a legitimate demand. If they forced you to adhere to the policy, you have legitimate grounds to feel coerced.

In contrast, suppose that you are part of a group deliberating about a policy that the group is contemplating adopting. The main advocate of the policy gives persuasive arguments that it is in the overall best interest of the community to adopt the policy. The policy runs counter to your own self-interest, but you see that the arguments are correct, and that the policy is in fact best for the community as a whole. The advocate is honest, and her arguments are good. You vote against it, but you lose. In this case, you don't really feel that you have a complaint. The policy was arrived at via fair deliberation. If the group demands that you adhere to the policy, you don't have legitimate grounds to feel coerced.

The first case we discussed, decision to allow fracking, was one in which an unfair process led to a policy that was bad for the community at large. The second case we discussed involved a fair process that led to a policy that was good for the community at large. These are what one might think of as *pure* cases. The deliberation and policy were both unfair and bad, or fair and good, respectively. What about the *impure* cases? That is, what about a fair deliberative process that leads, because of false beliefs due to a flawed ideology, for example, to a policy that is bad for the community? Or what about an unfair deliberative process that bypasses some of the community's unreasonable and irrational members to arrive at a policy that is good for the community? Democratic political theory divides over these impure cases.

According to *pure proceduralists* about democracy, such as John Rawls and Joshua Cohen, all that matters is that the *procedure* that leads to the policy is fair. The process of fair democratic deliberation itself leads to the formation of new preferences; democratic deliberation is an expression of one kind of autonomy, the autonomy that is found in rationally choosing one's duties. According to the main version of epistemic theories of democracy, of the sort defended by David Estlund and Hélène Landemore, both procedure and outcome matter.[9] The procedure matters insofar as it leads to outcomes that are better for the citizenry at large. Both the older, pure proceduralist view of democracy and the newer, epistemic version defend fair democratic deliberation. But according to advocates of the epistemic theory of democracy, fair deliberative procedures only have an instrumental value in leading to better overall policy. For pure procedural conceptions of democratic legitimacy, fair deliberation is valuable in and of itself. Both conceptions agree on the value of fair deliberation. One locates democratic legitimacy itself in such deliberation, connecting it to autonomy, while the other tries to explain the value of fair deliberation in terms of its correct outcomes. We will not need to decide between pure proceduralist conceptions of democracy and epistemic theories of democracy, since both rightly presuppose the value of fair joint deliberation. And it is fair joint deliberation that is placed in peril by propaganda.

The policies that result from discussion involving deception and trickery are not democratically legitimate. The person who loses out in a discussion subject to devious machinations is analogous to someone who has lost her freedom in an unjust war. Governance by the rules that emerge from such a process results in domination, rather than preservation of autonomy. In order for the principles decided upon by a group of autonomous agents to have binding force on each of them, without loss of autonomy, the procedure by which the joint decision is made must lend legitimacy to the result. As we have seen, if there is no constraint that the people who are party to the deliberation not simply mislead and lie and evade in order to further their own interests, the results of the deliberation will not be democratically legitimate.

Democracy requires that the policies that apply to everyone must be the result of fair deliberation and equal participation. The reason to impose this constraint is to ensure that the results of the agreement are something that can be the desires of the entire community, by virtue of being the results of such an agreement. The question of the ideals of public reason is the question of *what guiding ideals should be the norms of deliberation about laws*. It is clear that deliberation that allows deceit does not lead to democratic laws. One of the central questions of democratic political theory concerns the nature of the ideals governing the kind of deliberation that leads to genuinely democratic laws.

The difficulty of justifying a democratic state is that its citizens must live in a society and be governed by laws to which they must adhere while simultaneously preserving their liberty. In order to preserve the liberty of action of its citizens, the laws of a democratic country must be laws to which those citizens in *some sense* agree, via a process of joint deliberation. A central question, or perhaps *the* central question, of democratic political theory is what makes a joint deliberative process fair. The question is complicated by the fact that citizens of a democratic state are typically born into a state with already existing laws. Because of this, the deliberative process must take into account the fact that the laws will apply to people who did not have the opportunity to participate in their formation. The laws therefore must be crafted via normative ideals that take into account the views of those not yet born, as well as of children who, while not at that point capable of deliberation, one day will be among the people whose viewpoints need to be taken into account. What normative ideals should govern a deliberative process that results in laws of this sort, laws that can legitimately be taken as binding on individuals not yet born or too young to participate in their formation? This is the question of *the nature of the norms of public reason*. Any comprehensive list of the democratic ideals centrally includes the normative ideals of public reason.

Public reason is so important to the nature of democracy that on certain views of democracy, its chief virtue is most fully realized in deliberating about policy with one's fellow citizens. This is not Plato's view of the nature of democracy. In book 8 of *The Republic*, Plato describes liberty in terms of an unfettered unleashing of actions guided by random desires, motivated often by appetite. For example, Plato describes "the Democratic man" (561c, d), who is supposed to embody liberty, as living "his life day by day, indulging each appetite as it makes itself felt. One day he is drinking heavily and listening to the flute; on the next he is dieting and drinks only water." The fact that democracy is connected to this conception of liberty as fully unfettered action is at the basis of his critiques of the system of democracy.

Like Plato, Aristotle connects democracy with some conception of liberty. But the conception of liberty is very different. On Aristotle's view, one's true desires are the ones one arrives at via a process of deliberation with one's fellow citizens in the public square. On this conception, it is in following policies mutually agreed upon by a deliberating body of citizens that one is actually following the path of liberty. The classic modern discussion of these two distinct conceptions of liberty is in Benjamin Constant's famous lecture to Athénée Royal in Paris in 1819, "The Liberty of the Ancients Compared with That of the Moderns." The liberty of the moderns is what Plato is mocking as the chief virtue of democracy. The liberty of the ancients is what Aristotle argues is the chief virtue of democracy.[10] It is because of their different conceptions of democracy that Plato concluded that it was the least stable political system and Aristotle concluded that it was the most stable political system.

Many contemporary and modern American democratic theorists give a special role to political participation, suggesting that they have a conception of democracy that reflects the Aristotelian conception. In the great ode to democracy from 1903, *The Souls of Black Folk*, the American philosopher W.E.B. Du Bois repeatedly emphasizes that the nation owes its Black citizens three things: "the free right to vote, [the right] to enjoy civic rights, and [the right] to be educated."[11] Du Bois demands that "[n]egroes must insist continually, in season and out of season, that voting is necessary to modern manhood . . . and that black boys need education as well as white boys." Du Bois focuses on these three rights—voting rights, civic equality, and education—because he thinks of political participation as special among the liberties; education is important because only the educated citizen can participate well in civic life.[12]

I have emphasized throughout that there is no need for my purposes to choose between the different conceptions of liberty that democracy is supposed to embody. Whatever the conception of liberty underlying democracy is to be, the norms of public reason have a special role. Indeed, that role is so special that on perhaps the most compelling vision of the nature of democracy, the one championed by Du Bois, their role stands above all others.

Given that democratic ideals centrally include the normative ideals of public reason, an important form of propaganda in a democracy is speech that presents itself as embodying the normative ideals of public reason but that in fact contributes content that can be expected by a rational person in the situation to erode those very ideals. Propaganda in a democracy in fact often takes this form: speech that inhibits, rather than furthers, the ideals of public reason. To gain more clarity on the structure of propaganda in a liberal democracy, we must have a better sense of plausible normative ideals of public reason. Only then will we be able to assess various examples.

I will discuss three suggestions of standards for debate in public political forums. Any normative ideal of public reason should be *impartial* in the following sense: public political speech should not be of the sort that, in James Madison's words, "[divides] mankind into parties, [inflames] them with mutual animosity, and [renders] them much more disposed to vex and oppress each other than to co-operate for their common good." A norm of impartiality demands that the force of the reasons offered, and policies proposed, is not perspective-dependent. If someone is offering impartial reasons, their reasons "must be grounded in something that is independent of their stance, namely what is the case believer-neutrally."[13] This is the standpoint of the *impartial observer*. According to the ideal of impartiality, the claims politicians make in political debate must be from the standpoint of the impartial observer. All three different views of the normative public reason are impartial in this general sense.

The first is that debates in public political forums are guided by a norm of *theoretical rationality*. The second is that they are guided by a normative ideal of *practical* rationality plus ignorance in a sense I will characterize. The third normative ideal for public reason is that it is guided by equal respect for the perspective of everyone subject to the policy under debate. Following the recent political philosophy tradition, we shall call this the norm of *reasonableness*.

The first plausible normative ideal of public reason is to hold contributions up to a standard of *theoretical rationality*, what Jürgen Habermas famously calls "the unforced force of the better argument." A contribution to a political debate must be justified, and be assessed solely by its impact on the truth of the issue at hand. Let's say that *rational contributions to a debate* are legitimately justified claims (ones "backed up by evidence") that contribute to a rational resolution of the debate.

A claim contributes to a rational resolution of a debate only if it bears significantly on the likelihood of the issue under debate. For example, a claim would be a rational contribution to a debate about whether or not invading Iraq is the right thing to do if the claim was justified and provided evidence for or against the wisdom of invading Iraq.[14]

A claim may be a rational contribution to a debate, but have a nonrational effect on the debate as a whole. Take an example that was recently the subject of a *New York Times* Retro Report, from which the information to follow comes.[15] The example involves the expression "super-predator," introduced and popularized by academics—specifically James A. Fox at Northeastern University and John J. DiIulio Jr., then of Princeton University—in the mid-1990s as a description of the perpetrators of youth crime in the United States. In a television interview, DiIulio defined a super-predator as a "young juvenile criminal who is so impulsive, so remorseless, that he can kill, rape, maim, without giving it a second thought." In another television interview, DiIulio said, "We are talking about a group of kids that are growing up essentially fatherless, godless, and jobless." In an article from 1996, "My Black Crime Problem, and Yours," DiIulio wrote, "[A]s many as half of these super-predators could be young, black males."

The notorious "Central Park jogger" case in 1989, in which a group of Black children in New York City were arrested and convicted for the brutal rape of a jogger in Central Park, was used by Dan Rather to introduce the topic in a CBS news special on "super-predator theory" (the children later turned out to be innocent). During the presidential campaign in 1996, the Republican presidential candidate Bob Dole called for harsh new legislation for youth crime, saying (clearly of Black male children) that "experts call them super-predators." It is clear that the demagogic language of "super-predator" had an immediate, nonrational effect on the subsequent debate about the legislation of child crime. Over forty states swiftly enacted draconian new legislation cracking down on violent child crime. One can imagine, in this context, a politician using the phrase "inner-city youth" in favor of such legislation. But the debate had been polluted by the introduction of the language of "super-predator," which was inexorably linked to Black children. By being linked to the iconography evoked by the language of "super-predator," even rational contributions to the debate had a clearly nonrational effect. In fact, this was the very purpose of introducing the term "super-predator." As Fox acknowledges, his use of the "strong language" was intentional, since he meant to "sound an alarm about what might happen if we didn't act quickly."

In the context of the debate in the 1990s about child crime, terms like "super-predator" and "wilding" (introduced to describe the alleged actions of the youth accused in the Central Park jogger case) polluted subsequent debate by evoking negative stereotypes that impeded the subsequent employment of rational faculties. Even apparently fully rational contributions to the debate subsequently evoked such stereotypes. Such contributions thus ran counter to the normative ideal of theoretical rationality, because even speaking of Black youth crime evoked nonrational faculties, specifically fear, to end rational debate.[16]

If theoretical rationality is the normative ideal of public reason, then one paradigm class of cases of propaganda in a democracy will be uses of language that are masked as objective but that have a polemical effect. They have the effect of appeals to passions to cut off rational debate, in many cases without making a rational contribution to it. This unquestionably captures one kind of propaganda. Any account of the form of propaganda in a democracy must explain these cases as well.

Theoretical rationality as a normative ideal of public reason also explains the ubiquity of propaganda masked as embodying scientific ideals but conveying a content that runs counter to them. The propaganda involved in climate-science denial is typically of this sort.

If theoretical reason is the norm of public reason, then reasons advanced in public political forums are legitimate insofar as they play a role in a rational resolution of the issue. The issue under debate might be, for example, "Is it in the public interest to raise taxes on the wealthy?" Considerations for or against must weigh in on the resolution of this question (allowing compromises as a kind of resolution) in the sense of raising or lowering the likelihood of the truth of one of the options. So, for example, an opponent of raising taxes on the rich might provide empirical evidence that so doing will lead to an increase in unemployment.

According to the norm of theoretical reason, public political debate in a democracy is guided by reasons that bear on whether or not a particular policy is *for the common good*, or *in the public interest*. However, one might worry that a policy proposal might be in the public interest, yet run roughshod over the allowable personal liberties of a minority. This concern motivates a distinct normative ideal governing political debate. To introduce it, I will employ the thought experiment of the original position, from John Rawls's book *A Theory of Justice*, published in 1971.[17]

Practical rationality is "means-ends" reasoning: given a goal, what is the most rational way to achieve that goal, given one's beliefs? A norm of practical rationality on public reason is clearly not a version of impartialism. However, one can model the demands of impartiality by marrying practical rationality with the suspension of one's beliefs about *one's own position* in society, and hence one's particular perspective. One sees this model in the thought experiment involving "the original position" in *A Theory of Justice*. There, Rawls argues that the correct way to establish the principles of justice for a society is by imagining oneself into an "original position," where one does not know one's place in society, one's race or religion, or even one's intellectual and physical capacities. The laws governing the society will be the laws agreed upon by agents who are fully practically rational and have imagined themselves into "the original position." That is, in adjudicating the principles of justice, one must suspend belief about one's location in society, where society is conceived of as humanity, and employ one's practical rationality to decide what principles should govern a society in which one does not know where one is located. This is another possible view of the norms of public reason: a statement in a political forum is only acceptable if it is practically rational from the stance of someone ignorant of their place in the society. This is a version of impartialism; let us call it *practical rationality impartialism*.

Practical rationality impartialism may appear to rule out expressions of self-interest in public political forums. But it does not. Expressions of self-interest might even be evidentially *necessary* as a means of information that bears on reasons that are impartial.[18] A legitimate step in democratic deliberation on this picture is a reason that makes sense from the perspective of the impartial observer, who does not know her place in society. But this does not preclude expressions of self-interest, as they may contribute evidentially to the weight of one legitimate reason over another. For example, suppose we are debating about whether to build a bridge connecting an island to the mainland. The self-interest of those who live in the construction zone is relevant to the question of whether we ought to build the bridge. We need expressions of self-interest to provide that information, even though they themselves are not public reasons.

Practical rationality impartialism does not preclude expressions of self-interest in public debate. But such expressions are only relevant insofar as they bear on reasons that are compelling to all. The impartialist conception of public reason forces the elimination of any claim that has its source in self-interest that does not contribute to impartial reasons. And that is the right result, because claims that have their source in self-interest and are not useful from an impartial standpoint are paradigmatically the kinds of claims made in illegitimate attempts to gain power for a particular interest group.

For example, a senator wishing to do a favor for an oil company or a private prison company for the sake of a campaign donation might deliver a speech in favor of a piece of legislation that favors the source of the potential campaign contributor. From the perspective of people not benefiting from those campaign donations, the reasons the senator gives that come from his self-interest run counter to the impartialist norm of public reason. And that is the correct result.

Information about the self-interest of various parties is often indirectly relevant to debates about policy. So expressions of self-interest can be legitimate in political discussion, even if impartiality is the norm of public reason. But it is also the case that there are claims that do not bear on settling the debate, or do not provide relevant evidence in any way, but can still, according to the advocate of impartialism about public reason, be legitimate. These are claims that aid in satisfying the *preconditions* for public reason.

Practical rationality impartialism involves reasons that would make sense from the position of anyone in the society, if they did not know their place in the society. But it is not clear that one can argue, via impartial reasons, in such a way that would lead one to a more expansive conception of the inclusion conditions for the society. This kind of impartialist can allow claims that help facilitate the adoption of such a background. That is, the impartialist can allow for speech that helps to establish the background required to enable democratic deliberation. It may be that considerations that are not impartial are part of that background (such as reasonableness as a character trait, in the sense soon to be defined). So this kind of impartialist can grant the legitimacy of contributions that are not impartial, as long as they help foster the *preconditions* for the exchange of reasons that are impartial in this sense. The practical rationality impartialist is not so easily refuted.

Despite the appeal of practical rationality impartialism, it is not the most central ideal of public reason in democratic political theory, either historically or currently. Democratic political theory has long favored another ideal, according to which a democratic community is one that fosters certain kinds of attitudes toward one's fellow citizens. In *The Souls of Black Folk*, Du Bois brings our attention to this normative ideal of public reason by describing the consequences of its complete failure in his description of the political state in the American South after the Civil War:

> Can we establish a mass of black laborers and artisans and landholders in the South who, by law and public opinion, have absolutely no voice in shaping the laws under which they live and work? Can the modern organization of industry, assuming as it does free democratic government and the power and ability of the laboring classes to compel respect for their welfare,—can this system be carried out in the South when half its laboring force is voiceless in the public councils and powerless in its own defence? . . . It is pitiable that frantic efforts must be made at critical times to get law-makers in some States even to listen to the respectful presentation of the black man's side of a current controversy. . . . The laws are made by men who have little interest in [the Negro]; they are executed by men who have absolutely no motive for treating the black people with courtesy or consideration; and, finally, the accused law-breaker is tried, not by his peers, but too often by men who would rather punish ten innocent Negroes than let one guilty one escape.[19]

Du Bois's critique of the political system of the South during the several decades following the Civil War is that its laws are not democratically legitimate; they apply to some citizens, the Black ones, not as "laws and justice," but as "sources of humiliation and oppression." One obvious reason the laws lack democratically legitimacy is because Blacks were not allowed to participate in their formation. As Martin Luther King Jr. writes in "Letter from a Birmingham Jail," "A law is unjust if it is inflicted on a minority that, as a result of being denied the right to vote, had no part in enacting or devising the law." But Du Bois is not merely making King's point. He is rather bringing our attention to what he seems to regard as a more central reason the laws are not democratically legitimate. It is because those who created the laws did not have *empathy* for some of those subject to them, namely, their Black fellow citizens. The lack of empathy meant that the laws were crafted in such a way that did not reflect *respect* for the viewpoints of Black citizens; lawmakers will not listen to the "respectful presentation of the black man's side of a current controversy."

Du Bois is arguing that the laws in the South are illegitimate, and they are illegitimate because (a) Black citizens do not participate in their formation, (b) lawmakers will not take into account the reasonable perspectives of Black citizens, and (c) there is no empathy on the side of the lawmakers for the situation of Blacks subject to those laws. Du Bois is suggesting that underlying the kind of equal respect involved in taking into account reasonable perspectives of Black citizens is empathy.

A benevolently paternalistic society is one in which the policymakers have empathy with those who are subject to the policies, but do not treat them with equal respect. The difference between benevolent paternalism and a democratic culture is indicated by Du Bois's comments about the need in a free democratic society to take into account the "respectful presentation" of the perspective of alternative views.

Chapter 4 of the British philosopher Susan Stebbing's book *Thinking to Some Purpose*, published in 1939, is called "You and I: I and You." Stebbing calls attention to a failure common in public discourse, the "failure to see the point from the other man's position."[20] She recommends, in making assertions that apply to everyone, the "safeguard" of changing "you" into "I." That way, one can more easily see that the policy one is prescribing to others is a reasonable one. Stebbing is thereby suggesting that there is a norm of equality to public discourse. It is this that distinguishes mere paternalism from democracy.

The sociologist Manfred Stanley articulates the need in a democratic society for this kind of capacity to take the perspective of the other:

When a society evolves into a condition that is so complex and fragmented by social class and occupational specialization that great sociopsychic distance between population groups becomes a normal state of affairs, then insufficient compassion emerges as a distinct collective problem. . . . Mutual estrangement and stereotypical fantasy exist between the extremes of our class structure, between several ethnic and racial groups, and between considerable numbers of males and females. . . . The challenge is . . . one of bringing people to the point of understanding the objective historical and existing conditions of groups with whom they have had no personal life experience. Compassion presupposes the ability to "take the role of the other" in some particularly subtle and informed way.

But what is it to "take the role of the other" in the relevant respect? Stephen Darwall appeals to Adam Smith's notion of an "impartial spectator" to explain the notion of "being *someone* in the other's situation" and deliberating about what to feel from that perspective.[21] Stebbing is asking us, when proposing policy, to imagine being *someone* subject to that policy, with as many of the properties as those subject to the policies have, without losing the impartial stance suggested by the indefinite "someone." It is this ability, to imagine being someone in the situation of another, that underlies the capacity to give the perspectives of our fellow citizens equal weight. The difference between benevolent paternalism and a democratic attitude is that the latter presupposes the regular employment of this sort of imaginative capacity.[22]

I have sketched a democratic ideal that involves a certain cognitive capacity, that of imagining oneself as *someone* in the situation of another. Following Darwall, let's call this capacity *cognitive empathy*. It is not completely clear how to characterize cognitive empathy, since it is not completely clear what it is to imagine oneself as *someone* in the situation of another. The philosopher Laurie Paul has argued recently that it is not possible to imaginatively place oneself in the situation of others who have had dramatically different life experiences. It may be, if Paul is correct, that even cognitive empathy is excessively idealized as an affective base for a democratic ideal.

Paul argues that a certain class of experience makes it impossible to imagine being in that position.[23] One example Paul gives is the experience of having a child. She argues that having a child is a *transformative experience*, and that this entails that it is not possible to make a rational decision about choosing to be in that position. More needs to be said about Smith's impartial spectator before one can conclude that Paul's arguments show that a childless person cannot be an impartial spectator of a person with a child. But let's suppose, as it appears, that it is incompatible with Paul's arguments, that childless persons cannot imagine, in the relevant sense, what it is like to have a child. If so, then, on the conception of a democratic culture I have sketched, it is hard to see how any policies could be legitimate. Childless persons could not make policy that applies to those with children, in a democratically acceptable way. This is a not unfamiliar antiliberal position.

There are several options to the difficulties posed by Paul's arguments. One is to seek a norm of public reason that does not require cognitive empathy with the situation of others. For example, Sharon Krause has a suggestive discussion of perspective taking as "an exercise in moral sentiment," which involves taking into account the sentiments of those in different situations who would be affected by the policy.[24] Krause is suggesting that in order to gain an appreciation of the fact that others would be negatively affected by a policy I support, I do not need to be able to occupy their perspective, even in an impartial manner. One strategy in the face of the difficulties of perspective taking raised by Paul's work is therefore to seek a norm of public reason that captures a sense of impartiality, without requiring such a strong cognitive capacity as perspective sharing.

A different strategy is to take cognitive empathy as an *affective ideal*, which may function to regulate mutual policymaking,

without ever being actually embodied, or capable of being embodied, in practice. According to this strategy, the norms of
public reason are ideals. But ideals can perform a regulative
function while still being realistic. As we shall see at the end of
chapter 4, this strategy requires some account of what it is for an
ideal to regulate a practice.

When a political ideal is unrealistic in practice, one can either seek a weaker, more realistic ideal. Alternatively, one could
explore the thought that an unrealizable ideal can nevertheless
have regulative force. But for my purposes, these debates are
not relevant; this is not a project in ideal theory. My goal is
rather to use putative ideals to identify cases of propaganda.
Propaganda exploits all potential norms of public debate,
whether they are realizable or not.

A democratic culture is one in which citizens assume that
their fellow citizens have good reasons for acting as they do.
It involves, for example, questioning one's own perspective, if
one cannot make rational sense out of the actions of one's fellow citizens. It involves, as Du Bois argues, being open to the
"respectful presentation" of other perspectives.

Rawls usefully characterizes this conception of the ideals
governing democratic deliberation in a characterization of
what he calls "reasonableness":[25]

> Persons are reasonable in one basic aspect when, among
> equals say, they are ready to propose principles and stan-
> dards as fair terms of cooperation and to abide by them
> willingly, given the assurance that others will likewise do
> so. Those norms they view as reasonable for everyone to ac-
> cept and therefore as justifiable to them; and they are ready
> to discuss the fair terms that others propose.[26]

Reasonableness requires any contribution to political discussion, for example, in the form of a proposed policy, to be "justifiable" to all of those under whose purview it falls. Regarding
a reason one gives as justifiable to another presupposes "taking
the role of the other" in some relevant sense.

Let us set aside theoretical rationality and focus instead on the contrast between reasonableness and practical rationality, the kind of rationality exemplified in selecting the most effective means to further various ends (that are not truth or goodness). In contrast, a reasonable contribution is one that "we also reasonably think that other citizens might also reasonably accept."[27] An example from a *New York Times* column by the philosopher Amia Srinivasan provides a nice illustration of the distinction between practical rationality and reasonableness:

> Suppose that I inherited from my rich parents a large plot of vacant land, and that you are my poor, landless neighbor. I offer you the following deal. You can work the land, doing all the hard labor of tilling, sowing, irrigating and harvesting. I'll pay you $1 a day for a year. After that, I'll sell the crop for $50,000. You decide this is your best available option, and so take the deal.[28]

If I think of our bargain in terms of rational self-interest, then it is rational to offer you $1 a day, knowing that you have no other prospects. But I am clearly not being *reasonable*. I am not imagining someone in your situation, and then asking what would seem fair from that perspective. Rawls argues in *Political Liberalism* that the central norm of public speech is one that demands that contributions to public debate are *reasonable*.[29]

The importance of reasonableness as a norm for public discourse, and empathy as its foundation, is clear from the advice of successful propagandists. The state of Israel is in a constant asymmetrical battle with Palestinians, over whom they have the military upper hand. The constant stream of photos of dead Palestinian civilians poses a severe image problem for the country. The photos of the results of massively asymmetrical battle make Israel seem like it is an unreasonable partner in the peace process.

The Israel Project is an organization that promotes Israel's image abroad, particularly in the United States. During the war with Gaza in 2009, they commissioned the American propagandist Frank Luntz to create a pamphlet to aid in image repair. The 2009 Global Language Dictionary is an aid to Israel's public relations during a highly asymmetrical war with an enemy that involves the infliction of large civilian casualties. The document is titled "The Israel Project's 2009 Global Language Dictionary," and though intended to be secret, it was leaked to the public. Chapter 1 is "The 25 Rules for Effective Communication." The very first rule, indeed the beginning of the entire document, is "[p]ersuadables won't care how much you know until they know how much you care. Show Empathy for BOTH sides!"

Previously, in April 2003, The Luntz Research Companies, in collaboration with The Israel Project, created a similar document, titled "Wexner Analysis: Israeli Communication Priorities 2003." The report is an effort to find a way to communicate the message to American "opinion elites" that Israel is genuinely interested in peace and Palestinian well-being, while simultaneously undermining support for the Palestinian leadership. In polling, Luntz discovered that the sound bite "[w]e are hoping to find a Palestinian leadership that really does reflect the best interest for the Palestinian people" was an effective way to communicate the message that Israel is a reasonable negotiating partner, but the Palestinian leadership is not.

A good deal of the document from 2003 is spent trying to find a way to communicate reasonableness, while suggesting, without asserting, that the then unknown leader Mahmoud Abbas is untrustworthy. Luntz urges avoiding directly attacking Abbas, while simultaneously trying to communicate his untrustworthiness. He suggests finding a way to communicate that Abbas "was appointed to his current position by Arafat, which is suspect," and that he "has denied the Holocaust." Luntz's advice for Israel reflects the understanding that reasonableness in negotiations, undergirded by empathy for one's negotiating partners, is the expected norm of public discourse. His documents attempt to explain how to feign reasonableness while communicating a message that undermines the reasonableness of one's interlocutors in the eyes of third parties.

Rawls has a novel argument for reasonableness, what he calls "the fact of reasonable pluralism." A democratic society is one that allows *diverse reasonable perspectives* to be pursued by its citizens. The way to live an autonomous life is to "carve your way through the world," having your path governed by your decisions. If the decisions are autonomous, one's path will be one that is self-formed. The goal of a democracy should be to allow maximum freedom to develop along an individual path consistently with being reasonable toward one's fellow citizens. Thus, there must emerge, in a democracy, multiple reasonable full moral conceptions. You may decide to become Christian; I may decide to become a Scientologist; and a third friend may finally settle on atheism. These are all reasonable albeit incompatible paths. By imposing an ideal of reasonableness, Rawls is requiring reasons to not be drawn from the differing doctrines fellow citizens hold as a consequence of the decisions they made that formed a legitimate life path. On this view, it is not permissible for you to draw on your Christian beliefs in public debate, because, if you are reasonable, you are aware that Christian doctrine is not reasonable from my perspective.

In contrast, a normative ideal of theoretical reason for public deliberation allows any reason to be offered that potentially bears on settling the issue at hand. If one believes in the doctrines of Christianity, and their truth would settle the issue at hand, one could advance those doctrines in public debate and take oneself to be in accord with the normative ideal of theoretical reason.

If the central normative ideal governing public debate is theoretical reason, then one kind of paradigm case of propaganda in a democracy is an apparently rational contribution to a debate that makes it subsequently more difficult to follow the dictates of theoretical reason (and this consequence is not made up for by its positive contribution to the settling of the debate). If the central ideal governing public debate is reasonableness, a very different picture of the analogous paradigm case of propaganda emerges. If reasonableness is the central norm governing public debate, paradigm cases of propaganda will be ones that are presented as reasonable, but that subsequently *make it more difficult for the participants in the debate to be reasonable*. That is, paradigm cases of propaganda will be ones that represent it to be reasonable not to take certain perspectives into account.

To understand how a claim presented as reasonable could erode reasonableness, we need to look more at the notion of reasonableness and its emotional basis in humans. What is it to be reasonable? To be reasonable is to take one's proposals to be accountable to everyone in the community. A reasonable person only acts in ways that would be acceptable from every perspective; the reasonable person takes herself to be accountable to all her fellow citizens. Stephen Darwall argues that the emotional basis of accountability is guilt. Guilt is the emotion that we feel when we fail to live up to the demands of reasonableness.[30] But guilt is not the emotion that leads us to consider the perspectives of others. A community is reasonable if it is governed by norms of mutual respect and mutual accountability. A community governed by the normative ideal of reasonableness is one in which citizens have mutual respect for everyone else in the community and take their actions to be accountable to everyone else in the community. Possessing such an attitude requires, at least among humans, *empathy or the capacity to put oneself in another's shoes*.[31] One can therefore expect a characteristic form of propaganda in a liberal democracy to be a claim that is presented as reasonable, but that has the effect of eroding empathy for a targeted group.

Suppose that reasonableness is the normative ideal governing public reason. Those who contribute policy proposals to public reason that apply to everyone, or arguments for such policy proposals, must hold themselves accountable to everyone who may be subject to them. It is not reasonable to propose a policy that, from the perspective of another, is unreasonable. The normative ideal of reasonableness is the demand "to live politically with others in the light of reasons all might reasonably be expected to endorse."[32]

The normative ideal of reasonableness also explains why it is legitimate to take laws formed in a deliberation governed by reasonableness to be binding on those who did not participate in their formation. The demand of reasonableness requires those deliberating about policy to take into account the perspective of anyone who may be subject to those laws, including, for example, very young children. By taking into account the perspective of those not capable of participating in deliberation about policy, one ensures that the policies thereby formed are sensitive to their interests.

Adopting a second-personal attitude presupposes being accountable to others, and taking them in turn to be accountable to you. To take Darwall's favored example, when I ask you to step off my foot, I am adopting a second-personal standpoint to you, expecting that you will treat my request by treating me with *dignity*, which means considering my perspective. Second-personal attitudes thus centrally involve the notions of *dignity* and *respect*. If the adoption of second-personal attitudes is a precondition governing public deliberation in public political forums, then speech that is an affront to the dignity of other members of society runs counter to these ideals, and hence is the kind of speech that one expects to find masked paradigmatically by propaganda.

It is uncontroversial that propaganda, in the broad sense I have characterized, is bad. There is however a tradition in political philosophy dating back to Aristotle that advertises itself as *defending rhetoric*.[33] It is important to distinguish the aims of this tradition from an enterprise that would license propaganda, in the senses I have defined. In the rest of the chapter, I will demonstrate, just with the points I have developed up to this point, that there is a kind of propaganda that is politically necessary to use to overcome fundamental obstacles to the realization of democratic ideals. This kind of propaganda stands in a specific structural relation to demagoguery in liberal democracy.

We have seen Du Bois develop the point that overcoming barriers to democracy requires something like rhetoric or propaganda. W.E.B. Du Bois is plausibly taken to be appealing to the need for undermining propaganda, as works that directly address the distorted conception of Black fellow citizens will not sell. But it is also possible to take Du Bois as calling for particularly effective supporting propaganda that reveals Black humanity. This is a part of a classic debate he had during the Harlem Renaissance in the 1920s with the philosopher Alain Locke.

In "Criteria of Negro Art," Du Bois writes, "[I]t is not the positive propaganda of people who believe white blood divine, infallible and holy to which I object. It is the denial of a similar right of propaganda to those who believe Black blood human, lovable and inspired with new ideals for the world." Later in the essay, Du Bois expands on the desired effect of art used as propaganda: "[U]ntil the art of the black folk compells recognition they will not be rated as human. And when through art they compell recognition then let the world discover if it will that their art is as new as it is old and as old as new." Here, Du Bois uses "propaganda" to denote appeals to emotion, of the sort evoked by art, in the service of the message that Blacks deserve equal respect as humans and citizens.

In his response to Du Bois in 1928, the philosopher Alain Locke rejects this apparent call for supporting propaganda, while simultaneously providing a useful characterization of this nonpejorative sense of the term:

> My chief objection to propaganda, apart from its besetting sin of monotony and disproportion, is that it perpetuates the position of group inferiority even in crying out against it. For it leaves and speaks under the shadow of a dominant majority whom it harangues, cajoles, threatens or supplicates.

By "propaganda," both Du Bois and Locke mean a kind of speech that uses "haranguing, cajoling, threatening, or supplicating" as a method to force a dominant majority to expand the domain of respect and empathy to include a persecuted and ignored minority. In this sense, "propaganda" refers to a method of appealing to emotions to *increase* reasonableness. Locke's criticism of Du Bois's call for Black artists to engage in propaganda in this sense is that it places an undue burden on Black artists to advocate for themselves with the dominant white population, which is yet another burden stifling their freedom of expression.

Using the example of Du Bois, the political philosopher Melvin Rogers defends certain uses of rhetoric by appealing to its effect on the "cognitive-affective dimension of judgment."[34] Rogers does not here appeal to what I have characterized as undermining propaganda; in general, Rogers speaks less about the mechanisms. Rogers instead intends to illuminate the connection between the positive rhetoric tradition and a deliberative democratic ideal like reasonableness.[35] Rogers argues that Du Bois used rhetoric, of whatever kind, to force his audience to be accountable to Black citizens. It induced its audience to recognize their moral obligation to grant equal political participation to a group that had been invisible. The function of the discourse is therefore not to contribute to the rational resolution of a debate, in the sense of deciding the truth or falsity of the claim at issue. Its function is instead to force a reimagination of the presumed boundaries of that concept.[36]

As we have seen, reasonableness requires a framework of "relations of mutual respect and mutual accountability" between all citizens.[37] Du Bois clearly regards propaganda to be a method of increasing these "relations of mutual respect and mutual accountability" between all citizens, regardless of color. Public debate in Du Bois's time obviously fell well short of the ideals of reasonableness, since it did not include America's Black population within the framework of mutual respect and mutual accountability. Du Bois calls for Black artists to use their art to increase the reasonableness of public discourse, by forcing the recognition that the framework of mutual respect was too narrowly drawn.

Du Bois defends the necessity of rhetoric that *improves* the ideals of public reason. Du Bois is certainly not in the business of giving a defense of rhetoric based on its motivational powers to circumvent rational debate. Instead, he is, as Melvin Rogers rightly points out, defending the "aspirational" powers of rhetoric. A contribution to a debate can improve the subsequent reasonableness of the debate, even though the contribution itself is not a rational contribution, in the sense that its informational content contributes to the debate's resolution.

Assuming reasonableness as an ideal governing public speech, aspirational speech in Rogers's sense is, structurally, precisely the opposite of demagoguery. The person making a proposal in the public political sphere is reasonable if she can take herself to be accountable to everyone who is subject to that proposal. In most actual societies that regard themselves as liberal democracies, the laws are not reasonable from the perspective of certain groups. As Du Bois points out, the laws in the post-Reconstruction South were not reasonable, because they applied unreasonably to the Black citizens. An aspirational contribution is one whose effect is to yield an overall *improvement* of the reasonableness of a debate. A characteristic example of improving the reasonableness of a debate is to appeal to empathy and understanding to lead people to include the perspectives of some citizens whose perspectives had previously been ignored.[38] Here are some examples of civic rhetoric from American history; they will help us gain an understanding of the mechanisms by which civic rhetoric can be effective.

The Black American intellectual Fannie Barrier Williams published, in November 1904, an essay in *The Voice of the Negro* that is a classic example of aspirational speech, in Rogers's sense. It is a call for attention to the perspectives of Black women that elicits empathy for the situation in which they find themselves, the situation of having an unrecognized perspective. In a justly famous passage, she writes, of "the American Negro woman,"

> She is the only woman in America who is almost unknown; the only woman for whom nothing is done; the only woman without sufficient defenders when assailed; the only woman who is still outside of that world of chivalry that in all the ages has apotheosized women kind. Wars have been declared and fought for women; governments have been established and developed in the name of woman; art, literature and song have all conspired to make woman little less than angels, but they have all been white women.[39]

Fannie Barrier Williams used such passages to make the reader aware of the consequences to dignity and self-image of invisibleness.

Another example comes from the more recent past. Dr. Martin Luther King organized the Selma to Montgomery March of 1965 during the fight for voting rights in the American South. He insisted on nonviolence, knowing full well that the marchers would be met with extreme violence. Television viewers across the country saw nonviolent marchers who were asking only for political equality beaten and brutalized. It led to the increased visibility of American Blacks by eliciting empathy for their situation. The Selma to Montgomery March is a paradigm case of democratically acceptable propaganda: manipulation of the media to draw attention and empathy to the predicament of an otherwise invisible group.

What about the Kantian criticism of propaganda, discussed in the previous chapter? Is the form of propaganda that Du Bois urges still problematic on Kantian grounds? Is it a kind of manipulation of the rational will? Let's return to the example from chapter 2, John Coltrane's version of "My Favorite Things," as analyzed by Ingrid Monson. According to Monson, Coltrane lures the white listener into the song by appealing to white aesthetic ideals. Once the listener has been tempted into attention, Coltrane uses the song to reveal the previously invisible Black perspective. In some sense, this is misleading. But is it manipulation of the sort that would concern the Kantian?

In the case of Coltrane's version of "My Favorite Things" and the Selma to Montgomery March, some kind of manipulation is involved. In the first case, the listener expects to hear an example of a beloved tune that embodies certain aesthetic ideals, but instead discovers something else. In the second case, King manipulated white Southerners into revealing their hatred on national media, thereby turning the opinion of the country against them. But it is hard to see how *deception* is involved in these cases. No *lying*, for example, was involved in either case.

In the *Critique of Practical Reason*, Kant takes the sense of freedom attaching to the rational will to involve freedom via recognition of the moral law. There are, of course, many ways to understand Kant's view here. But it seems that propaganda used to awaken others to their moral responsibilities is in fact addressing their rational will, even if it does not appeal to their rationality, in some narrow sense of that notion. Such examples of propaganda are direct appeals to the practical freedom of one's fellow citizens.[40] The Kantian objection to propaganda would arise if one manipulated the rational will in the form of a lie; and so too, as I have argued with the case of Bernanke's use of "fiscal cliff," would the democratic objection to propaganda. Misleading people by expressing or implicating a lie has negative ramifications that lead well beyond the case at hand.

Du Bois and Alain Locke describe a species of propaganda that is speech that uses "haranguing, cajoling, threatening, or supplicating" as a method to force a dominant majority to expand the domain of respect and empathy to include a persecuted and ignored minority. There is a *structural* reason why this species of propaganda is a necessity in treating failures of liberal democracy. There are many times in which the perspectives of a group are invisible from the rest of the citizens.

This is so, for example, when there is excessive and irrational fear of that group, or excessive and irrational commitment to their inferiority. As we have seen, a result is that lawmakers do not hold themselves accountable to that group when proposing and passing laws. In such a situation, there is no obvious deliberative way to make that group visible, no method that appeals to reason to bring members of that group into equal political standing.

There is a structural problem in certain imperfectly realized liberal democracies that necessitates civic rhetoric. There is no obvious way that members of the group whose perspectives are invisible could use reasonable claims in public political discourse to compel their fellow citizens into recognizing their perspectives. After all, the same mechanisms that make a group's perspective invisible also silence their voices. Nor is it straightforward to see how the invisible perspectives of such a group could *come to be visible* from discussion among the citizens not in that group.[41] If the perspectives of a group are invisible to everyone else, their interests are not weighted in the forming of laws (this is why, for example, the ethical and political crisis posed by the prison situation in the United States seems particularly difficult to resolve). If the members of the excluded group are without property, they will remain so; if they are without political power, they will remain so as well. To recognize the invisible, democratic deliberation must often be circumvented by appeals to empathy of the sort Du Bois urges in his essay from 1926, which for that reason must be regarded as one of the great essays in democratic political philosophy.

Thus far, I have argued that there is a structural reason why civic rhetoric is required in certain situations. These situations are ones in which societies that take themselves to be guided by the liberal democratic ideals of autonomy, equality, and reason restrict the application of these ideals to one dominant subgroup of citizens (for example, white men). I have argued, following Melvin Rogers and others, that there is no obvious

way of using reason, or reasonable claims, to get members of
the dominant subgroup to extend the application of liberal
ideals to citizens who are not included (such as, in the history
of the American polity, Black citizens). What is required is extending the domain of cognitive empathy to include those citizens, and there is no obviously cogent *argument*, from the perspective of just those citizens who are included in the sphere
of liberal democratic ideals, to do so. But I have not addressed
the *method* by which the domain of empathy can be expanded.
Here too, following Rogers, I think close attention to the particular rhetorical tropes employed by Du Bois is revealing, as
in the following passage from *The Souls of Black Folk*:

> [F]ew men ever worshipped Freedom with half such un-
> questioning faith as did the American Negro for two cen-
> turies. To him, so far as he thought and dreamed, slavery
> was indeed the sum of all villainies, the cause of all sorrow,
> the root of all prejudice; Emancipation was the key to a
> promised land of sweeter beauty than ever stretched before
> the eyes of wearied Israelites. . . . The Nation has not yet
> found peace from its sins; the freedman has not yet found
> in freedom his promised land."[42]

Du Bois is here clearly employing civic rhetoric directed at a
white audience. The question before us is how the rhetoric is
supposed to work. What is the *mechanism* by which a passage
like this elicits empathy, and leads to the broadening of the
sphere of application of democratic ideals?

I think it is best to understand Du Bois here as employing *the liberal democratic ideals themselves*, against a certain understanding of their application. His goal is to undermine a
conception of liberal democracy that only extends freedom
to whites. His method is to appeal to freedom itself, that liberal democratic ideal that is so cherished even among a nation
in which it is restricted to whites. His rhetoric undermines
an understanding of those ideals thus restricted, by calling
attention to the fact that those ideals are deeply cherished

among nonwhites as well. The goal here is to elicit empathy, by drawing attention to the fact that cherished ideals among the whites are *also* cherished among Blacks. He is eliciting empathy by employing the problematically restricted ideals, and calling upon whites who cherish them to empathize with the plight of those who also cherish them, but to whom they have been consistently denied. The mechanism he is using is therefore a certain kind of undermining propaganda, one that targets the ideal *freedom just for whites*. His argument appeals to freedom, which is understand in the dominant group as *freedom just for whites*. He seeks to persuade them that if one values freedom, one must extend it to those who also value freedom just as much. *Freedom just for whites* is therefore incoherent as an ideal; freedom is an ideal for whites because it is cherished as the highest value. But then it is an ideal for Blacks as well, and must be extended to them. In this way, the liberal concepts can be used against restricted understandings of their proper application.

We have now seen that civic rhetoric is necessary to overcome certain situations that face societies striving to follow liberal democratic ideals, as well as some examples of civic rhetoric. But there is always a cost to bypassing deliberative ideals in discourse in such societies. Are the problems that arise from the invisibility of a group from political discourse worth bearing that cost? I will use the example of the situation of federal and state prisoners in the United States to illustrate the deep ethical and political problems raised for democratic societies by the existence of groups whose perspective has been made invisible.

Unlike in the majority of democracies, in the United States, prisoners cannot vote; they are barred from political participation. The United States is unique among Western democracies in barring some prisoners from voting even after they have been released.[43] As a consequence, there is no one recognized by the polity who can speak from the perspective of prisoners. Prisoners have become dehumanized as a consequence. They now serve as a strategic instrument in politics. A politician summons up crime to elicit fear, and then offers himself as the instrument to satisfy the desire for retribution (though the desire is for retribution of the fear caused by that very politician).[44] The disappearance from public political life of the perspective of the prisoner has resulted, in the view of many advocates, such as Chuck Colson, in an ethical crisis for the United States. Recent decades have borne witness to ever more draconian prison torture practices, including the extensive use of solitary confinement and inhumane prison-sentencing practices.

What is less often remarked upon is that the disappearance of the prisoners' perspective from public political discourse has resulted in another kind of crisis, a *political* crisis. The dehumanizing of prisoners has undermined our democracy. One example is the widespread practice in the United States of *prison gerrymandering*. In the many states that practice it, prisoners confined there also count as residents of the area where the prisons are. Many prisons are located in rural areas, and many of those areas have too few nonincarcerated residents to allow a representative to the state legislature. In the state of Pennsylvania alone, there are eight state legislative districts that have too few nonincarcerated residents to be state legislative districts without counting the nonvoting (and mostly urban) prisoners in their prisons. Prisons thus give the rural voters in the areas in which prisons are located vastly enhanced political power and money from the state. This, in turn, gives such voters extra incentive to promote brutal prison-sentencing practices to keep the prisoners incarcerated and bring more to their districts.

Prison labor also provides a salient example of the political crisis posed by dehumanizing prisoners. The Thirteenth Amendment, which banned forced unpaid labor, allows an exception in the case of prison labor. This has offered a large opportunity for states to replace good, high-paying public service jobs with often free prison labor. The governor of the state of Wisconsin in the United States, Scott Walker, in 2011 pushed through a law eliminating collective bargaining by public sector unions in Wisconsin, effectively destroying the unions in a state known for its history of union organizing. The law eliminated the ability of unions to label certain jobs as "union only" jobs. One effect was to allow high-paying union jobs to be replaced by privately contracted prison labor. This effectively incentivizes the state to seek more prisoners for cheap labor.

More generally, the widespread practice of dehumanizing those caught violating laws leads to a situation in which prisoners become a pawn in the hands of Machiavellian politicians who use the fear of crime to represent themselves as the people's protector.[45] Plato traces the weak point of democracy to the people's "propensity to elevate and glorify one man as the people's protector and champion" (565c). "[T]he tyrant's point of entry into the society" is his self-representation as "the people's protector" (565d). To win elections, politicians in the United States self-represent as being "the people's protector," by irrationally creating fear around crime and offering themselves as the ones who will deliver retribution. This erodes genuine democratic deliberation and facilitates the actions of demagogues. The disappearance of the prisoners' perspective from public debate in the United States is thus *both* a moral crisis and a political crisis.

Democratic countries do not have an official ministry of propaganda. Nondemocratic countries, such as Cuba, do. This distinction needs to be explained. We have seen that civic rhetoric is a legitimate, and even necessary, kind of propaganda in countries guided by incompletely realized democratic ideals. But this does not mean that a democratic country could have a ministry of civic rhetoric. The central purpose of Du Bois's and Locke's notion of propaganda is to make those contributing to public reason accountable to the perspectives of those of an oppressed group. In effect, it is to make an allegedly democratic state into a genuinely democratic state: to realize democracy. To have an official ministry of propaganda is to admit that the state is not democratic. It is to admit that there is still work to be done to incorporate some of those subject to the laws into the state as citizens. A state that considers itself already democratic could never have a ministry as an official state entity that delivers even propaganda of the sort called for by Du Bois. To do so would be to admit that the state has fallen systematically short of the minimum requirements for a democracy (which requires, minimally, awareness by the state that it has fallen short). The other function of ministries of propaganda is to bypass democratic deliberation to elicit support for a policy. Even if this is needed for a state emergency, or for furthering worthwhile secondary political goals, it is by its nature, as we have seen, nondemocratic. It is for these reasons that no democratic state can have a ministry of propaganda.

We can now also precisely identify the structural relation between propaganda that is in some sense useful to democracy and demagoguery. The account of propaganda I provide explains precisely why some kinds of propaganda are permissible, and perhaps even necessary, in societies that are guided by liberal democratic ideals, while others are not. The notion of propaganda at issue in the Du Bois–Locke debate, which *increases* reasonableness, is legitimate, even if it does not contribute to resolving the debate. Speech that appears reasonable but serves the goal of decreasing reasonableness by representing a group in the society as not worthy of empathy is always demagogic. It is demagoguery. Thus, propaganda of the sort that repairs wounds to democracy and propaganda that causes such wounds are systematically related.

Demagoguery in a democracy takes the form of a contribution that presents itself as exemplifying the norms of public reason but makes a contribution a rational person would recognize to be inconsistent with these norms. I have now given two examples of ideals of public reason. The first ideal of public reason centrally involves an ideal of theoretical rationality. On this conception, demagoguery is discourse that appears to make a rational contribution to the debate at hand, but instead serves to cut off rational debate by enlisting the forces of passion to make an impartial reasoned stance impossible. This fits Victor Klemperer's description of the effects of using the word "heroic" around those raised under the education system and moral values of the Third Reich. The second ideal of public reason centrally involves an ideal of reasonableness. The capacity to be reasonable requires, as we have seen, a disposition to take the perspective of others in the community in proposing reasons, to be empathetic to them, and to respect their dignity. A contribution to public reason is reasonable only if it takes into account the reasonable perspectives of all those citizens subject to the policy under debate. On this conception, demagoguery is discourse that appears to take every perspective into account but has the goal of rendering some reasonable perspectives invisible.

A salient feature of many paradigm cases of propaganda is that it is speech that owes its efficacy in ending rational debate not to its settling of the question, but rather to its erosion of second-personal ideals like reasonableness. In many paradigm cases of propaganda, its political effectiveness is initially thought of as explained by its effect in eroding the ideals of rationality, say, by cutting off debate. For example, in the first instance, linking Saddam Hussein to international terrorism after the tragedy of 9/11 raised fears that cut off rational debate. But it must be admitted that it is a possible explanation of why it was so *simple* to raise such fears in the absence of compelling evidence that Iraq was a threat to US security: these fears were embedded within a larger picture that excluded Arab Muslims from a framework of mutual respect. Whether or not this is what was happening in the debate about invading Iraq in 2003, it is undeniable that appeals to passions and fear are often more effective when wheeled against an enemy one considers to be morally repugnant, to lack the norms of humanity. In such cases, the effectiveness of discourse for halting ideals of theoretical rationality must be explained in terms of its effectiveness for ideals of reasonableness, or ideals sufficiently like reasonableness. The reason we cut off rational debate is usually because of a loss of empathy. It may be, for example, that the real explanation of the effectiveness of fear for the decision to invade Iraq was the lack of the average American's ability to imagine himself as a member of a population being invaded and heavily aerially bombed by a vastly more powerful military force, and that in turn was the consequence of stereotypes about Arab Muslims that robbed us of the capacity for empathy toward them.[46]

The mechanisms by which one erodes the normative ideals of public reason are often indirect. Consider the right to free speech. The right to free speech is justified by the fact that it is required for the demands of public reason. As John Stuart Mill famously argued, we cannot expect rational deliberation (including about policy) to end in knowledge unless we allow free speech. The case for government openness is also based on the role public reason plays in democratic legitimacy. It is after all not plausible to arrive via deliberation at the best decision even about which representatives to elect without knowing what the government has been up to and what those representatives have done about it. Given the role of the ideals of public reason in conferring democratic legitimacy on state policy, in a democracy, someone who ultimately seeks to bypass democratically legitimate processes to establish a policy will do so by eroding the ideals of public reason. As we have just seen, government transparency is a requirement of public debate in a democracy. Eliminating government transparency is a way to erode the ideals of public reason, by eroding the possibility of fully informed debate about policy.

If the guiding ideal of public reason in a democratic society is reasonableness, then it follows that a paradigm way propaganda in a democratic society manifests is by representing the perspectives of some of our fellow citizens as unworthy of consideration (and, in the international sphere, representing the perspectives of our enemies as such). But it must be acknowledged that much propaganda does not seem to be of this form.

For example, in the election in 2012, in South Carolina, Mitt Romney accused President Barack Obama of wanting to lift the work requirements of welfare. This was widely acknowledged to be propaganda, for example, it was clearly deceptive, since it was known to be false. But it appears to be economic rather than an attempt to exclude the perspectives of some of our fellow citizens.

To understand why claims about welfare programs are in fact fundamentally appeals to exclude the perspectives of some of our fellow citizens, it is worthwhile to bear in mind the chief Republican strategist Lee Atwater's famous comments, in a 1981 interview:

> You start out in 1954 by saying, "[N-word], [N-word], [N-word]." By 1968 you can't say "[N-word]"—that hurts you, backfires. So you say stuff like, uh, forced busing, states' rights, and all that stuff, and you're getting so abstract. Now, you're talking about cutting taxes, and all these things you're talking about are totally economic things and a byproduct of them is, blacks get hurt worse than whites.... "We want to cut this," is much more abstract than even the busing thing, uh, and a hell of a lot more abstract than "[N-word], [N-word]."

Subsequent research by the Princeton political science professors Martin Gilens and Tali Mendelberg has confirmed the success of the strategy of linking talk of welfare programs to the idea that Black Americans are unfit to have their perspectives taken into account. Their research shows that expressions like "welfare," "the poor," "food stamps," and "homeless" all introduce the thought that Black Americans are lazy. In his book from 1999, Gilens shows that "the belief that blacks are lazy is the strongest predictor of the perception that welfare recipients are undeserving."[47] There is a large amount of additional evidence that "welfare" has been connected with a flawed ideology of race, in addition to the studies Gilens himself has carried out. Gilens reports similar results from the "welfare mother" experiment from the National Race and Politics

Study of 1991: "[R]espondents are asked their impressions of a welfare recipient described as either a Black or white woman in her early thirties, who has a ten-year-old child and has been on welfare for the past year. Respondents are first asked how likely it is that the woman described will try hard to find a job and second, how likely it is that she will have more children in order to have a bigger welfare check."[48] The largest predictor of opposition to welfare programs was one's bias against Black welfare mothers.[49]

Lee Atwater's quotation shows that there was a deliberate attempt to appropriate the language of welfare to convey in a nonobvious way what racial slurs did in 1954. Subsequent research shows that the attempts of Atwater and those before him have been successful. Suppose that the implicitly recognized normative political ideal of public reason is reasonableness, and suppose that my characterization of propaganda is correct. It follows that one characteristic form of propaganda in a liberal democracy takes the form of claims that rely on flawed ideology to decrease empathy for a minority group (of course there are others as well). In the next chapter, I will explain the mechanism exploited by the kind of propaganda Atwater discusses, and why it is so effective at perpetuating dominant group ideologies.

In this chapter, I have explained the form of propaganda in a democracy. To preserve the character of democratic deliberation, those deliberating in formal and informal debate over policy are subject to a norm of reasonableness, which requires them to take the perspectives of others into account. Characteristically, then, negative propaganda, or propaganda, will take the form of a reasonable proposal, a proposal that seems to take everyone's perspective into account (for example, by calling attention to a public threat), in the service of a goal that, rationally speaking, erodes reasonableness. Civic rhetoric is an attempt to share the perspective of a group whose perspective has been made invisible, thereby preventing democracy; civic rhetoric is the tool required in the service of repairing the rupture.

LANGUAGE AS A
MECHANISM OF CONTROL

What are the mechanisms by which propaganda functions in a liberal democracy? Liberal democratic norms pose obstacles for the demagogue. If reasonableness is a norm governing public reason, how could one appear to be reasonable, yet nevertheless undermine reasonableness? In this chapter, I turn to the details of linguistic communication to describe one mechanism that I will argue is often exploited to overcome the problem raised by liberal democratic norms governing public reason. I conclude the chapter with a discussion about whether the phenomena I discuss raise worries for the practical possibility of deliberative norms.

There has been very little discussion in formal semantics and pragmatics on the effects of "code words" on discourse. This is problematic. We have an ideal picture of deliberation spelled out in semantics and pragmatics. That is, we have a specific, worked-out theory of how speaker and hearer can communicate effectively, which exploits a truth-conditional theory of meaning. An utterer can say something, which, if accepted, eliminates certain situations as possible. Eventually, speaker and hearer agree on a picture of the world. This truth-conditional, cognitivist framework gives us an elegant account of what happens when communication works.

What I will argue in this chapter is that the truth-conditional, cognitivist picture also gives us an elegant account of what happens when communication fails, due to propagandistic manipulation. Since the cognitivist, truth-conditional framework embodies an account of what happens when communication functions well, it allows us precise grasp of what happens when communications fails to function well. My worry with noncognitivist accounts, or accounts that are unsystematic at their core, is that, while they are sometimes well suited to explain failures of communication, they are ill suited to explain the contrast between well-functioning communication and poorly functioning communication.

If a group is deliberating about a policy or course of action that will affect everyone in the group, fairness requires regarding everyone's viewpoint as worthy of respect. But this is just to say that it is natural to expect reasonableness to be the norm governing any such deliberation, including those that are intended to issue in democratically legitimate policies. I will henceforth assume that the principle ideal of public reason is reasonableness, rather than theoretical rationality. To say that the principle ideal of public reason is reasonableness is not to deny that there are other ideals of public reason. Politicians must also be, for example, rationally consistent, objective, and logical.

One moral of the previous chapter is that demagoguery in a liberal democracy takes the form of a contribution to public debate that is presented as embodying reasonableness yet in fact contributes a content that clearly erodes reasonableness. This form of propaganda is not merely a deceitful attempt to bypass theoretical rationality, on this view. It functions via an initial selection of a target within the population.

A proposal is reasonable if it appears so from the perspective of each citizen of the state. A contribution is inconsistent with reasonableness if it undermines the capacity or the willingness to produce or be swayed by reasonable proposals. Reasonableness presupposes, at least in humans, the capacity for empathy for others. If I am right, we should expect paradigm cases of propaganda to have as part of their communicative content that *a group in society is not worthy of our respect.* So one characteristic way to convey that a target is not worthy of respect is to cause one's audience to lose empathy for them.

Demagoguery can take both linguistic and nonlinguistic form. Many of the paradigm examples of demagoguery, including demagogic propaganda, are posters, pictures, and architecture, rather than utterances of sentences. Any characterization of demagoguery, or propaganda more generally, that is focused specifically on language is clearly too narrow. My characterization of propaganda is accordingly perfectly general. It is not restricted to propaganda that takes linguistic form. Nonlinguistic images or movies clearly do exploit existing false ideological beliefs demagogically in just the way I have described. For example, pictorial representations of Roma in Hungarian articles about crime, or Blacks in American articles on this topic, will be demagogic if they are employed to justify brutal and unequal laws. But I am unable to give an account of the *mechanisms* by which this occurs.

There is a science of language and communication in place that enables us to gain some precision about the mechanisms underlying linguistic propaganda. I exploit that account to explain how some linguistic propaganda works. I suspect the same level of detail has not yet been achieved in our understanding of imagistic representation. Therefore, I will focus on the linguistic case. I expect that future research will be able to help us address how the perhaps more important imagistic case works.

I will use formal semantics and pragmatics to describe a specific mechanism by which demagoguery in linguistic form plays a role in bringing into the context false ideological beliefs that are apparently not part of the discussion. As we shall see, there is a great deal of evidence that there is such a linguistic mechanism. And perhaps there are analogous mechanisms in the case of images; indeed, the inspiration point in my analysis, Rae Langton and Caroline West's theory of pornography from 1999, employs similar formal semantic and pragmatic mechanisms to explain the phenomena of subordination with images. But it is not clear to me that all these *exact* mechanisms can function with images and movies, because it is not clear to me that one can make the distinction between at-issue and not-at-issue content that is at the center of the mechanism I describe. My focus is on explaining one way in which demagoguery exploits already existing nonpolitical mechanisms to be effective. This mechanism is well understood in the case of language, so we can describe it with precision.

A number of philosophers in the feminist tradition, including Catherine MacKinnon and Jennifer Hornsby, have argued that the function of certain kinds of speech (in their chosen example, pornography) is to silence a targeted group. The philosopher whose work has most inspired and influenced my own is Rae Langton. Langton argues, following MacKinnon and Hornsby, that pornographic material *subordinates* women and *silences* them.[1] In depicting subordination, Langton argues, pornographers subordinate women. Langton argues that the function of certain kinds of racist speech is "to rank blacks as inferior." Langton also argues that pornography silences women, by undermining the felicity conditions of their speech; it represents "no" as yes. My aim in this chapter is to explain some of these effects with the tools of contemporary formal semantics, by applying them to the case of propaganda.

Here is one model of how this could work; as is clear from her response to Judith Butler, it is a model from which Langton distances herself.[2] An imperative is a command to act a certain way. The imperative statement "eat your beets!" directed at a three year old is a command to the three year old to do something. Pornographic speech could function as a mechanism of subordination by delivering imperative-like orders of some kind. The thought here is not that imperatives bring about their truth. Commands must be associated with practical authority in order to have this function. But so too, as I will argue, does subordinating speech. The relation between imperatives and subordinating speech will be a theme of this chapter, as I will draw on both semantic and pragmatic features of imperatives in my analysis of subordinating speech. I will try to square this use of the semantics of imperatives with Langton's compelling "verdictive" account of subordinating speech.

Our discussion to this point suggests that there should be expressions apt for use in a debate that function to *exclude the perspective* of certain groups in the population. Since demagoguery, like undermining propaganda generally, is masked as embodying the ideals with which it ultimately clashes, we should expect these expressions to operate indirectly. That is, there should be systematic ways of genuinely or apparently *contributing* to debate, which simultaneously frame the debate in such a way as to exclude the perspective of a targeted group. The function of these expressions is to mask the demagogic nature of the contribution, by creating flawed ideological beliefs to the effect that the perspectives of a designated group are not worthy of reasonable consideration.

We should expect there to be linguistic means by use of which one can make an apparently reasonable claim, while simultaneously, merely by using the relevant vocabulary, wearing down the ideal of reasonableness. Because these linguistic means should be available for use to make any point whatsoever that may come up in debate about policy, we should expect that they function to exclude whether one takes the affirmative or the negative position on the debate. Indeed, if there were no linguistic means of excluding the perspective of certain groups from debate, while simultaneously representing oneself as contributing to the debate, that would raise the suspicion that reasonableness is not in fact the ideal of public reason.

If reasonableness is the norm of public reason, we should expect there to be linguistic mechanisms, that is, *expressions*, with the following three properties:

1. Use of the relevant expression has the effect on the conversation of representing a certain group in the community as having a perspective not worthy of inclusion, that is, they are not worthy of respect.

2. The expression has a content that can serve simply to contribute legitimately to resolving the debate at issue in a reasonable way, which is separate from its function as a mechanism of exclusion.

3. Mere use of the expression is enough to have the effect of eroding reasonableness. So the effect on reasonableness occurs just by virtue of using the expression, in whatever linguistic context.

Here is why my characterization of propaganda entails the existence of expressions with these properties. The expressions would have to have the first property, because that would be the property of eroding reasonableness. The expressions would have to have the second property, because they would have to be able to be used in discourse that appears to meet the ideal of public reason. The expressions would have to have the third property, because they would have to be apt for use, whatever one's stance on the issue at hand.

We will need some concepts in our analysis of particular cases of propaganda. The first set of concepts is from the branches of linguistics most relevant for our purposes, namely, semantics and pragmatics. We will also need the concept of social meaning, such as from the works of the legal theorist Dan Kahan. These will allow us to spell out how a claim can communicate an implicit message that runs counter to the ideals its explicit content seems to embody. The concepts we will need are somewhat technical. But this should not distract from the fact that the phenomena they are used to describe are very familiar.

The notion of a *linguistic context* is central in contemporary formal semantics and pragmatics. What a sentence of a natural language says depends upon the linguistic context in which it is uttered. In a context in 2014 in which President Barack Obama utters the sentence, "I am the president of the United States," what he says is true. In a context in which the time is 2007, or someone else is the speaker in 2014, what is said is not true. I will sketch some required concepts from the theory of formal semantics and pragmatics.

One notion we need in modeling linguistic context is due to the philosopher Robert Stalnaker. It is the notion of *the common ground* of a conversation: "Participants in a conversation begin with certain information in common, or presumed to be in common, and it is that body of information that the speech acts they perform are designed to influence. The content of an assertion will be a piece of information, and if the assertion is successful, then that information will become part of the body of information that provides the context for the subsequent discourse."[3] The common ground of a conversation is the "information in common, or presumed to be common," in a discourse.

On Stalnaker's view of content, which derives from Ludwig Wittgenstein's treatment of content in the *Tractatus Logico-Philosophicus*, a content is a *set of possible situations*, or "worlds." A proposition on this view is that set of possible worlds in which it is true. A common ground is, then, a set of propositions. On Stalnaker's model of content, the common ground can be thought of as the intersection of all of the propositions mutually presumed to be known by the conversational participants. This is itself a set of possible worlds, the set of possible worlds in which the conjunction of all of the propositions in the common ground is true. Given the model of a proposition as a set of possible worlds, this means that the common ground is the intersection of propositions, and itself is a proposition.

According to Stalnaker's account of communication, successful communication takes the form of *ruling out situations*. I ask you where the gas station is; you reply that it is to the right. You express a proposition, one true in just those possible worlds in which the gas station is to the right, and false in the others. When I accept your assertion, the common ground is updated. In the new common ground, all the possible worlds are ones in which the gas station is to the right. This is the common information. This is an elegant picture of successful communication. An assertion is made; it is a proposal to add a proposition to the common ground. It is debated and, if accepted, added to the common ground. This leads us to rule out possibilities that we had previously entertained.

In recent years, a basically Stalnakerian picture of communication has been altered to include a more complex notion of a context. The context is not just the set of propositions that are what is presumed by the conversational inquirers. It records more detailed information.

Stalnaker's model of a common ground is designed around declarative sentences, and the practice of *asserting* them. To assert a proposition is to represent oneself as knowing it, and to make a proposal to add that proposition to the common ground. But there are other speech acts that occur in conversation, such as questions ("Who went to the party?") and commands ("Eat your beets!"). To accommodate the contextual effects of these other speech acts, one must have a more complex conception of a context than just the common ground. The details of this more complex conception of context are front and center in more recent work on formal semantics and formal pragmatics. In Discourse Representation Theory, Irene Heim and Hans Kamp make contexts "structured," by appealing to the notion of a *file*, which records discourse information such as referents for later pronouns.

The work of the formal semanticist Craige Roberts has been very influential in recent thinking about context. According to Roberts, a context determines not only what is and what is not known to the participants in a discourse, but also a record of the questions that have been asked that direct the course of inquiry.[4] So Roberts adds to the common ground a record of the *questions under discussion*.[5] Roberts thus argues that contexts contain not just sets of propositions, but other elements as well. If so, linguistic meaning can change not just beliefs, but also other psychological states.

I will be applying these resources of formal pragmatics to model the workings of demagogic speech. But I am by no means the first to use them in an analysis of problematic political speech. As we shall see in what follows, the philosophers Rae Langton and Caroline West use Lewis's formal pragmatics to address the harm of pornography.[6] More recently, Ishani Maitra suggests the possibility that subordinating speech is or involves an act of *ranking*. Ranking is a speech act that, like Robert Stalnaker's account of assertion, involves adding a content to the shared background of a conversation. She argues that rankings don't merely seek to describe the world, but "constitute norms," and she sees that this may require a different account of their content.[7] She does not provide an account of the contents of rankings in her paper. Nevertheless, Maitra clearly sees here the possibility of extending the kind of dynamic account of conversation that is familiar from the work of Stalnaker and others in formal semantics and pragmatics to speech acts other than assertions. It is this basic model I am filling out and developing in this chapter.

The Dutch semanticist Frank Veltman, in his paper "Defaults in Update Semantics," published in 1996, adds to the context a preference ordering on possible worlds, meant to reflect "defeasible knowledge." The idea is that certain possible situations are conceived of as more likely than others, and hence to be epistemically preferred. Veltman's theory is meant to handle *generic statements*, roughly, generalizations that structure our expectations, making it easier to maneuver around the world. These are statements like "birds fly" or "dogs have four legs."[8] An utterance of "birds fly," if accepted, makes it the case that, when considering any given bird in context, the ordering on possible worlds is one according to which worlds in which that bird flies are closer than worlds in which that bird doesn't fly. This reflects the bias toward situations in which a given bird that one encounters flies.

Another notion we need, in addition to that of a linguistic context, is the distinction between *at-issue content* and *not-at-issue content*. Christopher Potts uses the following two examples to illustrate the distinction between at-issue and not-at-issue content.[9] The first involves what he calls a "supplemental expression," in this case "who lived in a working-class suburb of Boston," to make the distinction. The second involves what he calls an "expressive," in this case "damn," to make the distinction:

1. I spent part of every summer until I was ten with my grandmother, who lived in a working-class suburb of Boston.

2. We bought a new electric clothes dryer, and I thought all there was to it was plugging it in' and connecting the vent hose. Nowhere did it say that the *damn* thing didn't come with an electric plug!

As Potts writes, "[T]he supplementary relative *who lived in a working-class suburb of Boston* plays a secondary role relative to the information conveyed by the main clause. The issue is not where the grandmother lived, but rather the fact that the speaker summered with her as a child." The *at-issue content* is what is at issue in the debate. Supplemental constructions and expressives are "used to guide the discourse in a particular direction or to help the hearer to better understand why the at-issue content is important at that stage."

The at-issue content of an utterance is the information *asserted* by the utterance. When I utter (1), what I assert is that I spent part of every summer until I was ten with my grandmother. To assert something, as the linguist Sarah Murray describes, is *to propose to add it to the common ground*. To assert something is to advance it as something the speaker knows, and to thereby *propose* that its content be added to the common ground. Subsequent argument is debate about whether or not to accept the proposal.

In contrast, the claim about my grandmother, that she lived in a working-class suburb of Boston, is additional material that comments on what is asserted. It is not-at-issue content. The not-at-issue content of an utterance is not advanced as a proposal of a content to be added to the common ground. Not-at-issue content is *directly* added to the common ground. For this reason, not-at-issue content is in general "not negotiable, not directly challengeable, and [is] added [to the common ground] even if the at-issue proposition is rejected."[10] This characterization of not-at-issue content is supported by much linguistic evidence; the evidence mostly involves when it is legitimate to retract a claim. The not-at-issue content is often "semantic, part of the conventional meaning."

Rae Langton and Caroline West argue that not-at-issue content is involved in pornography.[11] Specifically, they argue that pornography has the effect of subordinating women, not by explicitly communicating a subordinating message, but by *presupposing* it. "In order to make sense of what is explicitly said and illustrated" in pornography, they argue, one must make the relevant sexist and subordinating presuppositions, or not-at-issue contents.

Langton and West were writing before the at-issue/not-at-issue distinction was drawn. Their theoretical model is linguistic presupposition, as described in David Lewis's seminal paper "Scorekeeping in a Language Game." Consider the examples:

3. It was John who solved the problem.

4. My wife is from Chicago.

Linguists generally hold that an utterance of (3) presupposes the proposition that someone solved the problem, and asserts that John solved the problem. Linguists generally hold that an utterance of (4) presupposes the proposition that the speaker has a wife, and asserts that she is from Chicago. One reason to think that this is the right account is that denying the speaker's claim is naturally understood as denying what is asserted, while agreeing with what is presupposed. So if someone asserts (3), and I respond with "that's false," the interpretation of my denial is as denying that John solved the problem, not as denying that someone solved the problem. Similarly, if someone asserts (4), and I respond with "that's false," then my denial is standardly taken to be a denial that the speaker's wife is in Chicago, not that the speaker is married. Presupposed content is a kind of not-at-issue content (roughly). Asserted content is at-issue content.

The linguist Sarah Murray argues that an assertion of a declarative sentence is a proposal to add the at-issue content to the common ground.[12] In contrast, the not-at-issue content is directly added to the common ground. Using the example of Cheyenne, she shows that there are explicit linguistic markers of not-at-issue content. In English, they are less obvious, but still present. For example, the expression "I hear" in (5) functions as a "hedge"; it introduces not-at-issue content:

5. The president is about to give a speech, I hear.

"I hear" functions to comment on the at-issue content that the president is about to give a speech. In the case of hedges like "I hear," Murray argues that they alter the at-issue content. The at-issue content of (5) is that it is *possible* that the president is about to give a speech. The not-at-issue content, that the speaker heard that the president is about to give a speech, is simply added to the common ground. Challenges to (5) are challenges to the at-issue content, but not to the not-at-issue content that the speaker heard the at-issue content. This raises the possibility that one can communicate a noneasily challenged meaning by attaching it to an expression as not-at-issue content.

Here is a final example of not-at-issue content, involving epistemic "must" in English:

6. It must be raining outside.

If someone utters (6), she communicates that she did not herself experience rain, that she *inferred it indirectly*. Kai von

Fintel and Anthony Gillies have convincingly argued that this feature of "must" is like the evidential markings in other languages. (Von Fintel and Gillies's view is unsurprising, because epistemic "must" is of course by definition, like evidentials, epistemic.)[13] That the agent did not witness the event of raining is *not* part of the asserted content of an utterance of (6). For example, it is not easy to deny this content. It is difficult to respond to (6) by responding with "that's wrong, you are soaking wet." The communicated content *that the agent did not witness the rain herself* is something that would be very odd and rude to challenge. So doing would suggest that the agent is deficient in some way, rather than merely ordinarily misinformed. It is not-at-issue content, rather than at-issue content.

Some kinds of not-at-issue content are easier to recover than other kinds. The kind associated with epistemic "must" is "baked" deeply into the meaning of the modal auxiliary "must." Other kinds, such as those found in explicit supplemental expressions, are more easily targeted and identified. The properties associated with being not-at-issue come in degree.

Here is a property of presuppositions that makes them not suitable for analysis as classic not-at-issue content. A presupposition of a word or a linguistic construction can be "filtered" from a larger construction containing it. Sentence (1) presupposes that the problem was solved. But (7) does not presuppose that the problem was solved.

7. If the problem was solved, it was John who solved it.

In this case, the presupposition that the problem was solved has been "filtered" by the antecedent of the conditional, the sentence following "if," namely, "the problem was solved." Similarly, (8) presupposes that John smoked, but (9) does not:

8. John stopped smoking.

9. Bill believes that John stopped smoking.

In contrast, not-at-issue content cannot be "filtered."

One kind of linguistic propaganda involves repeated association between words and social meanings. Repeated association is also the mechanism by which conventional meaning is formed; it is because people use "dogs" to refer to dogs, repeatedly, that "dogs" comes to refer to dogs. My claim in this chapter is that when propagandists use repeated association between words and images, they are forming connections that serve as the basis of conventional meaning. Typically, the conventional meaning is not-at-issue content. As is the case with conventional meaning generally, the links between word and meaning are a matter of degree, vague, and negotiable. The word "Madagascar" originally referred to part of the mainland of Africa, but, because of changing usage, came to refer to an island off the coast of Africa. We see the same possibilities for change and resisting change with the kinds of repeated associations that propaganda involves.

When the news media connects images of urban Blacks repeatedly with mentions of the term "welfare," the term "welfare" comes to have the not-at-issue content that Blacks are lazy. At some point, the repeated associations are part of the meaning, the not-at-issue content. The negative social meaning associated with "welfare" functions like the content that the agent has not directly witnessed the event that is associated with "must," as in (6). This does not mean that someone hearing the term "welfare" automatically comes to believe that Blacks are lazy. It does mean that they may have to shift to different vocabulary, or consciously resist the effects of the association, in conversation or otherwise, to deter the propagandistic effect.

Langton and West, in their account of pornography, explain how presupposition can be used to smuggle in content that one would not necessarily accept if it was presented as the content asserted. This is a significant discovery about how problematic messages are communicated, either intentionally or not. However, I will replace their appeal to presupposition with the related category of not-at-issue content. The fact that not-at-issue content is, in Murray's words, "directly added" to the common ground is what makes it rife for propagandistic abuse. The fact that the not-at-issue content cannot be canceled is what makes it so effective.

Those who have theorized about not-at-issue content tend to represent not-at-issue content as content of the same sort as at-issue content, but playing a different role. Our discussion of reasonableness suggests that this approach may be incorrect. The effect of propaganda in a liberal democracy is to erode respect for a targeted group. In humans, respect for a group or a person is characteristically based upon empathy for them. One characteristic effect of propaganda in a liberal democracy will be to erode empathy for the perspectives of a group in a population, while presenting itself as not so doing. This means that there will be expressions that have normal contents, which express these contents via a way that erodes empathy for a group.

How should we think of the mechanism by which a contribution is in the service of the erosion of empathy for a group of people? In an important series of papers, Sarah-Jane Leslie has connected generics to problematic social stereotyping of groups. Leslie establishes that generics are *cognitively fundamental generalizations* that are acquired very early in life.[14] She argues that generics are one mechanism, perhaps a key one, by which we come to form social essentialist views about groups.[15] In "The Original Sin of Cognition," she provides an explanation of the epistemic problems that acceptance of a generic engenders; it leads us to generalize the surprising properties of some members of a group onto the group as a whole (as in "Muslims are terrorists").[16] One does not need to accept all of Leslie's theory to accept the argument that generics plausibly play the role of *stereotypes*, including racial stereotypes, in many theories of stereotype (including Walter Lippmann's original notion, to be discussed in a subsequent chapter). I am going to use Leslie's insights, together with the mechanisms discussed by Veltman in his theory of generics, to explain various features of propaganda. I am thereby exploiting Leslie's important insight that generics are or can play the role of stereotypes, and the existence of a semantic account of at least one effect of generics that I find persuasive.

Here is one way in which a contribution can erode empathy for a group. The contribution could communicate a certain claim about that group, such as that *Jews are the enemy*, that *women are submissive*, that *Blacks are violent*, or that *immigrants are criminal*. A claim could have a perfectly ordinary at-issue content, but erode empathy by having such a proposition as its not-at-issue content. For example, if someone utters in a political speech in the United States, "There are Jews among us," it expresses a perfectly ordinary at-issue content, one that is in fact true. There are Jews in the United States. But it equally clearly conveys the not-at-issue content that Jews are the enemy, by suggesting that Jews are enemy invaders distinct from the "us" of the polity. Let us call this *the content model of propaganda*. According to the content model, one kind of paradigmatic propaganda in a liberal democracy would have a normal at-issue content that seems reasonable, and would also have a not-at-issue content that is not reasonable.

Here is another way of thinking of the mechanism by which a contribution could lead to an erosion of empathy for a group. The contribution could express a perfectly ordinary at-issue content, but cause a decrease in empathy or respect directly, as part of its not-at-issue function. The idea here is not, as on the content model of propaganda, that there is a not-at-issue content, acceptance of which decreases empathy for a group. It is rather that words have direct not-at-issue emotional *effects*. Let us call this *the expressive model of propaganda*. According to the expressive model, one kind of paradigmatic propaganda in a liberal democracy would have a normal at-issue content that seems reasonable, and would also have a not-at-issue effect that would decrease empathy for a group. Since decreasing empathy for a group runs counter to reasonability, its not-at-issue effects would be unreasonable.

The division in the theory of meaning between expressivist theories and content theories is central in twentieth-century philosophy. For example, theorists of value who hold that there are no ethical facts treat ethical assertion as expressive, rather than contentful. Thus, they free themselves from commitment to a domain of moral facts. The problem facing expressivist theories has always been that they cannot explain the kind of linguistic behavior that shows that our interpretation of the relevant sentences is governed by formal rules. For example, the "Frege-Geach Problem" is that declarative sentences can be embedded in more complex constructions. For example, "If you make a lot of money, then you ought to give some money to solve social injustice" is a perfectly well-formed sentence of English. Yet the mechanisms required to explain the process by which the meaning of one sentence contributes to the meanings of larger sentences containing it, the so-called problem of compositionality, all employ models of meaning that assign contents to words and sentences. Expressivists about certain kinds of language have had a very difficult time describing the mechanisms by which what are by their lights sentences that lack content can nevertheless have a systematic effect on larger linguistic constructions that embed them.

Recent work in formal semantics and the philosophy of language has broken down the decades-long impasse between expressivist and content-based models. Imperatives have something to do with *ordering*; an imperative orders actions into a certain hierarchy. "Eat your beets" places the action of eating the audience's beets ahead of the action of not doing so. (As the linguist David Beaver remarked to me, "It can't be an accident that we call commands 'orders.'") The philosopher William Starr, in his paper "A Preference Semantics for Imperatives," produces a formal analysis of the effects of imperatives on the common ground. The details of his analysis are not essential to us. But the basic point of Starr's paper is that it is possible to represent imperatives as having a perfectly formally articulable effect on the context set, without representing that effect as adding a *content*. In short, one can accommodate the contextual effects of an imperative without representing them as a proposal to add a proposition to the common ground.

As in Frank Veltman's analysis of the contextual effects of generic statements, Starr represents contexts as containing a preference ordering on worlds. According to Starr, the effect imperatives have on the common ground is to impose a *preference ordering* on possible situations. An utterance of "eat your beets!" structures the context in a way that ranks possible worlds in which you eat your beets to be preferable to worlds in which you do not eat your beats. Starr shows that there is no obstacle to a full articulable formal implementation of this view.

Veltman and Starr employ preference rankings in different ways. On Veltman's account, "birds fly" has the effect of ranking worlds more closely, in the sense of *more likely*, in which a given bird flies than worlds in which it doesn't; worlds in which birds one encounters fly are closer than worlds in which they do not. On Starr's account, a command has the effect of making worlds preferable in which the command is obeyed. These are different orderings on worlds. Subordinating speech employs both.

Langton distances herself from an imperative account of subordinating speech.[17] The reason she does is that there is an important distinction between a command and the effects of subordinating speech. A command is an order to change the world in a certain way; it is an order to change the world to fit it. In contrast, much subordinating speech aims to fit the world; it aims to describe the world as it actually is, rather than change it. "Blacks are lazy" is not a command to *change* the world to make Blacks lazy; it is rather an attempt to *describe* the world. The preference relation relevant to imperatives (commands) has another direction of fit, that of desires. Imperatives tell the hearer to *change* the world. The preference relation appealed to in Veltman's analysis is of the former kind; it aims to fit the world by describing it. An utterance of "birds fly" has the effect of leading one to think that worlds are more likely in which a bird one encounters flies. Langton is correct that subordinating speech is not adequately characterized in terms of the preference orderings employed in the semantics of imperatives, because it aims to fit the world by describing it. But it is adequately characterized by the preference ordering in Veltman's analysis of generics. A use of the term "welfare," for example, leads one to update one's preferences, by thinking that a Black person one meets is more likely to be lazy than not.

It is no doubt too simplistic to assume that the only effect of subordinating speech is to change epistemic preference orderings. We can enrich contexts both with epistemic preferences orderings, which order worlds according to their likelihood, and with desire-like preference orderings. A word like "inner city" or "super-predator" can have an effect on both; it can tell you that worlds in which young Black teenagers are violent threats tend to be closer than ones in which they are not, and it can order you not to associate with them.

Imperatives are also implicated in the way I have suggested in explaining the force of certain speech acts, which can be taken as commands to update one's epistemic preferences. The mechanism here is familiar from the literature on ideology. Figures in the media, as well as teachers in schools, exploit their position as epistemic authorities to issue assertions that are not supposed to be taken as proposals, but as commands. The newscaster telling the audience something like "austerity is needed to cut down debt" is an order to each audience member to add it to her stock of beliefs. It cannot be a proposal to add it to the common ground, because the relation between the newscaster and the audience is fundamentally asymmetric. He is *telling* me things, not proposing things that he may himself give up when I present him with a good counterargument. *Telling* someone something from a position of authority is a *command*, not an assertion; it is what Pierre Bourdieu and Jean-Claude Passeron call a "game of fictitious communication."[18] The social studies teacher in school is not genuinely proposing her claims for debate.

There are many other resources in formal semantics that can be used to model the effects of subordinating speech. A great deal of formal semantics and the philosophy of language has been devoted to understanding anaphoric pronouns, like the occurrence of "he" in the discourse "A man walked in. He was wearing a hat." It has become typical to add to the context a ranking of salience on objects in the domain, and to treat certain expressions as affecting that ranking. Similarly, we can imagine rankings of groups of people as parts of context. Subordinating expressions would alter these rankings in different ways.

These mechanisms from formal semantics can be used to model in a rigorous way an expressivist account of the function of words that erode empathy. We can think of the not-at-issue meaning of such words, on an expressivist view, as imposing a preference ordering on possible situations in the common ground. We can think of a derogatory word as imposing a preference ordering that ranks groups in a hierarchy. There is no doubt a plethora of ways in which this occurs. In Veltman's theory, the preference order is epistemic. An utterance of "birds fly" makes the context such that, for any given bird, possible worlds in which that bird flies are closer (to be epistemically preferred) than possible words in which that bird doesn't fly. But we can also imagine a preference ordering that holds between worlds that is not epistemic, but rather has to do with what one desires. Certain derogating speech might lead one to accept a preference ordering in which worlds in which one is socializing with members of one's own group are to be preferred, in the sense of more desirable, than worlds in which one is socializing with members of the derogated group.

It is plausible that a word like "welfare" has, in the American political context, as its not-at-issue content, a generic content like *that Blacks are lazy*, as Leslie's view would perhaps predict. On Veltman's view, the result of using the term "welfare" would be to change the preference ordering over worlds in the linguistic context so that, for any given American citizen of African descent, worlds in which that person is lazy are closer than worlds in which he is not lazy. In this way, uses of the term "welfare" change the context in ways that go beyond simply adding propositions to the common ground, or proposing to add them to the common ground. They change the context in a formally tractable way that reflects the expressivist's insights.

In certain characteristic cases in which epistemic authority and practical authority come together, assertions have an imperative-like force. Examples, as I have mentioned, are teaching, media, and the news. In such cases, an authority figure's proposal to add something to the common ground brings with it, in some sense, command-like features, which can be formally modeled. We can make some of this more precise by reflecting on Sarah Murray's account of assertion. Murray argues that an assertion is a *proposal* to add something to the common ground. Proposing is something one does with an equal. When I tell my three-year-old son to add something to the common ground, say, that the Earth is the third planet from the sun, I am not merely *proposing* it to him. I am *ordering* him to add the content to his set of beliefs. When there are asymmetrical authority relations, a proposal may become a command. When I tell my three-year-old son, "beets are good for you," I order him to add it to his common ground.

One cannot command another person to believe something, unless one simultaneously presents evidence for the belief that is to be adopted. I cannot successfully command you to believe that you are on Mars right now. However, in combining epistemic and practical authority, my assertion can have the effect of a command to change one's beliefs. This is what happens when we are in school listening to teachers or watching the news. One can command someone to believe something, by presenting *oneself* as an epistemic authority, whose expert testimony is sufficient to back up one's practical command.

As we saw previously, Samuel Huntington's solution to the problem of "an excess of democracy" in the United States in the 1960s and 1970s was to recommend "claims of expertise, seniority, experience, and special talents" in order to "override the claims of democracy as a way of constituting authority." We can now see the mechanisms at play behind Huntington's proposal. By representing oneself as an "expert" on a topic, one gains the authority to command someone to believe something, presenting one's status as an epistemic authority, an "expert," as the basis for testimonial justification.

An apt description of the derogatory effect of derogatory words is that in addition to conveying not-at-issue contents, they alter the contextually salient preference ordering, perhaps via the generic nature of the not-at-issue contents. On this view, the word "kike" just has Jewish persons as its at-issue content, and it has as its not-at-issue content that Jews are greedy (for example). This has the effect of altering the preference relation in the context, so that, for any given Jewish person, possible situations in which he is greedy are closer than ones in which he is not. My own view is that derogatory words like "kike" have not-at-issue meanings that are both contents, and impose preference orderings of this sort and others. My view is therefore *neither* a pure content model nor a pure expressivist model. A word can erode reasonableness in either of these ways.[19]

Rae Langton famously calls to our attention the fundamental *asymmetry* of subordinating speech. Subordinating speech only works when it is employed by one of the dominant groups in society against a negatively privileged group. In short, it is at least prima facie plausible that subordinating speech must be delivered from a position of *authority*. A homeless, penniless man from Appalachia cannot give commands to managing directors on Wall Street. For the same reason, he cannot engage in speech that has even the possibility of successfully establishing a preference ordering among worlds that ranks him higher than managing directors on Wall Street. Nor can he make assertions that can function as commands; his proposals to add things to the common ground can never, given his lack of practical authority, rise to the point of being *tellings*. This is *the problem of authority*, which has received much discussion in the literature on subordinating speech.[20]

Let's return to the structure of deliberation, any deliberation, about a policy that is to govern a group. As we have seen, reasonableness is a norm governing such deliberation. We should expect to find dialectical methods to cut off reasonable debate that naturally emerge in any society involving group deliberation, in other words, any human society. The most obvious candidates to play this role are *slur words*, such as the N-word (as used for Blacks), "kike," "Kraut," "Spic," and so on. The word "kike" contributes to the at-issue content, the same denotation as "Jewish person." But the effect of its use is to guide the discourse in a particular direction, by eroding empathy for the group the word denotes. If one is speaking with a Jewish person, after "kike" has been mentioned, one cannot help but think that it is more likely that she is greedy than not.

In an unpublished paper written in 1897, "Logic," the German logician Gottlob Frege drew our attention to the relation between the German translations of the words "dog" and "cur":

> If we compare the sentences "This dog howled the whole night" and "This cur howled the whole night," we find that the thought is the same. The first sentence tells us neither more nor less than does the second. But whilst the word "dog" is neutral as between having pleasant or unpleasant associations, the word "cur" certainly has unpleasant rather than pleasant associations and puts us rather in mind of a dog with a somewhat unkempt appearance. Even if it is grossly unfair to the dog to think of it in this way, we cannot say that this makes the second sentence false. True, anyone who utters this sentence speaks pejoratively, but this is not part of the thought expressed. What distinguishes the second sentence from the first is of the nature of an interjection.

Frege's insight is that the word "cur" means the same thing as "dog," but contributes a negative association. Moreover, it contributes this negative association wherever it occurs in the sentence. This is a general property of slurs; the negative association remains, no matter where in the sentence it occurs. For example, negated slur words also erode reasonableness:

4. Jason is not a kike.

5. Bernhard is not a kraut.

Despite the presence of "not," the effect of the use of "kike" and "kraut" remains. One cannot use (4) and (5) to deny that Jews and Germans should not be slandered. By using (4) and (5), one is endorsing the effect of these slur words. The slurring effect of slurs persists, in any linguistic context, even under quotation:

6. "Kike" is a slur for Jewish people.

Since group deliberation about what to do is a feature of human society generally, we should expect slurs to occur in every human society, not just in liberal democracies.

The standard view of slurs is that they express contempt for the targeted group. This is no doubt true; describing a Jewish person as a "kike" conveys contempt toward Jews. But it is not clear how contempt relates to the framework of second-personal relations that underlies the preconditions for joint deliberation on policies that apply to all. Here is the kind of account of slurs I find plausible; versions have been proposed independently by Lynne Tirrell and Elizabeth Camp.[21] Camp argues that slurs "signal allegiance to a perspective: an integrated, intuitive way of cognizing members of the targeting group."[22] Similarly, Tirrell argues that slurs, the category into which her chosen focus of deeply derogatory terms falls, have the function of creating an "insider/outsider" distinction: "the terms serve to mark members of an out-group (as out), and in so doing, they also mark the in-group as unmarked by the term."[23]

Camp argues that while slurs do involve an attitude of contempt, this is not their central function:

Although it is undeniable, and important, that slurs deni-
grate, I think an associated feeling of contempt is less important and explanatory than is usually assumed. Rather,
I think the association with contempt largely falls out of
a more basic one: that the perspective is distancing in the
sense that the speaker signals that he is not "of" or aligned
with Gs; and more specifically, that it is *derogating* in the
sense that the speaker signals that Gs are not worthy of
respect.

According to Camp, a slur like "kike" has, as its at-issue content, Jewish people. Its not-at-issue content is the effect she describes, of decreasing reasonableness, by placing the targeted
group outside the second-personal framework of "mutual
respect" that underlies the possibility of reasonableness. Different slurs are associated with different generic contents that
structure the preference relation accordingly. In each case, the
preference ordering will be such as to make it the case that it is
much more likely that given members of the targeting group
have some property that excludes them from the domain of respect. This is precisely how one would expect slurs to function,
if they are to be of use in excluding a certain perspective from
policymaking in joint deliberation.

Camp describes the not-at-issue content of a slur as "signal-
ing allegiance to a perspective," one that distances itself from
the targeted group. As we will see, this kind of identification
with a group is a notion that lies at the root of the notion of a
flawed ideology.

It is by now clear that the topic of slurs is extremely important in understanding the mechanism by which genocide
occurs. David Livingstone Smith reports a Japanese veteran of
the Rape of Nanjing, one of history's most indescribably brutal massacres, as describing the Chinese as "chancorro," meaning like bugs or animals.[24] In her paper "Genocidal Language
Games," published in 2012, the philosopher Lynne Tirrell describes in detail how "[t]he use of derogatory terms played a

significant role in laying the social groundwork for the 1994 genocide of the Tutsi in Rwanda." Hutu extremists used two slurs, or "deeply derogatory terms," for Tutsis. The first was the word for cockroach, *inyenzi*; the second was the word for snake, *inzoka*. Snakes are a danger in Rwanda, and killing them is a rite of passage for boys. Their heads are cut off and they are cut into pieces. By describing Tutsis as *inzoka*, Hutu propaganda was connecting long-standing social practices in the villages to instructions to Hutu militias on how to kill their victims. As Tirrell clearly brings out, the purpose (what we will call the "social meaning") of calling someone *inzoka* was that it became a legitimate and indeed socially useful act to kill that person in the way one kills a snake.

David Livingstone Smith argues persuasively that genocide is often preceded by dehumanization expressed in linguistic and pictorial form. The deeply derogatory terms represent the targeted group as a public health threat, by linking them with animals and diseases, especially of the sort that elicit disgust, such as rats (in the case of Nazi propaganda about Jews) and snakes (as in the Rwandan genocide). Public health warnings are of course an embodiment of reasonable discourse. Dehumanizing propaganda is of course much more ubiquitous than genocide. But the well-established link between dehumanizing propaganda and genocide should make all of us wary when a group of our fellow humans is represented as subhuman animals, insects, or vermin. The message of such representation is to legitimate the kind of treatment our society recommends for the relevant kind of animal.

There is, however, a problematic assumption behind the small philosophy literature on slurs. It is that slurs are *special*. The focus in the literature is on describing their special properties. But expressions with the linguistic properties imputed to slurs are *not* special. As we have seen in previous chapters, the distinctive danger of propaganda in a liberal democracy is that it goes unnoticed. It is hard to think of a better way to exhibit this distinctive danger than by reflection on the fact that philosophy professors in liberal democratic societies assume that there is a distinctive and easily identifiable class of words the function of which is to decrease reasonableness, which have this effect wherever they occur in a sentence. Standard slurs for ethnic groups are too widely recognized as slurs to occur in political debate in a liberal democracy. As liberal democracy breaks down, as in the case of modern-day Hungary, explicit slurs become more acceptable.[25] In a liberal democracy, slurs just are not a central problem, which is why of course work on the topic of slurs flourishes in philosophy departments in liberal democracies. The problem is, rather, with words that *function* in discourse as slurs, but are not explicitly slurs.

Failure to grasp the fact that the supposedly distinctive features of slurs are in fact ubiquitous is not merely an oversight. It undermines views of prominent recent theories of the functioning of slurs. Luvell Anderson and Ernest Lepore argue against "content theories" of slurs, of the sort that I favor. Their argument is that no "content theory" of slurs can explain why slurs *always* carry their negative connotations. Anderson and Lepore claim that the only possible account of this fact is their nonsemantic, deflationary account, according to which slurs carry negative connotations because they are on a *list of banned words*. The explanation of why slurs always carry problematic connotations, according to Anderson and Lepore, is that their use is prohibited. Because their use is prohibited, any use of them is a violation, and hence carries problematic connotations.

I am sympathetic to Anderson and Lepore's claim that explicit slurs belong on a list of banned words, in liberal democratic cultures. In fact, I think that their insight reveals a feature of what a liberal democratic culture is; it is one that, among other things, does not tolerate *explicit* degradation of its citizens. But, as I argue below, not only politics but also everyday discourse involve apparently innocent words that have the feature of slurs, namely, that whenever the words occur in a sentence, they convey the problematic content. The word "welfare," in the American context, is not on any list of prohibited words. Yet the word "welfare" always conveys a problematic social meaning, whenever it is used. A sentence like "John believes that Bill is on welfare" still communicates a problematic social meaning.

In this chapter, following Sally Haslanger, I will show that even apparently unproblematic words like "mother" also convey harmful social meanings whenever they are used. The words "welfare" and "mother" are not on any lists of banned words. Yet "welfare" and "mother" have exactly the property that slurs have, possession of which Anderson and Lepore maintain is only explicable on the hypothesis that the words with those properties are on a list of banned words. Therefore, their analysis fails. The Anderson and Lepore analysis is in tension with the existence of propaganda.[26]

The attempt to introduce words that function as slurs is a regular and systematic feature of political debate. This is the point of the quotation from Lee Atwater in 1981 with which we concluded the last chapter. The Princeton political scientist Tali Mendelberg, in her monumental study from 2001 of racial appeals in American politics, *The Race Card*, gives a detailed explanation of the mechanisms involved in implicit racial appeals.

The racial predispositions of white Americans are very well documented; they appear in fact to be a permanent feature of the American psyche. The belief that Blacks are excessively prone to criminality and inherently lazy is a central feature of white American ideology dating back at least two hundred years. As Mendelberg writes, the supposed propensity of Blacks to engage in criminal behavior "was deemed to go hand in hand with a propensity to avoid honest work. Each was taken to originate in inherent laziness."[27] Even abolitionists in New Jersey at the end of the eighteenth century were committed to the view that Blacks were inherently lazy.[28] The racial views of white Americans explicitly dominated political campaigns for the entire history of the American republic. But in the 1960s, what Mendelberg calls "a norm of racial equality" emerged in the American body politic. Mendelberg's expression "norm of equality" is however highly misleading. What is true is that certain kinds of previously acceptable, *very explicit* forms of racism began to elicit strongly negative reactions from white Americans. It remained the case that claims that are legitimately regarded as racist remain an acceptable part of American public political discourse. It perhaps still remains acceptable in the United States for a politician to say, for example, that Black Americans have a problematic culture that leads to failures of character. This is not speech that is by any stretch of the imagination aptly described as falling under a "norm of equality." But it is clear, as the Lee Atwater quotation we have seen attested, that *certain* kinds of previously acceptable racist claims became unacceptable in the late 1960s.

The new, less racist norms of public political discourse forced political propagandists to seek a way of reaching the racial biases of Americans without explicitly and obviously violating the new structure of explicit norms surrounding race. Lee Atwater was by no means the first to pursue the search for implicit means of communicating disrespect for Blacks. It had been a central communication strategy of the Republican Party for at least a decade. For example, President Richard Nixon's chief of staff, H. R. Haldeman, wrote in his diary, "President emphasized that you have to face that the whole [welfare] problem is really the blacks. The key is to devise a system that recognizes this, while not appearing to. . . . Pointed out that there has never in history been an adequate black nation, and they are the only race of which this is true."[29]

After the Civil Rights Movement, the vast majority of Americans consciously adhered to a norm that made very explicit racist expression impermissible. However, Americans retained the racial biases that are so central to the national identity of the country. These facts led political strategists to appeal to words that were not obviously slurs, or even obviously references to Black Americans, but functioned in exactly the way Camp describes the function of slurs, by removing respect from Black Americans.

Mendelberg and her Princeton colleague Martin Gilens have both studied the effects of the use of the term "welfare" on political opinions. They have discovered that the use of the term "welfare" leads to a priming of white racial bias. In other words, the mere use of "welfare," and presumably also "food stamps," as well as some other expressions referencing social spending programs, primes racial bias against Blacks. A conclusion from this research is that "any allusion to a racially tinged issue like welfare may racialize a campaign, even if it alludes to white recipients."[30] Most interestingly for the topic of slurs, Mendelberg, via a compelling experiment with nonstudents in Michigan, shows that the racial-bias effects actually *decrease* if a candidate's message is made explicitly racial in character.[31]

Studies that document the effects of priming are helpful for telling us about various effects. They are less helpful about the *mechanisms*. My goal here is to describe the linguistic mechanisms that underlie the sorts of effects discussed by Mendelberg and Gilens. It is in effect to say what it is to prime racial bias with words, once those words have been propagandized, within a framework that allows us to see when political debate can be successful.

Slurs for Black Americans are obviously explicitly racial. In the presence of Mendelberg's so-called norm of equality, slurs are much less effective than nonslurs in having the kind of effect that philosophers assume is indicative of slur words. More generally, in a liberal democracy like the United States, especially after the Civil Rights Movement, implicit messages are vastly more effective in achieving the results that philosophers attribute to slurs. Philosophers working on slurs, particularly Camp, have arrived at an elegant description of how propagandistic language functions. But to attribute the effect to slurs is to locate the phenomenon in the wrong place. In the presence of a norm of racial equality, the effects on reasonableness are most dramatic in cases in which the group is only *implicitly* targeted. In the United States at least, the focus philosophers have placed on explicit slurs is misplaced.

In the case of "welfare" and "entitlement" and similar language surrounding social welfare programs, there was a deliberate attempt to link them with not-at-issue contents that are racial in character. But many expressions carry with them not-at-issue content that is political in nature. The problem with the literature on slurs is that it suggests that there is a clear dividing line between expressions with the properties of slurs and expressions that are not slurs. This assumption is false. Many and perhaps most expressions have the properties that only slurs are supposed to have, not-at-issue content that cannot be denied and is directly added to the common ground. Most words carry with them, in all of their occurrences, not-at-issue meanings that cannot be easily expunged, if at all.

Politics involves a constant search for words that do not appear to be slurs, but that carry a not-at-issue content that prejudices political debate. Consider the recent legal debate about the expressions "illegal immigrant" and "illegal aliens." There is an obvious worry that these expressions carry not-at-issue content that frames debates about immigration in a way that fails to take into account the perspective of the immigrants. In 2006, the National Association of Hispanic Journalists urged the news media to cease using "dehumanizing terms," such as "illegals" and "illegal aliens."[32] In the words of the article, "[T]he association has always denounced the use of the degrading terms 'alien' and 'illegal alien' to describe undocumented immigrants because it casts them as adverse, strange beings, inhuman outsiders who come to the US with questionable motivations." Despite this and subsequent pleas, the supreme courts used the expression "illegal immigrant" in a dozen cases. In her very first decision in 2009, Justice Sonia Sotomayor introduced the expression "undocumented immigrant" into a decision in place of "illegal immigrant." In a decision by the California Supreme Court filed on January 2, 2014, in a long footnote, the court followed suit, making a note of its use of "undocumented immigrant," which "avoids the potential problematic connotations of alternative terms."[33] In politics, as Carl Schmitt noted, terminological questions are of the highest importance.

On the picture I am sketching, certain words are imbued, by a mechanism of repeated association, with problematic images or stereotypes. One can use these words to express ordinary contents, and explicitly deny complicity with the associated problematic image or stereotype. For example, in a debate during the Republican primary presidential campaign in 2012, Juan Williams asked a candidate, Newt Gingrich:

> You recently said, "black Americans should demand jobs, not food stamps. You also said, "poor kids lack a strong work ethic," and proposed having them work as janitors in their schools. Can't you see that this is viewed, at a minimum, as insulting to all Americans, but particularly to black Americans?

Gingrich answered, "No. I don't see that," and received a loud ovation from the audience. He then proceeded to deliver a bromide on the value of hard work, and examples of people who worked extremely hard from an early age. The audience gave him an immense ovation. Williams followed up by pointing out to Gingrich that expressions such as "lacking work ethic" were associated with negative racial stereotypes. He defended his point by saying that Americans across the racial divide understood the associations here, and it was disingenuous for Gingrich to deny them. The audience loudly booed Williams's response.

The interest of the exchange is the intensity of the audience's reactions. Clearly, this was the most emotionally charged moment of the debate. This is precisely because of the racially loaded not-at-issue content of the discourse, expressions like "work ethic" and "food stamps." Gingrich was allowed to act responsible just for the at-issue content of his utterance, and feign ignorance of the racial overtones of the expressions.[34]

What is important to note is that even the act of raising the expressions to salience by Juan Williams conveyed the negative social meanings, inspiring characteristically strong emotion in the audience. This is how propaganda works. It is possible to challenge its effects, but even using the expressions to do so runs the risk of invoking these very effects.[35]

A further concept is going to be essential to explain the mechanisms that propaganda exploits. The concept is that of *social meaning*, as it is found, for example, in the works of legal theorists such as Dan Kahan, who advance the expressive theory of law. The institution of marriage is a good example of something with a clear social meaning. The social meaning of marriage, as the philosopher Ralph Wedgwood has argued, involves "sexual intimacy (which in heterosexual couples often leads to childbirth); it involves the couple's cooperation in dealing with the domestic and economic necessities of life (including raising children if they have any); and it is entered into with a mutual long-term commitment to sustaining the relationship."[36] Marriage is an institution that has a powerful social meaning. An example Kahan uses of social meaning in the law is The Flag Protection Act of 1989.[37] The social meaning of the law was to emphasize patriotism. Given the fact that hardly anyone ever burns flags in protest, its only purpose in fact was to express this social meaning. Expressive theorists of law bring our attention to the social meaning of laws. Social meaning does not need to take the form of truth-evaluable contents. The social meaning can take the form of a command, an instruction to prefer certain situations above other situations. We have already explained how to model formally social meanings that are nontruth conditional in this way.

Institutions and laws have social meaning. Words too have social meanings. As Michael Walzer writes, "[T]he words *prostitution* and *bribery*, like *simony*, describe the sale and purchase of goods that, given certain understandings of their meaning, ought never be sold or purchased."[38] Propaganda characteristically involves attaching problematic social meanings to seemingly innocuous words that are used to describe policy, in effect making the word "welfare" like the word "prostitution." The social meanings of these words are not-at-issue content. Because they are not-at-issue contents, they are "not negotiable, not directly challengeable, and are added [to the common ground] even if the at-issue proposition is rejected." In short, even evaluating the proposal means that one must accept the social meaning. It is odd to challenge the social meaning; the social meaning associated with a word is accepted even if the claim made with the associated word is rejected.

Recall Victor Klemperer's description of the associations with the word "heroism" during National Socialism at the beginning of this book. The media associated these words with specific images: the racecar driver, the tank commander, the Storm Trooper. The images the media associated with these words became part of the social meaning of the term "heroism" for those raised under National Socialism. As with Frege's description of the images associated with the term "cur," it was impossible for those raised under National Socialism not to have the word evoke those images. The Republican "Southern Strategy" was to associate the language surrounding social welfare programs with images reinforcing the stereotype of urban Blacks as lazy.

Linda Taylor was a Black woman in Chicago in the 1970s who appears to have been a serious criminal.[39] She was arrested on charges of welfare fraud, of fraudulently filing welfare claims under four separate aliases, and charged with stealing $8000 from the government. In reporting on the case, the *Chicago Tribune* described her as a "welfare queen" who rode a Cadillac to pick up her fraudulent welfare checks. This was a crime for which Taylor was sentenced to prison. Welfare fraud was, however, the least of her crimes.

When Ronald Reagan ran for the presidency in 1976, he appropriated the expression "welfare queen" to raise the specter of massive Black fraud. In a campaign rally, he said, "In Chicago, they found a woman who . . . used 80 names, 30 addresses,

15 telephone numbers to collect food stamps, Social Security, veterans' benefits for four nonexistent deceased veteran husbands, as well as welfare. Her tax-free cash income alone has been running $150,000 a year." This was nowhere near an accurate description of the case, and welfare fraud was not a central source of Taylor's income (robbery was). But the image of the Black, Cadillac-driving welfare queen turned out to be very powerful, and was the dominating motif surrounding political debate about social welfare programs in the United States for decades to come. As with the case of "heroism" for those raised under National Socialism, it is scarcely possible for Americans raised during this time not to find the image of a Cadillac-driving Black urban woman popping into their head when they hear the word "welfare."[40]

The word "welfare" in the United States of America denotes a range of state and federal programs that provide "cash benefits to the able-bodied, working poor," an example of which would be Temporary Assistance for Needy Families (TANF, formerly AFDC).[41] The contribution the word "welfare" makes to the explicit claim made by assertions of sentences containing it is these programs. So a politician using the word "welfare" can appear to be making eminently reasonable claims; after all, a politician is supposed to be talking about government programs. Furthermore, politicians who militate against welfare usually do so with the appearance of primarily caring about the well-being of their Black fellow citizens.

In March 2014, US Representative Paul Ryan released a 204-page report titled "The War on Poverty: 50 Years Later." The report argues that welfare programs have removed incentives from work. Welfare programs have created a "poverty trap." Summarizing its findings on Wednesday, March 12, 2014, Representative Paul Ryan said on Bill Bennett's "Morning in America" show, "We have got this tailspin of culture, in our inner cities in particular, of men not working and just generations of men not even thinking about working or learning the value and the culture of work. There is a real culture problem here that has to be dealt with." US Representative Barbara Lee responded, "My colleague Congressman Ryan's comments about 'inner city' poverty are a thinly veiled racial attack and cannot be tolerated." Lee said in an email to reporters, "Let's be clear, when Mr. Ryan says 'inner city', when he says 'culture', these are simply code words for what he really means: 'black.'"

Ryan's proposal sounds on the face of it very reasonable. He devoted a great deal of time to writing a two-hundred-page piece all about the problems of the "inner city." It argues, using the language of economics, that welfare programs are to blame for these problems, chief among them lack of a "work ethic." It will help those in the inner city to be forced to work. It will improve their "work ethic." This sounds like a reasonable proposal, devoted to helping those in the "inner city" improve themselves.

Of course, the widespread American view that those in "the inner city," that is, Black Americans, lack a "work ethic" could not possibly be due to social welfare programs, which, after all, originated only in the 1960s. As Tali Mendelberg shows, stereotypes of Black Americans have remained constant throughout the history of the republic. The justification for slavery was that Black Americans have a lack of "work ethic," and as a result need special incentives to work. Ryan is simply suggesting that the special incentive be starvation, rather than slavery. It is hardly a proposal he would offer to those not in "the inner city."

In the United States, the language that names federal aid programs has acquired a social meaning that expresses disdain for Black American citizens. It communicates that Blacks are lazy. For example, in Appalachia, there is serious multigenerational poverty and unemployment. Yet I suspect few Americans would describe impoverished white Appalachian residents as "lazy." If so, then to claim that multigenerational poverty among urban Blacks is a cause of, and is caused by, laziness is to endorse a racial difference between poor whites and poor Blacks. This racial difference is the social meaning of the word "welfare." In other countries, federal assistance programs have acquired similar social meanings connected to immigrant groups. This is one general mechanism by which propaganda functions, especially in situations in which there is a norm against the social meaning being explicitly expressed.

We are now in a position to see the illiberal nature of propaganda, in the way it makes democratic deliberation impossible. The Republican Party, via its Southern Strategy, associated the terms for certain social programs with long-standing American racist stereotypes. This makes democratic deliberation about the merits and problems with such programs more difficult; it requires first fighting about vocabulary. Raising doubts about such programs requires using the standard terminology for them. But the standard terminology affects the discussion by making salient these long-standing racial stereotypes. It therefore becomes difficult to criticize these programs without seeming to be a racist. Republican Party propaganda has made democratic deliberation about the merits of these programs more complicated. This explains the puzzling phenomenon to which Jonathan Chait brought our attention, discussed in the very first few pages of this book.

We can also now understand the quotation from Victor Klemperer about the effects of the word "heroism" on those who grew up under National Socialism. The National Socialists successfully linked the term "heroism" to various symbols of Teutonic hegemony. These symbols, that of the Storm Trooper or the racecar driver, were the social meaning of "heroism." The concepts of liberalism are universal and neutral; no one group is singled out. In contrast, National Socialist ideology is profoundly illiberal, as it singles out the Teutonic race and the Jews for special treatment. Klemperer notes that as soon as "heroism" was mentioned, the people in the class lost all ability to grasp the concepts of liberal democracy. The reason is that the word "heroism" has a social meaning that is profoundly illiberal. Given the nature of not-at-issue content, that social meaning is immediately accepted by those raised under

National Socialism once the word "heroism" is mentioned. Accepting the social meaning of "heroism" leaves one in a speech context with a common ground (in the sense explained) that is incompatible with the presuppositions of liberalism. That explains Klemperer's comment that "it was impossible to have a proper grasp of the true nature of humanitarianism, culture, and democracy if one endorsed this kind of conception, or to be more precise misconception, of heroism."

Propaganda is of course not just aimed at those who share the propagandist's ideology. Propaganda is very often aimed at those who are its targets. We will see, in subsequent chapters, that propaganda is the means by which the highly privileged group in a society controls negatively privileged groups. I will explain some psychological and epistemological mechanisms underlying its efficacy. But we now are in a position to see the *linguistic* mechanisms of efficacy. The notion of not-at-issue content is one way negatively privileged groups come to accept the dominant ideology. As we have seen, the way not-at-issue content works is that it is added to the common ground, that is, accepted, even for further discussion to take place. The dominant group tries to place members of the subordinated group in a position so that merely engaging in debate requires accepting certain claims about their own inferiority. Members of subordinate groups may not believe the not-at-issue content, but to communicate with the chosen words they must act like they believe it.

None of this is to deny that the use of these terms may be challenged or reappropriated. For example, in the United States, the term "Obamacare" was initially introduced as a means of referring negatively to the Affordable Care Act. But then it was reappropriated as a nonnegative way of referring to the act. However, such challenges require sufficient control of media and other instruments of power that are often outside the control of members of the subordinated group. Successful challenge and reappropriation very often can take place only in the context of something approximating equal social footing.

The linguistic mechanisms at work explain why in conversations between members of the dominant group and members of the subordinate group, the members of the subordinate group feel pressure to accept the negative stereotypes of their own group. For example, when a white US citizen is speaking to a Black US citizen about the "problems in the inner city," there will be pressure, just to move the conversation forward, for the Black citizen to say that she recognizes that many people in the inner city are in fact lazy and violent. So there will be pressure, just for conversation ease, to accept the stereotype of one's group, and of course then to personally distance oneself from that stereotype. Subordinate group members may be led to accept, however provisionally, the negative stereotype of their group, *simply to enter smoothly into any conversation about their group with members of the dominating group*. This is a consequence that follows straightforwardly from the linguistic mechanism involved.

Dominant group propaganda will typically propagate negative stereotypes of subordinate groups, via exploitation of not-at-issue content. It will represent members of that group as not worthy of reciprocity. So propaganda will lead to diminished self-respect on the part of subordinate groups. If self-respect is, as John Rawls has argued, "perhaps" the most important primary good, then propaganda will lead to diminished self-respect. So propaganda leads to inequalities in perhaps the most important of all primary goods. Any political philosopher concerned with inequalities in the social basis of self-respect must therefore worry about propaganda.[42]

The social meaning of "welfare" in the United States is something like "Blacks are lazy." The view that Blacks are lazy is a flawed ideological belief, in a sense to be explained in subsequent chapters. The word "welfare" has become propagandized, because it has been attached to this social meaning. But the employment of ideological social meanings as not-at-issue contents is not the only way in which propaganda that erodes reasonableness works.

Which claims one makes with the sentences one utters vary, depending upon the context in which they are made. If one person says, "I am angry," another person is not contradicting her by saying, "I am not angry." They are making claims about different people. This kind of context-dependence is due to the English first-person pronoun "I," which can contribute differently to the claims made by sentences in which it occurs, depending upon the context. The same is true of the first-person plural pronoun "we." Someone's use of "we" can refer to the people in this room, or it can refer to the inhabitants of Berlin, or the inhabitants of Europe. One can exploit the context-dependency of natural language to erode reasonableness.

One kind of context-dependence in natural language is related to the quantifier words, such as "every" and "some." A sentence like "every student speaks Mandarin" makes different claims, depending upon the domain for the quantified expression "every student." If the domain is the students in the room, it makes one claim. If the domain is the students in the school, it makes another. Domain restriction of quantifiers can be used as a mechanism to erode reasonableness. If a politician in Italy speaks of "every citizen," she means every citizen of Italy, not every citizen of any state in the world. But if that politician says, "every citizen thinks laws are needed to keep Italy traditionally Italian," then she is excluding those who don't come from traditional Italian heritage from the domain of quantification.

We are all familiar with strategic uses of the domain of quantification. One place they emerge is in the use of the first-person plural pronoun, "we" or "us." A strategic use of "we or "us," one that erodes reasonableness, is one that clearly does not include some members who are subject to the laws of a nation. Eric Acton and Christopher Potts remark in a paper that "there is preliminary evidence" that Sarah Palin, the Republican vice presidential candidate in the United States in 2008, is a much more frequent user of the first-person plural pronoun than other politicians; for example, in Palin's vice presidential debate with democratic vice-presidential candidate Joe Biden in 2008, 3.49 percent of her words were the first-person pronoun, whereas only 2.21 percent of Biden's were. Acton and Potts also cite the following remarkable sentence from that debate, which contains five occurrences of the first-person plural pronoun: "Let's do what our parents told us before we probably even got that first credit card: don't live outside of our means." The first-person plural pronouns here seem not to refer to every American, but only to those who were raised with two-parent families and who self-identify as "family values" voters. Politicians often use "we" and "us" and their equivalents as devices of exclusion.

Chapter 13 of Victor Klemperer's *The Language of the Third Reich* is called "Names." It concerns the practice that became ubiquitous in Germany under the Third Reich of naming one's children explicitly Teutonic (Germanic) names, such as "Baldur," "Dieter," "Detlev," "Uwe," and "Margit" (names in fact familiar to those of us who have lived in Germany and met members of the generation born during the Third Reich). To have such a name meant you were one of the citizens of the country. It meant inclusion in the "we" of the people. You had a traditional Germanic name. You were safe.

Propaganda that erodes reasonableness is not just used to derogate groups. It is often, in liberal democracies, used to raise doubts about individuals. Miranda Fricker argues that when a social meaning to the effect that the target is "less than fully human" is communicated, its purpose is often to impugn the *credibility* of the target.[43] Fricker divides epistemic trustworthiness into two components: *competence* and *sincerity*.[44] Political propaganda is generally in the service of challenging one of these two components of the credibility of its target. When President Obama is described as being Muslim, the not-at-issue content, or social meaning, of the use of the term "Muslim" is of course related to terrorism, or some kind of anti-American sentiment. This is an attempt to challenge the president's sincerity, and thereby his epistemic trustworthiness. Similarly, descriptions of Sarah Palin as a "hick" and of President George Bush as a "frat boy" are attempts to impugn their competence.

Among the documents released from the archives of Edward Snowden are reports of something called The Joint Threat Research Intelligence Group (JTRIG), a secret UK government operation under the auspices of GCHQ, the British signals intelligence agency. The stated goal of JTRIG was to use social networking and blogging for "propaganda," "deception," "mass messaging," "pushing stories," "alias development," and "psychology."[45] It is a primer in the production of propaganda. Some of it is devoted to the production of motivated reasoning via, for example, identity protective cognition, by reinforcing membership in a nonthreatening or pro-government group ("affirming one's membership in an important reference group," as in Dan Kahan's work). For example, one of the reports is called "The Art of Deception: Training for Online Covert Operations"[46] and has instructions on bringing groups together (via "shared ideology") and tearing them apart (sowing "ideological difference"). But other parts of it are devoted to "discrediting targets." There is one slide on discrediting individuals, and another on discrediting corporations. The way to discredit individuals is to make them seem personally repugnant, to destroy their personal reputations (for example, "write a blog purporting to be one of their victims"). Fricker's point that the social meaning "less than fully" is regularly used to impugn the credibility of a target receives a good deal of corroboration from the fact that the manuals of propaganda that are in use in some prominent Western democracies appeal to that very method of undermining credibility.

Speech that communicates the social meaning "less than fully" is generally illiberal, because it represents an individual or group as unreasonable, that is, as having claims that are not worthy of our attention. When in a liberal democracy such speech also exploits the norm of reasonableness, it typically manifests as a characteristic form of demagogic propaganda.

Focusing on demagogic uses of reasonableness, we have looked at a diversity of methods that language uses to foment propaganda. Our discussion raises the question of whether it is plausible to ban propaganda, while retaining the freedom of speech, as one might ban slurs. It is too large of a topic to take on here. But it is worth briefly reflecting upon the difficulty of the task.

Social meaning is ubiquitous. Elizabeth Anderson and Richard Pildes provide a number of good examples of how judges and lawyers employ social meaning to prejudice debate.[47] Their description reveals how social meaning is used to prejudice debate in a characteristically propagandistic way. It also reveals the pervasiveness of the use of social meaning in deliberation. In describing the debate about federalism, they write, "In *Printz*, Justice Scalia characterizes Congress as having 'dragooned' state officials and as having reduced the states to '[p]uppets of a ventriloquist Congress,' which hardly seems consistent with the '[p]reseveration of the States as independent political entities.'"[48] In a debate about whether or not the states were being unfairly subordinated, Justice Scalia employed expressions with a social meaning that conveys "degradation, subordination, and domination," thereby attempting to bias deliberation that is intended precisely to establish whether or not improper degradation and subordination are in fact occurring.

As the description given by Anderson and Pildes shows, it will not be obvious in advance which words have political not-at-issue contents that shape debate in problematic ways, or how they do so. In her APA Presidential Address in 2013, Sally Haslanger made the point that while the slur word "slut" has an obvious political not-at-issue content, the seemingly innocuous word "mother" also has a political not-at-issue content, one that involves the presupposition that "one's sex is relevant to one's parental nurturing."[49] We can think of the effects of "mother" either as adding a certain content to the common ground or as imposing a preference relation on possible worlds that ranks worlds in which mothers have these features as preferable. Haslanger's point is that a great many words have some kind of social meaning, that is, not-at-issue content, even a word as innocuous as "mother." These social meanings, like the social meaning of slurs, cannot be divorced from the use of these expressions either. The words with the most political efficacy are presumably going to be the seemingly innocuous ones, those words that do not appear to be slurs but are associated with a social meaning that is disabling in some way.

What are the prospects of coming up with a method of banning social meanings that operate in illiberal ways? I am skeptical. Think of replacing "my wife" and "my husband" with the expression "my marriage partner." There is so much social meaning conveyed by the former expressions that is lacking in the latter; these social meanings are embedded into a lived illiberal practice. The only way to eliminate the problematic social meanings is to undermine the illiberal practices that slot *being a wife* and *being a husband* into such different social roles.

We can think, if we wish, of words as names for properties and things. But if we do so, we must simultaneously remember that words are not *just* names for properties and things. In his essay "General Semantics and Propaganda," published in 1939, S. I. Hayakawa writes:

> In fact, there is nothing that can be named, let alone described, without invoking the wraiths of an entire contextual system. What is "money"? What is a "house of correction"? What is a "professor"? What is a "musician"? . . . a "tom-boy"? . . . a "mortgage"? . . . a "cat"?[50]

The word "professor" truly applies to a range of human beings. This may lead us to think that calling someone "professor" is simply to include her among these human beings. But including her among those human beings *in that way* is also to do a number of other things. It is to make salient in the conversation a range of presuppositions about the institution of the university, presuppositions that may naturally lead to the belief that she teaches students. It is also to convey a certain social meaning: perhaps someone with liberal political views, who is practically incompetent. The fact that words are the product of human culture means that reasoning is nowhere near as straightforward as it appears from logic textbooks to be.

The fact that there are multiple effects of an utterance of a sentence on a context makes it possible to say something that is reasonable yet alter the context in such a way that is unreasonable. It therefore explains how to appear reasonable while being unreasonable. But it might be natural to infer a more drastic conclusion from the ubiquity of social meaning and institutional presuppositions associated with words. It is tempting to infer that the complexities in communication show that it is not really possible to approximate *any* ideal of public reason. Perhaps this stronger conclusion is true. But it is at this stage unwarranted; it would just be a guess.

Just as it is natural for some to think that the stronger, pessimistic conclusion that communication according to ideal norms is impossible follows from the diverse ways in which utterances affect beliefs, it may also be natural to think that to avoid the stronger, pessimistic conclusion, one needs to speak in some kind of ideal language, which lacks this feature. But the search to make ordinary communication akin to reasoning with schematic letters in logic is futile. And in any case, an ideal language for communication is not necessary to avoid the pessimistic conclusion. All the different ways in which utterances affect context do not necessarily cancel one another out, as they do with propaganda.

The use of the tools of logic and semantics to understand communication and how it is impeded is often thought to carry with it the presupposition that natural language is like the bare forms of logical languages. It is folklore that David Lewis named one of his pioneering papers in formal semantics "General Semantics" in partial mockery of the program of General Semantics, by Alfred Korzybski, between the two world wars. Korzybski sought to describe how propaganda worked, and to devise methods to avoid it, by reflection on logic and psychology. But as Rae Langton, Mary Kate McGowan, and Ishani Maitra have showed, the formal tools described by Lewis, especially in his paper "Scorekeeping in a Language Game," are in fact immensely helpful in isolating problematic effects of language.

My chapter as well is an exercise in showing how the tools of semantics and pragmatics are helpful in understanding the linguistic mechanisms of subordination. The usefulness of the truth-conditional framework at the core of the tools I have employed is that it gives us an account of how deliberation works, when it is successful and straightforward. Successful deliberation is a matter of proposing a content to be added to the common ground, which is then debated. If the participants in the debate accept the assertion, then they eliminate possible situations in which it is false and continue to the next question at issue. This cognitivist framework allows us a clear sense of one part of the *structure* of deliberation.

Many utterances communicate information that is not directly "up for debate." In the main, these are harmless contents. For example, when I speak, it is not "up for debate" that I am speaking. When I say, "that damn table," it is not "up for debate" that I have a negative attitude toward the table. When I say, "it must be raining," the debate is about whether or not it is raining, not whether I inferred it indirectly. We can challenge the material that is "not up for debate." But so doing typically distracts from the topic being discussed.

Because the truth-conditional framework allows us at least to see how the core structure of unbiased communication works, it might be thought that its employment suggests that we could communicate in a way in which that ideal was realized.[51] But the fact that we can usefully describe the way that propaganda uses linguistic complexity with precise or simple tools does not mean that our ordinary discourse consists of words that are precise or simple tools. A straightforward example is an ambiguous word that can be described in two precise, nonambiguous ways. This chapter has been an exercise in the use of the tools of formal semantics and pragmatics to describe various propagandistic effects. I have tried to show that the effort to systematize the unsystematic ways in which language operates can help us understand when it is used deviously in communication.

The multifarious effects of ordinary speech do, however, raise an important theoretical issue in political theory, about the role of ideal norms of public reason. John Rawls has argued that ideal conceptions must be "practically possible." Given just the linguistic complexity I have described, is it even practically possible to follow norms such as reasonableness, objectivity, and theoretical rationality? This is a large question with no straightforward answer. The reason is that we must have a better grasp of *what is it for a discourse to be guided by a norm*.

We can think of reasonableness, or theoretical rationality, as ideal deliberative norms guiding discussion. The question at issue is whether the complexity of actual human communication makes such deliberative ideals hopeless or useless. What role do norms of public reason have when communication is so often indirect and complex?

The most salient examples of shared norms guiding communicative acts are the norms governing speech acts, such as *assertion* and *promising*. It is widely agreed that in order for there to be a practice of assertion or promising in a community, there must be a regularity within certain ordinary contexts of speakers taking what Habermas calls an "interpersonal binding and bonding relationship" with their audience.[52] Different speech acts determine different such relations, which are the norms guiding the relevant speech acts:

> The binding and bonding relationship into which the speaker is willing to enter with the performance of an illocutionary act signifies a guarantee that, in consequence of

her utterance, she will fulfill certain conditions—for example, regard a question as settled when a satisfactory answer is given; drop an assertion when it proves to be false; follow her own advice when finds herself in the same situation as the hearer. . . . *Thus, the illocutionary force of an acceptable speech act consists in the fact that it can move a hearer to rely on the speech-act-typical obligations of the speaker.*[53]

As Habermas here makes clear, the existence of a speech act in a community depends upon the existence of a regularity in the community, perhaps constrained to a range of regularly encountered and identifiable contexts, in which speakers fulfill the obligations of that speech act. Timothy Williamson makes a similar point when he notes that the speech act of assertion can only exist if there is "at least general sensitivity" to the violation of its governing norm. If it is rare for people in a community to be sanctioned for the act of uttering false sentences in utterances of declarative sentences, or (perhaps equivalently) if it is rare for people to live up to the commitment of uttering truths (or known propositions) when using declarative sentences, then we may conclude that there is no speech act of assertion in that community.

The complexities of communication we have surveyed do not undermine, for example, standard suggestions for norms for assertion. What is asserted is the at-issue content of an utterance. I have argued that propaganda typically affects the not-at-issue content of an utterance. It enters into the common ground by routes other than assertion. In fact, this is key to the kinds of demagoguery I have in this chapter discussed; the assertion must express a reasonable at-issue content in order for the act to be effective qua propaganda; propagandists seek to retain reasonableness (or any other deliberative ideal) at the level of assertion, but violate reasonableness at another level.

There is widespread agreement that in order for a certain kind of speech act to exist in a community, there must be norms in place in that community, in the way Habermas describes. This suggests that a parallel story can be told about democratic ideals, which are, after all, norms governing public communication. On this account, the degree to which a society satisfies a democratic ideal of rationality or reasonableness can be measured by the degree to which those who enter public political discourse commit themselves to following these ideals, and the degree to which those who deviate from it are sanctioned.

One might, however, worry, given just the complexity about communication surveyed in this chapter and the pervasiveness of propaganda, that no actual state would count as democratic to any reasonable degree, if norm guidance was like what is at issue in the norms governing speech acts like assertion. Given the complexity we have discussed, perhaps no deliberative ideal of public reason has ever been strictly adhered to in the passing of any policy in the United States; certainly for the vast majority of policies it has not. As we have seen from Anderson and Pildes, discussion in the Supreme Court regularly involves the communication of unreasonable social meanings. In contrast, if most utterances of declarative sentences were known to be false by the speaker and never sanctioned, there would be no speech act of assertion. Is there a less demanding model of norm governance available for the task?

In his book *The Public and Its Problems*, published in 1927, John Dewey confronts one of the main problems for democracy posed in Walter Lippmann's book *The Phantom Public*, published in 1925. Lippmann there argues that there is no public, or at best there is a *phantom* one. The facts of the division of labor, of geographical location, and so on threaten the idea of an intersection of interests in a large, geographically diverse population. Anything that holds 51 percent of the people together is not a common good, a set of important and valuable common interests, but rather an appeal to emotion, a "call to arms." There is no interesting notion like that of a public, a democratic community, or a democratic society. Arguing for the common good is arguing for nothing at all.

The problem Lippmann raises is that if there is no set of interests to be taken as the public's interests, one cannot choose to be bound by the result of a public deliberative procedure aimed at furthering the common good, that is, the good of the public. But something like this is Dewey's deliberative ideal. In the face of arguments Dewey admits are cogent in support of the view that there is no public or public interests, Dewey suggests considering the characteristic elements of democracy to be ideals that ought to guide our behavior if we want our society to become more democratic:

> [Democracy] is an ideal in the only intelligible sense of an ideal: namely, the tendency and movement of some thing which exists carried to its final limit, viewed as completed, perfected. Since things do not attain such fulfillment, but are in actuality distracted and interfered with, democracy in this sense is not a fact and never will be. But neither in this sense is there or has there ever been anything which is a community in its full measure, a community unalloyed by alien elements. The idea or ideal of a community presents, however, actual phases of associated life as they are freed from restrictive and disturbing elements, and are contemplated as having attained their limit of development.[54]

Thus, Dewey suggests that democracy functions as an ideal. Dewey even has a particular suggestion about how these ideals ought to regulate the behavior of an actual society struggling with "the ills of democracy." When confronted with the daily reminders of the nonrealistic features inherent in the ideals of democracy, we should nevertheless adhere to the ideals, which means trusting our fellow deliberators and abiding by the outcome of the deliberative process. If this is what it is to follow a deliberative ideal, it is possible to follow it despite its persistent failure to match reality. This attitude is aptly described as *having faith in the democratic process*. That it is so natural to appeal to such language is evocative of John Dewey's contention "that the cure for the ailments of democracy is more democracy."[55]

As we have seen, what Dewey means is that in the face of the fact that "democracy [in the ideal sense] is not a fact and never will be," we must nevertheless have faith in democratic ideals in our political deliberations. By this, Dewey meant that the ideals should in some sense guide our actions. But in which sense?

Lara Buchak has usefully provided a characterization of faith, which can help us understand more precisely the notion at issue. Her characterization is meant to be perfectly general, by which I mean that it is intended to apply to all the different relations that count as faith: faith between people, faith that a proposition is true, and so on.

> A person has faith that X, expressed by A, if and only if that person performs act A when there is some alternative act B such that he strictly prefers $A\&X$ to $B\&X$ and he strictly prefers $B\&\sim X$ to $A\&\sim X$, and the person prefers {to commit to A before he examines additional evidence} rather than {to postpone his decision about A until he examines additional evidence}.

Let us provisionally say that a process is democratically legitimate if it exemplifies reasonableness or rationality, or comes close enough (this is here irrelevant). To exhibit faith that a process is democratically legitimate, or, in this case, that a process is sufficiently close to the ideal deliberative procedure, is to endorse an action over an alternative action that one would prefer if the process were not democratically legitimate.

The idea that participation in democratic deliberation requires faith that the process was governed by an ideal of public reason is much weaker than the norms governing speech acts. Even if *no* procedures by which policies are passed in fact exemplify, or come close to exemplifying, the norms of public reason, the measure of a democracy can be taken by the proportion of participants in its deliberations who have faith that the procedures exemplify those ideals (and hence act on that supposition).

However, the Deweyan conception of norm guidance as faith is too problematic to be adopted. The problem is that *faith in democratic ideals* leads us to *blindness about their violations*. To simply assume that policies based on appeal to bias and special interest were democratically legitimate risks overlooking too many concrete instances of injustice. This is simply too large a risk to take.

One might also reject the demand for ideals to be practically possible in order to be useful. Even practically impossible scientific ideals are nevertheless useful in science.[56] However, this defense of political ideals is tendentious. Scientific ideals, as Kwame Anthony Appiah has argued in unpublished work, are useful because the details from which they abstract are unimportant to our overall picture of the physical world. However, political ideals are not at all like this. The details from which they abstract are concrete instances of social injustice. Scientific ideals abstract from friction; political ideals abstract from the existence of oppressed minorities.[57]

Still, there are many possible models of norm guidance that are left open. In the face of the complexities we have discussed, perhaps a reasonable way to adhere to ideal deliberative norms, for example, the norm of objectivity, may be to adopt *systematic openness to the possibility that one has been unknowingly swayed by bias*. If so, the mark of a democratic culture is one in which participants in debates regularly check themselves for bias, and subject their own beliefs and unthinking use of language to the same critical scrutiny as they do the beliefs and utterances of others. The question of the practical possibility of deliberative ideals then becomes the question of the practical possibility of such policing. It is not just a matter of attending to our own discourse. Since whether or not discourse is propagandistic depends upon flawed ideological belief, the practical possibility of deliberative ideals ultimately rests upon our capacity to be sensitive to the effects of flawed ideologies on our own belief system.

In the next two chapters, I turn to the topic of ideology. I will suggest that democratically problematic ideology is virtually inevitable in societies with substantial inequality. This suggests that the practical possibility of the democratic ideals we have discussed depends upon whether or not humans are capable of mitigating the effects of inequality.

IDEOLOGY

Undermining propaganda is a claim that is presented as embodying a political ideal, but that is in the service of the kind of goal that tends to undermine that ideal. What this means is that the success of undermining propaganda depends on two things. First, it depends on people having beliefs that are resistant to the available evidence, the evidence that reveals the tension between goal and ideal. Secondly, since undermining propaganda conceals a contradiction of sorts, the beliefs that are resistant to evidence must themselves be flawed in some way.

In this chapter, I will spell out a characteristic way in which beliefs are resistant to evidence. The philosophical puzzle of ideological belief has always been to explain how we could come to have beliefs that are resistant to evidence in this way. It is the philosophical puzzle at the heart of, for example, David Hume's philosophy. For instance, the philosophical puzzle raised in "Of Skepticism with Regard to the Senses" is not, as is sometimes thought, external world skepticism. Hume does not view external world skepticism as a philosophical puzzle. The philosophical puzzle is rather that as soon as we reflect upon our belief in external things, we realize that it is inconsistent with the available evidence. But we nevertheless continue to believe that external objects exist. The philosophical puzzle

Hume takes himself to be addressing is this: why is our belief in external things resistant to rational revision in light of available evidence? The purpose of "Of Skepticism with Regard to the Senses" is to answer this question. Why we have a class of beliefs that are peculiarly resistant to evidence is one of philosophy's traditional questions.

The cases that tend to interest philosophers are ones in which the source of our inability to rationally revise a belief is some kind of confusion or error. Thus, the most puzzling cases of ideological belief are what I will call *flawed ideological belief*. In the case of "Of Skepticism with Regard to the Senses," the flaws that explain our ideological belief in external things lie in individual psychology. But in the cases of central interest to us in this book, they lie in society, in the form of social injustice. Hume devotes "Of Skepticism with Regard to the Senses" to explaining the mechanisms by which a certain kind of flawed individual psychology inevitably gives rise to flawed ideological belief. I am engaged in a structurally similar project, except my concern is with *flawed social structures*, rather than flawed psychology. The goal of the next two chapters is to explain the mechanisms by which flawed social structures give rise to flawed ideological belief.

David Hume's interest in "Of Skepticism with Regard to the Senses" was to explain flawed ideological beliefs, the source of which lies in flaws in our individual psychology. His explanation for why we cannot revise what he regarded as the flawed ideological belief that there are external things is that we cannot change the flaws in our psychology that necessitate possession of that belief. My aim is different. I will be concerned with flawed ideological beliefs whose source is flaws in *society*, that is, social arrangements. In the cases of interest to us in this book, the reason why a belief is resistant to rational revision is because of structural features of the society in which the agent is located.

I will argue that societies with flawed social structures tend to give rise to flawed ideological belief, in a similar (yet perhaps less inevitable) way to the manner in which Hume takes our flawed psychology to lead to what he thinks of as our flawed ideological belief in external things. We are capable of setting this belief temporarily aside, according to Hume, when we explicitly rationally reflect upon its justification. But as soon as we return to ordinary life, we slip back into believing in external things. In a similar way, when we explicitly rationally reflect upon the flawed ideological beliefs that are caused by living in a society with structural injustice, we often reject them. But when we return to ordinary life, we nevertheless slip back into the flawed ideological beliefs.

A goal of this book is to provide an argument for equality by showing that one central cause of effective propaganda is inequalities, both material and political. Inequalities tend to result in flawed ideology, which explains the effectiveness of propaganda. To eliminate the kinds of flawed ideologies that are particularly problematic democratically, we need to seek a society that embodies equality at the structural level. My goal in this chapter is to elucidate the sense of flawed ideology that mediates between the facts of substantive inequality and the effectiveness of antidemocratic propaganda.

There is a danger that must be immediately addressed, which is that my claim will be taken as somewhat trivial. Suppose that a flawed ideology is one that is fundamentally morally or politically bad, and suppose that inequality of any kind, even material inequality, is morally or politically bad. From the perspective of the view that justice requires material equality, and a moral conception of flawed ideology, it is not surprising that the ideology of a materially unequal society looks to be problematically flawed. And it is not surprising that a materially unequal society will give rise to the ideology that a just society can tolerate substantial material inequality. Because I am interested in arguing for a stronger claim than this, my focus is not on a political or moral notion of flaw. It is on a purely epistemic notion of flaw. My argument will be that certain ideologies have epistemic flaws, in addition to what one might regard as the epistemic flaws of all ideological beliefs. These are flawed ideologies. Among these flawed ideologies are ones that are particularly problematic democratically (as I will argue in the next chapter).

My argument would also be trivialized if I were *presupposing* that material inequality is democratically problematic. If I were presupposing this, then it would not be a surprise that the ideological belief that material inequality is democratically acceptable would be democratically problematic. But I am not presupposing that material inequality is democratically problematic. I am *arguing* that it is, and my argument does not require its conclusion as a presupposition. Substantive inequalities, including material inequalities, are democratically problematic because they typically result in democratically problematic flawed ideologies, which contain the beliefs that make demagoguery effective. And as I have showed in the introduction, effective demagoguery is an obstacle to all varieties of democracy.

Epistemic practices that are *partial*, in the sense of biased toward the interests of one party, lead to characteristic failures of rationality in one's reasoning about what to do politically. Partiality in some domains is necessary for ordinary cognitive functioning. For example, one of the key experiments for my discussion involves the mistakes in rationality made by fans of a sports team. Another example I use involves the mistakes in rationality made by members of a family who do not wish to condemn their parents. But this kind of partiality is just an effect of the normal functioning of being a sports fan and being a member of a family. By not being partial in one's reasoning in these ways in being a sports fan, or by not being partial to one's family members, one is not engaged in the practice in the right way.

It is a familiar point about liberalism that it requires a division between the personal and the political. Liberalism is consistent with partiality in judgments, as long as it remains in the so-called personal domain, examples of which are plausibly domains such as sports fandom and family relations. But liberalism condemns certain kinds of partiality that are natural and even desired within these domains when they are imported to reasoning about public policy. The standard liberal political theorist has no quarrel with a billionaire's partiality to her son. However, liberalism condemns the billionaire when she seeks to affect public policy in ways guided by the desire to advance her son's interests over the interests of others.[1]

I will explain, in what follows, how a certain kind of partiality undermines the kind of deliberation we expect when people are thinking about public policy for everyone. It is not just any partiality; it is not, for example, a rational preference for one's self-interest. One special class that will interest us involves beliefs that are *connected to one's identity*, characteristically by *legitimating* it. We all have such beliefs, and not all of them are democratically problematic. They become democratically problematic when they prevent us from perceiving important parts of reality, characteristically social reality. When the identity tied up with an ideology is one that benefits from being ignorant of some parts of social reality, the ideology will often be of this sort.

Here is a possible example of the kind of problematic partiality in question; I do not claim it is a description of how things are. I considered in the introduction the possibility that political party affiliation is a method to deceive citizens to import partiality that is a normal and healthy part of certain practices, such as being a sports fan, into a realm in which it is not appropriate, namely, political decisions. If so, then political party affiliation is illiberal. Beliefs that are connected to one's identity will be difficult to abandon. So it will be difficult to abandon the beliefs connected to one's identity as a political party member. But these will be politically important beliefs, which will now be much less resistant to rational revision. An ideology that is partial becomes democratically problematic when it affects political judgment about policies that might address the injustices that the ideology overlooks. As long as a partial perspective is kept within its proper domain—for example, sports talk radio—it is not flawed. But as soon as it is imported into discourse and reasoning about the public good, it functions as illiberal.

Running through this book is a detailed argument for equality. Conditions of inequality tend to give rise to flawed ideologies, which make the kind of demagoguery that imperils democracy particularly effective. One half of this argument is the account of propaganda I provided in previous chapters. The other half is the account of flawed ideology I provide here. My accounts of ideology and propaganda are independent, but they are mutually supporting in the book's argument for equality.

I began this chapter by noting that the explanation of ideological belief is the central problem in the works of the Scottish Enlightenment philosopher David Hume. We have already discussed how it features in his most famous contribution to epistemology; it is just as clearly at the heart of Hume's naturalistic account of religious belief. Hume argues that enthusiasm and superstition are the result of "the intrusion onto the formation of our beliefs of *hope* and *fear*, respectively."[2] Hume's account of superstitious belief (under which he includes religious belief) is that "emotion leads to excessive credulity in judgment—an unwillingness to amend judgment in the light of reflection."[3] Superstitious and enthusiastic beliefs are ideological, because they arise out of the passions, in particular hope and fear, rather than reason. This is at the basis of Hume's naturalistic explanation of religious belief.

It is natural to present Hume's critique of religious belief as focused solely on individual psychology as the locus of its origin: he is critiquing religious belief by arguing that it arises from fear and superstition, which are natural features of humans. But social practice, in the form of custom and habit, clearly plays a role even in the ideologies he discussed. After all, it is religious social practices that maintain religious belief. No doubt Hume recognized that flawed ideologies can be maintained by social practices and do not just rest on flawed psychology.[4]

Our focus is on the puzzles raised by societies that tolerate large inequalities. Many such cases, though perhaps not all, are instances of social injustice. The classic source for the notion of ideology whose source is social injustice is the work of Karl Marx. There are distinct views of ideology in Karl Marx's classic paper "The German Ideology." The one that is most useful for our purposes is embodied in Marx's famous quotation from there: "The ideas of the ruling class are in every epoch the ruling ideas: i.e., the class which is the ruling *material* force of society, is at the same time its ruling *intellectual* force."[5] On this view, the ideological beliefs are the ruling classes' self-legitimation, or self-justification, of the expectations that make up their ideologies. Both Hume and Marx emphasize troubling epistemological features of ideological belief that arises from flawed sources. But Marx focuses on certain ideologies in particular, which are among the ones that I will argue are most democratically worrisome.

Marx's focus in this passage from "The German Ideology" is on the ideology formed by "the ruling material force of society," the legitimation narrative they tell themselves about why they are deserving of their position. Here is the concept of ideology I favor, which is influenced principally by Sally Haslanger, but also by Tommie Shelby.[6] The beliefs that are part of an ideology are the record of expectations of various goods built out of regularities of convention. They are the beliefs that unreflectively guide our path through the social world. In this sense, everyone in the world has an ideology, since everyone has a social world. Because our ideologies are guided by a desire to retain a sense of normalcy, especially when normalcy is pleasant, they characteristically lead to beliefs that are connected to one's positive self-image, in the way Marx describes. These problematic beliefs are characteristic examples, maybe *the* characteristic examples, of flawed ideology that has its source in flawed social structures.

Traditionally, philosophers have spoken of *ideological belief*, and I will as well. However, focusing on belief as the nexus of ideology is dangerously misleading. The distinctive feature of ideological belief is that it is very difficult to rationally revise in light of counterevidence. This is the feature of beliefs that a theory of ideology is devoted to explaining, a feature that is especially troubling in the case of flawed ideological belief, cases in which a bit of explicit rational reflection may lead us to reject it in light of the evidence. In his nonpolitical writings at least, Hume was concerned to explain the mechanisms by which flawed psychology leads to flawed ideological belief. But in the cases that interest us, the source of both the ideology and the flaws is society. The danger of focusing on ideological *belief* as what is to be explained is that we will be tempted into the view that there are two kinds of mental states that are intrinsically different qua mental states: the kind that is rationally revisable (normal beliefs) and the kind that is not (ideological beliefs). We may even be led into thinking the latter are a different kind of mental state altogether. But there is no reason to think that this is so, in the kinds of cases that concern us.

One main source of the unrevisability of certain beliefs is that they are connected to *social practices*. The beliefs are ones I need to have in order to remain in those practices. Following Dan Kahan, I will argue that one central source of ideological beliefs is our social identities. We value our social identities. Social identities are constituted by the practices and habits in which we engage; those we engage with are our community. We must at least act as if certain propositions are true in order to engage in those practices. To abandon these beliefs is to abandon certain practices and habits that constitute our social identity. To abandon these beliefs is therefore to abandon one's community, to leave everyone with whom you identify behind. This is very difficult for an individual person to envisage; usually they can only perform the experiment of setting beliefs aside that are so connected to their social identities when they explicitly are asked to rationally reflect upon them. But as soon as they slip back into ordinary life, they reengage in the practices that make them who they are.

What this means is that revision of flawed ideological belief whose source is flawed social structure is very hard, perhaps almost as hard as revising flawed ideological belief the source of which is flawed psychology. If this is right, then it's not correct to try to solve the puzzle of why even obviously flawed ideological belief is hard to revise by looking just at intrinsic features of the beliefs themselves, or even the overall mental structure of individuals. Many ideological beliefs "look mentally" just like nonideological beliefs. The reason individuals are loathe to abandon them is that they don't like to leave their friends behind.

Because of this, I am skeptical about the search for a psychological strategy individuals can use to "protect themselves" from problematic ideological belief on a case-by-case basis. The distinctive feature of ideological belief often arises from being embedded in a practice together with people like you, your friends, and family. What is needed to eliminate problematic ideological belief is to change the practice of a large group of people simultaneously over time, to alter a social identity many people share. It would be hard to see how this would work by assigning to individuals individual psychological curatives to employ.

It should now be clear that while I theorize with a category of ideological belief, and defend this choice in what immediately follows, this does not mean that I think that being ideological is an intrinsic property of mental states (though I will argue that there are certain interesting, self-reinforcing mental mechanisms implicated in the maintenance of such beliefs). In sketching my account of what makes a belief ideological, I will emphasize that many of the interesting properties that a theory of ideology must explain require looking at practices. As a result, on my account, it is an *accidental* and not an intrinsic feature of ideological beliefs that they are ideological.

The philosopher Tamar Gendler has argued that much of the philosophical role played by ideological belief is better played by a notion she introduces called "alief." In her work, Gendler introduces novel, everyday, nonpolitical examples of the most striking feature of ideological belief, namely, its puzzling resistance to rational revision. For instance, in "Alief and Belief," Gendler begins by describing a transparent walkway over the Grand Canyon, consisting of many layers of glass that make it completely safe, and obviously so. Gendler points out that our knowledge that the walkway is completely safe does nothing to dislodge an attitude that seems to control our behavior as the belief that it is dangerous to walk on the walkway would. Taking it as obvious that in such a case we believe that the walkway is safe, and that we would not explicitly hold contradictory beliefs, Gendler argues at length that we should recognize a distinct category of mental state that she calls *alief*. The person standing on the glass skywalk believes that the walkway is safe (if she did not, she would not risk her life by voluntarily perching there), but her behavior is also governed by a contrary alief: that she is in mortal peril. No matter how convincingly she rehearses to herself that she is in a situation of complete safety, her behavior will be tempered by her disavowed alief.

The distinctive and controversial property of ideological belief is its resistance to rational revision. Skeptics about the theory of ideology tend to hold that those motivated to theorize about belief-like mental states that are rationally resistant to revision just have a hard time accepting that beliefs they reject have large independent plausibility. Such skepticism about ideology faces the threat of incoherence; after all, the skepticism usually takes the form of the charge that theorists of ideology are incapable of rationally evaluating beliefs that have large independent plausibility. And it is the theory of ideology that studies just this. Though standard versions of skepticism about the project of ideology critique are incoherent in just this way, there is no denying that such skepticism is widespread. What Gendler's work shows is that the skepticism is misplaced, at the level of uncontroversial example. There are entirely mundane examples of mental states that have the most controversial feature of ideological belief. In the face of the ubiquity of such examples, there is no remaining case for skepticism.

Gendler's work is a remarkable contribution to the theory of ideology; it should settle a lengthy philosophical debate about the presuppositions of that theory. It is also a rich source of insight into the structure of ideology, upon which I draw in the next two chapters.[7] But I disagree with the motivations for her novel ontology of the mental. In particular, my concern is with Gendler's appeal to "immediate rational revisability" as a criterion for a mental state to be a belief, in her argument that alief is distinct from belief. On my conception, a belief is ideological insofar as it is connected with one's various identities. And connection with, for example, one's social identity comes in degree. It is possible but hard to resist the conclusion that whether or not a belief is ideological also depends upon degree. Some beliefs are more ideological than others: the ones that are more closely connected to one of the agent's identities. That ideology comes in degree is hard to pair with a binary opposition between rationally revisable states and non-rationally revisable states.

More importantly, the conception of ideological belief I will defend sits uneasily with the thought that the failure to rationally revise in light of available evidence is a direct measure of whether or not a state is a belief. It is natural to think that some beliefs are connected to our identity and others aren't; this for me is the source of the incapacity for rational revision, rather than the failure to be a belief. Beliefs that are connected to one's identity, which one shares with others, will be hard to revise one by one, because it is hard simply to abandon one's identity.

In her rejoinder to the kind of position I defend, Gendler draws attention to its apparent incompatibility with a norm governing belief: "whatever belief is—it is normatively governed by the following constraint: belief aims to 'track truth' in the sense that belief is subject to immediate revision in the face of changes in our all-things-considered evidence."[8] Gendler here argues from the premise that the normative ideal for belief is the modal notion of *tracking the truth* to the conclusion that the belief must have the property of being immediately revised, were the available evidence to suggest it to be false. I will not question the validity of the inference. My objection is rather to her assumption that among the normative ideals of belief (perhaps derivatively, via knowledge) is the property of tracking the truth.

There are many ways to spell out the notion of tracking the truth. One way involves what epistemologists call sensitivity: if one believes that p, then were p to be false, one would no longer believe that p. It is widely agreed that sensitivity is not a plausible normative ideal for belief; there are too many counterexamples. But there is a weaker way to construe truth-tracking: if one believes that p, then were one to be presented with rationally compelling evidence against p, one would revise one's belief. Even this weaker version faces counterexamples. As Timothy Williamson has compellingly argued, there are counterexamples to any straightforward counterfactual analysis of an epistemic ideal.[9] Following Williamson, I will argue that there is a more compelling alternative picture of the normative ideals for belief that does not involve truth-tracking.

Let us first suppose the antecedently plausible view that knowledge is the normative ideal for belief: belief aims at knowledge.[10] What are the conditions under which a belief is knowledge? One alternative to sensitivity that has arisen in analytic epistemology is the notion of safety, developed in different ways most prominently by Ernest Sosa and Timothy Williamson.[11] Because I am convinced by Williamson that there is a general worry with counterfactual analyses, I will adopt his exposition of the safety condition on knowledge.

One formulation of Williamson's safety condition is "if one knows, then one could not easily have been wrong in a similar case."[12] Here is the kind of example that motivates it. Suppose that I am in a stadium with exactly 10,387 people. I can come to know by looking that there are more than 1,000 people. I can come to know by looking that there are less than 100,000 people. But I cannot come to know by looking that there are exactly 10,387 people. Even if I guess correctly, I could have easily been wrong in a similar case (where there were, for example, 10,388 people). We do not need to investigate the details of this debate in epistemology to see that the view that knowledge is the aim of belief, together with the safety condition on knowledge, does not entail that immediate rational revisability is a normative ideal of belief. My identity might be connected to social practices that involve beliefs that could not have been easily wrong in similar cases, even if I fail to revise these beliefs in sufficiently *dissimilar* cases. Knowledge is in the first instance about being connected to the world in the right way. It is not in the first instance about features of my underlying epistemic character that would be revealed in distant counterfactual situations. Immediate rational revisability may be part of having a good overall epistemic character. But it is not a normative ideal of belief.

The central puzzle of the theory of ideology is this: why is our behavior so often guided by states that do not seem to be sensitive to available evidence? There is much more to say on either side of the debate that Gendler's work has initiated on the ontology of ideology. But perhaps I have said enough here to indicate why I remain with tradition in theorizing about the puzzle primarily in terms of the category of ideological *belief*.

Gendler's theoretical focus is on the mental ontology of the theory of ideology; she argues that in order to explain ideology's distinctive features, we need a new mental category. Other theorists of ideology place their ontological focus elsewhere, in social ontology. Theorists such as Althusser, Bourdieu, and Haslanger urge that ideologies include *social practices*, which should be theorized independently of the mental states of agents embedded within them.[13] A theory of ideology is there to explain certain puzzling behavior: in the most interesting cases, behavior that seems to run contrary to what is rational, given what the obviously available evidence strongly suggests or even demonstrates. These theorists argue that a theory of ideology that does not pay substantial theoretical attention to social structures ignores central issues of explanatory concern.

A theory of ideology that restricts its explanations to the mental states of members of society does not just risk missing the *source* of the most worrisome kinds of ideology, which arise from unjust social structures, for example, the relations of oppression described by Haslanger.[14] It also risks analyzing the problematic feature of ideological beliefs in terms of intrinsic features of mental states. But it is still possible to theorize with a category of ideological belief. It is just necessary to insist that notions like *resistance to rational revision*, as well as the deficiencies that attend such resistance in conditions of social injustice, should not be expected to be explained on the level of intrinsic features of mental states. This is a feature of the account to follow, which is framed in terms of an account of ideological belief.

I am going to argue that there are certain ideological beliefs that are particularly problematic democratically. I am not the first to identify these as the most democratically problematic. In book 5, part 2, of *The Politics*, Aristotle provides "the universal and chief cause" of revolution; in fact, Aristotle provides two chief causes. The first is "the desire of equality, when men think that they are equal to others who have more than themselves." The second is "the desire of inequality and superiority, when conceiving themselves to be superior they think that they have not more but the same or less than their inferiors." Aristotle notes that these are "pretensions which may and may not be just." In the case of *unjust* revolutions, either "[i]nferiors revolt in order that they may be equal," or "equals that they may be superior." Aristotle's two "universal and chief" causes of unjust revolutions are the two examples of democratically problematic flawed ideological belief I will discuss. They are precisely the flawed ideological beliefs that arise in conditions of substantive inequality (as Aristotle recognizes). The argument of this book is not new.

One of Aristotle's chief causes of injustice requires believing that humans are fundamentally naturally unequal. Suppose this is so, and consider a group of people who are not as meritorious for some reason. As a result, they end up without resources. The social scripts that guide them through life involve difficult searches for food and housing. They are unwilling to blame their failures on themselves, as this would involve impugning their self-respect. They come then to blame their predicament not on themselves, but on an unjust distribution of resources in society. They then develop the flawed ideological belief that those who have gained fortunes have done so illicitly.

If there were to be a society in which the wealthy have gained their fortunes legitimately, those who acquire the flawed ideological belief that the wealthy have gained their fortunes illicitly will be hard-pressed to abandon it, even in the face of clear evidence to the contrary. For example, when presented with evidence that everyone can in fact succeed in the society, if they make the correct choices, they will reject the evidence as unconvincing. Giving it up will force them to admit to themselves that their choices were poor and their struggles their own fault. They would be filled with jealousy and anger at the ruling classes, jealousy that is difficult to justify but no less real for that.

Marx's example of an ideology is of the second variety: the self-legitimations of those who control the material goods of society. This is a flawed ideology, in the sense I will elucidate. The example I will give is one in which the self-legitimation is clearly unjust. Consider a prosperous family in the Antebellum American South who lives on a plantation that has provided a high level of income for the family for several generations. The family owns slaves who maintain and cultivate their plantation, and slaves who work in the house doing domestic chores. The members of the family have grown up with the expectation that slaves will cook their meals for them, slaves will clean the house and raise the children, and slaves will work on the plantation at no cost to provide for their well-being, as well as the well-being of future generations of that family.

I will take the ideology of this family to be the beliefs they have that guide them through their social lives, as well as the concepts they use to structure reality around them. The beliefs that are part of this ideology are beliefs like (i) the belief that slaves will cook them dinner, (ii) the belief that slaves will clean the house, and (iii) the belief that slaves will work in the field and collect the cotton that is sold on the market for the family's gain. These are beliefs that constitute the ideology of this family. They are, as Haslanger writes, "representations of social life that serve in some way to undergird social practices."[15] It is because of the expectation of a dinner without labor that they arrive at the table without first cooking in the kitchen. It is because of the expectation of slaves cleaning the house that they retire to bed without doing any household chores. It is because of the belief that slaves should do the fieldwork that they spend the day in the house rather than laboring in the hot sun. These beliefs are the ones that explain their everyday behavior. This is what I will provisionally at least take to be their ideology.

Now that we have a sense of the ideology of this particular family, I will explain how their ideology can be expected to include, and give rise to, beliefs that will prevent them from gaining knowledge about their social world.

The family has, for several generations, relied on the work of slaves to create and maintain their fortune, as well as their daily existence. If the institution of slavery is unjust, then their wealth was not properly obtained. Furthermore, their ancestors, including their own parents, were the ones who built and maintained that wealth by exploiting the institution of slavery. So if slavery is deeply unjust, then their own immediate ancestors were perpetrators of great wrongs. If slavery is deeply unjust, then the comfortable aristocratic manner of living to which they are accustomed, relying as it does on the institution of slavery, is unjustifiable.

It is very difficult to view one's own parents as evil. It is also difficult to contemplate giving up luxuries that one has spent one's life enjoying. It is therefore natural to expect the members of the plantation family, by virtue of the ideology they have, to form beliefs that protect them against considering the hypothesis that slavery is an unjust institution. One might expect the ideology to lead the members of the plantation family to believe that Blacks are inherently lazy and require the institution of slavery to instill in them a work ethic that they naturally lack. One might expect their ideology to lead them to believe that Blacks, by virtue of culture or genetics, are not capable of self-governance. One might expect them to believe that Blacks are inherently violent and dangerous and require harsh punishment and control to keep them from posing a threat to civil society. One might expect them to believe, as a result of all of these beliefs about Blacks, that the institution of slavery is just and required by the inherent nature of Blacks.

The ideology of the family can be considered to be the social practices they engage in, together with the beliefs that guide their behavior in these practices. These include their ordinary daily expectations about their social life: expectations of a clean house and food without labor, of free labor for their financial gain, and so on. These expectations lead them to adopt a *justification* for their expectations. It is justified to expect Black slaves to prepare one's dinner, clean the house, raise the children, and labor in the hot sun for free, because Blacks are lazy, incapable of self-government, and a danger to civil society. The institution of slavery is good for society, and good for the Black slaves as well. The philosopher Christopher J. Lebron calls these expectations *legitimizing myths*; they have importance as "the means by which ascendant groups assign to themselves positive social value while portraying others . . .

as justifiably possessing lower standing. Without legitimizing myths, hierarchy is merely stratification. With legitimizing myths, hierarchy becomes grounded in superiority and inferiority and formal distinctions become laden with norms."[16]

The notion of a stereotype, as developed by Walter Lippmann in *Public Opinion*, is his surrogate for an ideology, in the sense I have described. As he there writes:

> [Stereotypes] are an ordered, more or less consistent picture of the world, to which our habits, our tastes, our capacities, our comforts and our hopes have adjusted themselves. They may not be a complete picture of the world, but they are a picture of a possible world to which we are adapted. In that world people and things have their well-known places, and do certain expected things. We feel at home there. We fit in. We are members. We know the way around. There we find the charm of the familiar, the normal, the dependable; its grooves and shapes are where we are accustomed to find them. And though we have abandoned much that might have tempted us before we creased ourselves into that mould, once we are firmly in, it fits as snugly as an old shoe.
>
> No wonder, then, that any disturbance of the stereotypes seems like an attack upon the foundations of the universe. It is an attack upon the foundations of our universe, and, where big things are at stake, we do not readily admit that there is any distinction between our universe and the universe. A world which turns out to be one in which those we honor are unworthy, and those we despise are noble, is nerve-racking.

Lippmann here is clear that stereotypes are the social scripts that guide us through the world, make sense of it, and legitimate our actions within it.[17] He also provides an explanation of why stereotypes are resistant to rational revision: it is emotionally unsettling, perhaps in a distinctive way, to abandon them. They are connected to our identity. Return to the example of the slave-owning plantation family in the Antebellum

American South. Members of the family have certain beliefs, which arise from *self-interest*. They arise from the family's desire to maintain their aristocratic lifestyle, without moral condemnation of themselves or their ancestors. Insofar as their identity is connected to their lifestyle, the beliefs are also connected to their identity. They support that identity.

Susan Stebbing usefully describes ideological beliefs as *cherished beliefs*.[18] A cherished belief, as she writes, is a belief that "we want to retain; it is a pleasant belief to hold." She warns that "[w]e have to be on our guard against supposing that a belief that is cherished could not be false because it would be so dreadful if it were." This echoes Lippmann's description. The disturbance of a stereotype seems like "an attack upon the foundations of the universe." Stebbing's vocabulary, "cherished belief," reflects a feature that Lippmann's "stereotype" lacks. A cherished belief is one that *we will be reluctant to give up*. Stebbing's vocabulary brings out an important feature of ideological belief; it is one that is resistant in a distinctive way to rational revision. Both Lippmann's and Stebbing's discussions bring out the connection between ideological belief and identity; Stebbing's vocabulary additionally calls attention to the fact that beliefs that are connected to our identity will be emotionally dear to us in ways that beliefs unconnected to our identity are not. As a consequence, they will not be easy to abandon.

Stebbing's term "cherished" suggests a kind of individualism about ideological belief: that an individual's *emotional attachment* to a belief is what makes it difficult to rationally revise. This risks the temptation of explaining the puzzling features of ideological belief in terms of intrinsic features of an individual's mental states. We must resist this temptation. The fact that a belief is cherished in the relevant sense can be constituted by social reality. A social identity could be thought of as a set of practices and habits. If we think of those practices as external social relations between persons, it may be that the various social relations that make up those practices prevent the revision of certain beliefs. An individual might be habituated to a practice and, in virtue of the structure of that practice and the costs of breaking the habits it involves, may not easily abandon certain beliefs. There might be nothing in the beliefs that is intrinsically cherish-worthy. But the beliefs are preserved by dint of their connection to certain cherished *practices*. The relation of the agent to the practice is what is fundamental in the case of the flawed ideological beliefs at issue in this book.

While Stebbing's vocabulary and description of the phenomenon could mislead as to its source, it is nevertheless deeply insightful. What Stebbing brings out in her discussion is that the unrevisability she is interested in explaining has its source in *identity*. Beliefs connected to that identity are more difficult to rationally revise. But not all ideological beliefs, in this sense, are problematic. Here is an example. Suppose that my identity involves sensitivity to the diversity of reasonable perspectives; it is a tolerant identity. The practice of tolerance is connected to my identity; it is a "cherished" practice, in Stebbing's sense, and therefore difficult to revise. But it is *not epistemologically problematic*. In fact it may be a good belief-forming policy to have this identity, in the sense that having this identity may lead to more true beliefs and fewer false ones. I may be more open, in virtue of having this identity, to revising my beliefs in accord with evidence.

There are different ways in which an ideology can be problematic. Ideologies can, for example, be morally or politically problematic. However, my focus is on epistemologically problematic features of certain ideologies.

In some sense, ideological belief, since it is resistant to rational revision, is *by its nature* epistemologically defective. But despite its possession of this apparent epistemic defect, we should *not* think of ideological belief as a fortiori epistemologically defective. Ideological beliefs can be true, and can be instances of knowledge (see Thomas Kelly, "Following the Argument Where It Leads"). What is puzzling are cases in which the available evidence suggests that the puzzles raised

by ideological beliefs that philosophers have mulled over involve a subclass of ideological beliefs. It is tempting therefore
to think that when one singles out a subclass of ideological
belief as flawed, the flaw must be moral or political. However,
my interest lies in singling out a subclass of ideological belief
that is epistemologically flawed. Its moral and political flaws
are a consequence of these epistemological defects.[19] Given
that all ideological beliefs have features that make them prima
facie epistemologically suspect, what is the basis for thinking
that there is a subclass worth attending to that has additional
epistemological defects? Perhaps there are just the epistemic
defects associated with all of ideology, and then moral and political defects? If so, this would be a problem for the project
of my book. The argument of my book is that there are certain ideologies that become politically problematic in a liberal
democracy. These ideologies have negative epistemic features
that other ideologies lack. What are these negative epistemic
features?

I have argued that not all ideologies are epistemologically
disabling. Flawed ideologies are, however, epistemologically
disabling; this is why they are flawed. Flawed ideologies prevent us from gaining knowledge about features of reality, including social reality. Some flawed ideologies specifically are
about features of reality that are the characteristic domain
of democratic policy. Such ideologies are epistemologically
disabling about the domain of democratic decision making.
What makes the flawed ideologies that I discuss in the next
chapter democratically problematic is that they concern central domains of democratic decision making.

Let's consider some examples of ideologies that are flawed,
in the sense that they involve false ideological beliefs that prevent us from gaining knowledge about otherwise obvious features of reality.

Suppose that my identity involves the false belief that the
French are untrustworthy. My belief that the French are not
trustworthy will be difficult to revise. This will, for example,

close off French people from being sources of information, which will further prevent my acquiring evidence that it is false. An identity that involves the false belief that the French are untrustworthy will make it much harder to acquire evidence against that belief (for example, trustworthy French people). This is an ideological belief that is flawed in the sense I am after: a difficult to abandon false belief the presence of which hinders the acquisition of knowledge. Flawed ideological belief also characteristically contributes to its own unrevisability.

Here is another example of the additional epistemically problematic features of ideologies that are flawed, in the sense I am characterizing. Suppose that I am brought up in a religious cult that cultivates the rejection of all of the physical and biological sciences. It is easy to imagine that having this identity may block me from acquiring knowledge and contribute to false belief. It will also contribute to its own unrevisability, if one needs to trust some of the physical and biological sciences to evaluate it.

Just as a belief can be *ideological* in virtue of structural features of society that inhibit its revision, so too can an ideology be *flawed*, because of flawed structural features of society that inhibit the rational revision of preexisting false belief, to preserve a desirable situation for a privileged group. Indeed, it is plausible that this often occurs. According to the Yale historian David Blight, "In 1860, slaves as an asset were worth more than all of America's manufacturing, all of the railroads, all of the productive capacity of the United States put together."[20] The belief that Blacks were inherently fit for slavery presumably was widespread in the Antebellum South because those who challenged it were sanctioned. White children in the South were raised with the belief from birth. Debate about it was prevented. If debate with others is prevented, it is hard to revise a belief. Structural features of a society can inhibit rational revision of belief to preserve desirable outcomes for the group privileged by that structure. There are many other ways in which structural features of a society can inhibit the rational revision of beliefs.[21] An individual might have a flawed ideology, because she is a member of such a society, though someone who shared all of her mental states, in another society, does not have a flawed ideology. Structural features of a society are not merely the *cause* of flawed ideology; they also may *constitute* it.

I am arguing that there is a specific subclass of ideologies that have additional epistemological flaws, and so warrant being considered flawed. Perhaps all ideologies have varying degrees of these additional flaws; if so, then all ideologies are at least somewhat flawed. An ideology, in the sense I use, is simply a social "script" that governs one's expectations, normative and practical. We all have ideologies, in this sense, and only some of them are flawed in the relevant sense. The ones that are flawed in the relevant sense are the ideologies that are genuine barriers to the acquisition of knowledge.

Of course, considered simply as nonideological false beliefs, the beliefs in question would *also* be barriers to the acquisition of knowledge. But the reason flawed ideologies are so problematic is that they are *ideologies* that include beliefs that are barriers to the acquisition of important knowledge. Ordinary false beliefs are revisable in ways that ideological false beliefs are not. It is the combination of rational unrevisability with additional epistemic defects that makes flawed ideological belief epistemologically problematic.

I have shown why ideological belief is hard to rationally revise. An ideological belief is connected to identity and/or self-interest, and tends to contribute to its own maintenance. I have argued that there are certain cases in which the beliefs in an ideology are particularly epistemologically problematic, for example when they seal us off from good testimony. But there are other ways for an ideology to be flawed; because of the concepts it contains (or fails to contain).

In her essay "The Idea of Perfection," the philosopher Iris Murdoch considers the example of a mother-in-law, whom she calls M, who disapproves of her son's marriage to D.[22] She regards her daughter-in-law D as "lacking in dignity and refinement," "noisy," and "vulgar." As time passes, M reconsiders her judgment. M decides to think about whether these judgments issue from M's being "old fashioned and conventional," "prejudiced and narrow minded," or "snobbish" and "jealous." She decides to rethink her judgment, eventually realizing that D is "not vulgar, but refreshingly simple," "not undignified but spontaneous." What has happened to allow M to move from a false picture of reality, one resistant to evidence, to one that accurately reflects the facts?

Murdoch calls our attention to the role played in this change of view by the "normative-descriptive words," such as "vulgar" and "spontaneous."[23] Murdoch notes that it is characteristic of normative descriptive words to belong to "sets or patterns without an appreciation of which they cannot be understood."[24] Words like "vulgar" express concepts that belong to a conceptual scheme—a set or pattern of concepts—that orders the social world in a certain way. M came to realize that this conceptual scheme was "old fashioned and conventional." She also came to realize that her attachment to this conceptual scheme was motivated by jealousy (a form of self-interest).

M's change to a more accurate way of perceiving the social world is the result of her abandonment of a conceptual scheme that involves the concepts *vulgar, common*, and *undignified*. These concepts belong to a hierarchical and problematic conception of the social world. Possession of this conceptual scheme prevented M from acquiring knowledge about it. In its place, M adopts a conceptual scheme, a pattern of concepts, including concepts such as *spontaneity* and *joy*, which do not presuppose problematic social hierarchies. Adoption of this new conceptual scheme enables M to see that what she regarded as vulgar is in fact a sign of being spontaneous, what she regarded as "noisy" and breaking the polite calm a decent household should have was in fact joyousness. M thus came to see her social world more accurately.

What Murdoch is arguing is that just as self-interest can lead us to hold and retain *beliefs* in the face of contradictory evidence, self-interest—in this case in the form of jealousy—can also lead us to *retain certain conceptual schemes*, ones that involve normative concepts that mislead us about our social world. M solved her problem, on Murdoch's view, by replacing self-interest with a desire for justice or love, which leads to the "substitution of one set of normative epithets for another."[25] In short, just as social identity and self-interest can lead us to hold and retain flawed beliefs, self-interest can lead us to adopt a set of concepts that prevent us from gaining knowledge about the social world. Murdoch urges us to replace self-interest with love in our relation to others. Murdoch's discussion clearly brings out that the sources of flawed ideological belief, such as self-interest, are sources of flawed concepts, as well as flawed ideological beliefs.

It is not just that a set of concepts, a conceptual scheme, can be flawed because the concepts misrepresent social reality, for example, by imputing to it a fictional hierarchy of worth between people. As Murdoch's discussion brings out, a pattern of concepts can be flawed because it *lacks some concepts entirely*. Miranda Fricker has recently provided a striking example of the phenomenon by which a conceptual scheme lacks a crucial concept. It is from a memoir of the women's liberation movement. The story involved a woman working for Cornell University who was systematically sexually harassed over a period of years. Yet the concept of sexual harassment had yet to be articulated. So she could not conceptualize or understand her "ongoing mistreatment." This is a clear example in which the failure of her ideology to have a concept robbed her of the tools to understand her own oppression. This clearly brings out the sense in which failure to possess a concept can be, in Fricker's words, "epistemically disabling."[26]

On May 13, 2013, the Chinese government issued a secret document, entitled "A Report about the Current Situation of Ideology," to university administrations. The report was leaked by Gao Yu and published in the German magazine *Der Spiegel* in August 2013. The document demands that university professors refrain from discussing seven topics. The seven topics are universal values, free press, civil society, civil rights, historical mistakes of the Chinese Communist Party, crony capitalism, and independence of the judiciary. This is a clear attempt to ensure that students lack crucial political concepts, precisely the ones possession of which would enable them to critique Chinese government policy. It is an attempt to instill a flawed ideology in Chinese students by ensuring that they lack crucial political concepts.

These examples suggest a view according to which negatively privileged groups are hindered from acting in their own self-interest by their failure to have the right conceptual scheme, a scheme that would isolate and explain the oppressive social contexts in which they find themselves. Fricker is assuredly correct that this is a distinctive kind of hermeneutical injustice. But Murdoch's discussion of a conceptual scheme involving concepts such as "vulgar" and "noisy" brings out that privileged subjects also often suffer from flawed conceptual schemes.[27]

Self-interest or jealousy can motivate one to adopt and retain a particular conceptual scheme. It is perhaps even easier to see how concepts can become ideological by being connected to one's identity. Certain ways of conceptualizing the world will clearly be connected to one's identity: the concept of atonement is connected to Catholic identity (on the effects of which, see Kathryn Pogin, "Conceptualizing the Atonement"). Just as beliefs connected to one's identity will be hard to rationally revise and will contribute to their own maintenance, certain concepts will be hard to abandon, and their existence will contribute to their own maintenance.

Iris Murdoch's discussion of M's problematic conceptual scheme, containing concepts such as *vulgar* and *noisy* as "descriptive-normative concepts" of persons, shows that *concepts* can be flawed. In Murdoch's example, the conceptual scheme of the mother-in-law M prevents her from recognizing the true nature of her daughter-in-law.

One of the most famous critiques of a concept is the Black American intellectual Sojourner Truth's discussion of the concept of *woman*, in her speech "Ain't I a Woman?," delivered to the 1851 Woman's Convention, in Akron, Ohio:

> That man over there says that women need to be helped into carriages, and lifted over ditches, and to have the best place everywhere. Nobody ever helps me into carriages, or over mud-puddles, or gives me any best place! And ain't I a woman? Look at me! Look at my arm! I have ploughed and planted, and gathered into barns, and no man could head me! And ain't I a woman? I could work as much and eat as much as a man—when I could get it—and bear the lash as well! And ain't I a woman? I have borne thirteen children, and seen most all sold off to slavery, and when I cried out with my mother's grief, none but Jesus heard me! And ain't I a woman?

Sojourner Truth here calls attention to the fact that the concept of a woman is supposed to be connected to feminine helplessness. However, she presents herself as an example of a woman who does not meet any of these criteria, despite undoubtedly experiencing the worst travails women, and only women, can experience, a "mother's grief." Sojourner Truth in her famous speech is arguing that the concept of *woman* is flawed. Let's explore ways in which concepts can be flawed in this way by preventing the acquisition of knowledge about the social world.

A concept is a *way of thinking* of a property. For example, the concept expressed by "table" is a way of thinking of the property of being a table; the concept of water is a way of thinking of the property of H_2O. Let us say that a concept is empty if there is no property it denotes. For simplicity, I shall stipulate that a property only exists if there are things that did or do fall under it. The concept of being a unicorn is empty, since there are no unicorns, nor have there ever been unicorns.[28] In contrast, the concept of a table is not empty, nor is the concept of water.

I shall use the term "proposition" for the content of a belief. So, when someone believes that Tyrone is about to become CEO, she stands in the belief relation to a proposition, the proposition that Tyrone is about to become CEO. We will take propositions to be built out of *concepts*, rather than the properties or objects they denote. Someone can believe that unicorns have horns, despite the nonexistence of the property of being a unicorn, because the proposition that unicorns have horns is constituted out of concepts, rather than properties.

To explain one model of flawed concepts along these lines, it is helpful to use one theory of concepts, the *inferential role* theory of concepts. According to the inferential role theory of concepts, one possesses a concept if and only if one is disposed to make certain characteristic inferences. The property denoted by a concept is the property that makes those inferences valid.

Here is an example of an inferential role treatment of the concept of conjunction, that is, the concept expressed by "and." According to the inferential role theorist, the concept expressed by "and" is the concept of a property that licenses inferences from the proposition that P and Q to the proposition that P, the inference from the proposition that P and Q to the proposition that Q, and from the proposition that P and Q to the proposition that P and the proposition that Q. The concept of conjunction denotes a *truth-function*, a function from truth-values to truth-values, characteristically supplied by a truth table. The truth-function denoted by the concept of conjunction is the one that makes these inferences valid. What would an account of flawed concepts look like on the inferential model of concepts?

Following Sojourner Truth's famous analysis, let's suppose hypothetically that the concept expressed by "lady" licenses the following inferences: the inference from "x is a well-dressed white woman" to "x is a lady," and the inference from "x is a lady" to "x is submissive and in need of care." This concept is flawed in two ways. First, it is flawed because it leads to false beliefs. Well-dressed white women are not in general submissive and in need of care. Second, it is flawed because such concepts are empty. The inferences it licenses are not valid. Therefore, a fortiori, there is no property in the world that makes these inferences valid. So the concept expressed by "lady," as I have defined it, is *empty*, in the sense that it does not denote a property. One model of an ideologically flawed concept is a concept that both is empty and leads to false beliefs of a certain sort.

According to the inferential role account of flawed concepts I have just sketched, concepts that are flawed are empty of content. For example, the term "lady" that was stipulated to license the inferences described does not denote any property. In chapter 4, I argued that there are words that express concepts that have content, yet that also in some sense express flawed concepts. This is necessary to treat propaganda, which often involves the use of ordinary terms that have been associated with flawed concepts or beliefs.

We can also speak of *terms* being flawed. The discussion in chapter 4 revealed another possible account of how our terms may express flawed contents, one that does not involve them having empty contents. Perhaps "lady" denotes the property of being gendered female, but is associated with another kind of flawed content, one that licenses the inference that anything that is gendered female has properties such as being submissive and in need of care. On this account, "lady" would license the inference, of a particular woman, that she is submissive and in need of care. But "lady" would still denote a normal content, namely, persons who are gendered female.

Here is a third way a concept can be flawed. Let us say that a concept's aptness is determined by whether or not its employment facilitates or impedes the acquisition of knowledge (even if indirectly, via emotional associations). The more a concept impedes one's acquisition of knowledge, the less apt it is. An explanation of what it is for a concept to fail to be apt would explain one way in which flawed ideologies lead to flawed ideological beliefs. We have seen one model of failure of aptness, namely, when the concept is empty and leads to ideologically flawed belief. But it is possible for a concept to fail to be apt, even if it does denote a property.

The nineteenth- and twentieth-century German logician Gottlob Frege is best thought of as an archrationalist. His philosophical goal is to show that analytic judgment alone, definitions and logic, could lead to fruitful extensions of our knowledge. In sketching out his rationalist program of showing how definitions could lead to genuine extensions of knowledge, Frege writes of "the really fruitful definitions in mathematics," such as "that of the continuity of a function":

> What we find in these is not a simple list of characteristics; every element in the definition is intimately, I might almost say organically, connected with the others. A geometrical illustration will make the distinction clear to intuition. If we represent the concepts (or their extensions) by figures or areas in a plane, then concept defined by a simple list of characteristics corresponds to the area common to all the areas representing the defining characteristics; it is enclosed in segments of their boundary lines. With a definition like this, therefore, what we do—in terms of our illustration—is to use the lines already given in a new say for the purpose of demarcating an area. Nothing essentially new, however, emerges in the process. But the more fruitful type of definition is a matter of drawing boundary lines that were not previously given at all. What we shall be able to infer from it, cannot be inspected in advance; here, we are not simply taking out of the box again what we have just put in.[29]

Frege here speaks of concepts that aid us in beneficial ways, which aid our reasoning by helping us to see patterns that we could not otherwise see. But one can then easily see the possibility of definitions of concepts that fool us into thinking that there are patterns that are not there. To take an example from mathematics, the concept *x is divisible only by 1 and 17* is not a particularly fruitful concept. If we thought it was mathematically central, we would be confused about the actual patterns of mathematics. The fruitful number-theoretical concept is *x is divisible only by 1 and x*, that is, the concept of a prime number.[30]

Frege's discussion of fruitful concepts shows us that concepts may mislead us about the structure of reality. We can imagine a definition that is not fruitful in this sense, that occludes, rather than illuminates, the "dependence of propositions" on one another. This is one way in which a concept can be flawed. If an ideology contains such concepts, it will prevent the rational acquisition and revision of belief, in much the same way as a mathematical ideology containing the concept *x is divisible only by 1 and 17* and not the concept of a prime number. Iris Murdoch's discussion of M's conceptual scheme, involving concepts such as "vulgar" and "refined," is intended to provide a case in which certain conceptual schemes are obstacles to the rational acquisition and revision of belief about the *social* world.

Given the conception of flawed ideology I have sketched, and their myriad sources, it is natural to expect that no actual human ideology is completely nonflawed. As theorists of ideology from Lippmann to Gendler emphasize, it is part of natural functioning to have stereotypes that allow us to act rapidly, given limitations of working memory. These stereotypes will help us, but they will also lead us into cognitive error. Similarly, it is hard to imagine an actual human ideology that does not contain some flawed concepts. We all have flawed ideologies, that is, beliefs or concepts that hinder us from gaining knowledge in the normal way in some domain.

We are now in a position to characterize what Manfred Stanley calls *the ideology of technicism*.[31] This is an ideology that excludes (for example) narrative claims about personal experience as reasons for action or belief. The ideology of technicism is one that restricts genuine reasons in the public sphere to those whose contents contain only scientific or quantitative concepts. The ideology of technicism does not contain concepts for personal experience; it therefore consigns them, in Stanley's words, to the status of mere "convenient rhetoric."

Manfred Stanley argues that the ideology of technicism undermines democracy, by undermining the autonomy of those who are unfamiliar with the technicist concepts. The ideology of technicism makes citizens feel unqualified to participate democratically in the formation of the laws that govern their behavior. Patricia Hill Collins and Khalil Muhammad have argued that the ideology of technicism is what underlies discounting personal narratives as explanations of patterns of statistics that paint minority groups in an unflattering light. If these theorists are right, the technicist conceptual scheme is typically adopted as an *ideology*. It is employed by those in power to disenfranchise and subordinate those who are not in power, and hence is connected to a distinct social identity, the identity of ruling elites.

Patricia Hill Collins describes the ideology of technicism as the conceptual scheme of "Eurocentric Knowledge Validation Processes."[32] Collins's choice of vocabulary echoes the Senegalese philosopher Léopold Sédar Senghor, who contrasts the European tradition of reason, with the African tradition, as follows:

> However paradoxical it may seem, the vital force of the Negro African, his surrender to the object, is animated by reason. Let us understand each other clearly; it is not the *reasoning-eye* of Europe, it is the *reason of the touch*, better still, the *reasoning-embrace*, the sympathetic reason, more closely related to the Greek logos than to the Latin ratio. . . . At any rate, Negro-African speech does not mold the object into rigid categories and concepts without touching it; it polishes things and restores their original color, with their texture, sound and perfume; it perforates them with its luminous rays to reach the essential surreality in its innate humidity—it would be more accurate to speak of subreality.

> European reasoning is analytical, discursive by utilization;
> Negro-African reasoning is intuitive by participation.[33]

As we have seen, theorists such as Stanley, Collins, and Muhammad make a further claim. They argue that the employment of such a radically impoverished conceptual scheme as the technicist one is not just an accident of history. The idea that public reason should be constrained to technocratic concepts is there for a specific purpose: to serve the interests of the ruling elite. In the face of Samuel Huntington's appeal to employ the language of expertise more widely as a mechanism to deal with the "excesses of democracy," it is difficult to reject this further claim. If so, then the technocratic conceptual scheme is very often put to ideological purposes, in the sense of ideology I have laid out in this chapter. It is a flawed ideology, because, by denying us access to narrative accounts and personal testimony, it blocks us from an understanding of the human suffering that explains the statistics, even when the statistics are factually correct.

Since Aristotle philosophers have held that there are some particularly important flawed ideologies that threaten democracy. A persistent worry about democracy is that these democratically problematic ideologies seem inevitable, and so democracy will invariably be threatened by their existence. What I have attempted in this book is to develop this ancient worry about democracy in detail. My account of persuasion and manipulation, that is, my account of propaganda, is that it depends for its effectiveness upon the existence of flawed ideology. Any identity that is connected to the belief that a group of one's fellow citizens does not have a perspective worth taking into account will make unreasonable policy appear reasonable. Other kinds of flawed ideologies will make irrational proposals appear rational. Given that there will be the sorts of flawed ideologies Aristotle discusses, in the seemingly inevitable situation of substantive inequality even in democracies, one can see why this has been regarded as an existential problem for democracy since the Ancient Greeks.

It may be easy to see how various features of society may lead someone to acquire a legitimation myth that prevents them from recognizing what is really happening, or to fail to acquire the right concepts to think about reality. But it might be thought that *perceptual belief* is safe from this process. Perhaps the perceptual concepts are simple enough, and given a direct enough relation between experience and belief, flawed ideology cannot affect perceptual belief. If so, by restraining ourselves to a foundation of perceptual belief, we can avoid the kind of cognitive errors that result from flawed ideology.

However, recent work in philosophy of mind and psychology has called into question the idea that perceptual belief is isolated from cognitive error due to bias and prejudice. Our perceptual mechanisms themselves can mislead us by delivering misleading information, resulting in systematically flawed perceptual belief. Our perceptual faculties are now, as is widely agreed, affected by background beliefs. There is a relatively uncontroversial sense in which there is "cognitive penetration" of background belief on perception. As a result, perception itself can be a source of flawed ideological belief.

There are various versions of this thesis, to be distinguished below. But all versions are troublesome. We do think of perception as providing us with the "facts," upon which we build our theories. But if our perceptual mechanisms are themselves affected by bias, then we are at risk of appealing to biased mechanisms to build our theories of the world, yet naturally assume that these mechanisms are not biased. What results from such a situation are biased beliefs that are assumed to be objective.

The notion that perceptual belief is affected by ideology, and can thereby serve to reinforce that very ideology, even when it is flawed, is found quite explicitly in Walter Lippmann's introduction of the notion of stereotypes in *Public Opinion*. There, he writes, about Aristotle's description of slaves:

This is the perfect stereotype. Its hallmark is that it precedes the use of reason; is a form of perception, imposes a certain character on the data of our senses before the data reach the intelligence. The stereotype is like the lavender window-panes on Beacon Street, like the door-keeper at a costume ball who judges whether the guest has an appropriate masquerade. There is nothing so obdurate to education or to criticism as the stereotype. It stamps itself upon the evidence in the very act of securing the evidence.

Lippmann asserts here that stereotypes affect perceptual beliefs by affecting the route from perception to belief. His notion of stereotype here is ideology in the sense that I have characterized; it is resistant to rational revision (obdurate to education and criticism), and contributes to its own unrevisability by stamping itself "upon the evidence in the very act of securing the evidence."

In 2001, in a now famous experiment, Keith Payne first showed that Americans when primed with Black faces more rapidly identify guns than when primed with white faces. In a second experiment in the same paper, he showed that Americans, when under time limits, more often misidentify hand tools and handguns when primed with Black faces. Payne's work shows that stereotypes affect perceptual judgment. The perceptual mechanisms of Americans are affected by their flawed ideological belief that Blacks are violent. It suggests that the perceptual belief *that is a gun* or *that person is dangerous* can be a flawed ideological belief, which justifies the heightened sense of panic and fear associated with an encounter with the other.

I have argued, following Lippmann, that ideological beliefs, or stereotypes, are generalizations that aid us in acting when under time constraints.[34] Given that we are by our nature under time constraints, we need beliefs that have this feature. Lippmann is clear that this means that stereotypes also affect perceptual judgment, which is what Payne's work confirms.

Payne's work provides strong evidence that stereotypes affect perceptual judgment. But there are different ways in which stereotypes could affect perceptual judgment. The most dramatic interpretation would be that many Americans *literally see* a hand tool as a handgun; on this view, the stereotype affects the content of the perception. On a less dramatic interpretation, bias enters in on the route between unbiased perceptual experience and perceptual belief. On this less dramatic interpretation, we have the perceptual experience we would have in seeing a hand tool, but in moving from perception to belief, the salience of the belief that Blacks are violent (the social meaning) makes us leap to an unwarranted belief that what we are seeing is a handgun. Given the rapidity with which we move from perceptual experience to perceptual belief, however, even on the less dramatic version, *we end up with biased beliefs that we wrongly take to be unbiased*.

Jennifer Eberhardt et al., in terms echoing Lippmann, provide evidence that stereotypes "operate as visual tuning devices by determining the perceptual relevance of stimuli in the physical environment. That is, given the processing capacity limitations that all perceivers face, these associations determine which information is important and worthy of attention and which is not. So, for example, the association of Blacks with crime renders crime objects relevant in the context of Black faces and Black faces relevant in the context of crime."[35]

Eberdardt et al. subliminally primed subjects with either Black faces, white faces, or no faces. They then presented the subjects with highly degraded pictures of guns or knives. They discovered that being primed with Black faces enabled the subjects to recognize the degraded pictures of guns and knives much more rapidly than in the other two conditions. In another study, they found that priming with pictures of guns, knives, and other crime-relevant objects greatly facilitated identification of a signal inside Black faces, as opposed to whites faces. This shows that stereotypes, as Lippmann astutely predicted, direct visual attention. It does not show that the experiences themselves are biased, but it shows that *which experiences we have* is a function of our prior beliefs, including our stereotypes.

In a paper published in 2008, Goff, Eberhardt, and two other colleagues ran a series of experiments on undergraduates at Stanford University to test implicit perceptual connections between Blacks and apes.[36] They ran four studies. Their first study, run on 121 Stanford students, showed that priming with Black faces facilitated the identification of images of apes. The authors' summarize the results as follows:

> Simple exposure to Black faces reduced the number of frames participants required to accurately identify ape images. This Black-ape facilitation effect was observed among White and non-White participants alike. And this effect was not moderated by participants' explicit racial attitudes or their motivation to control prejudice. Surprisingly, participants not only exhibited a Black-ape facilitation effect but also exhibited a White-ape inhibition effect as well.[37]

Their second study showed that priming with ape images produced an unconscious attentional bias toward Black faces. In their fifth study, involving 121 white male undergraduates at Pennsylvania State University, subjects primed with images of apes were more likely to judge police beatings of Blacks as justified than subjects primed with images of big cats. Priming with images of apes had no effect on judgments of police beatings of whites. Goff and his colleagues conclude that a "bi-directional association between blacks and apes that can operate beneath conscious awareness" can "significantly affect perception."[38]

There is by now a large enough body of research indicating that stereotypes affect the information we acquire via perception. The mechanism by which perceptual judgments are formed is itself a source of flawed ideological belief. It is furthermore a particularly nefarious source of biased belief, because of the strong pull to treat perceptual judgments as unbiased (hence "eyewitness testimony"). We do not, for example, even ordinarily think that what we pay attention to in perception is affected by our background biases. We consider ourselves as having taken in the whole scene at once.

Susanna Siegel calls the phenomenon by which structural social prejudice against out-groups affects perceptual judgment "perceptual farce." She writes, in terms that evoke Lippmann:

> In all of these cases, a perceiver ends up either perceptually experiencing what she already suspects or fears to be the case, or forming beliefs on the basis of perception that confirm her suspicions or fear. We might say that they are all cases of *perceptual farce*. The farce is that perception seems to open our minds to the things around us, but doesn't. It purports to tell us what the world is like, so that if need be, we can check our beliefs, fears, and suspicions against reality and can use it to guide our actions—but it doesn't.[39]

It is now clear that all sorts of unconscious processes affect the formation of even perceptual beliefs.

As we have seen, there are stronger and weaker forms of the thesis that bias affects perceptual belief. According to the strongest form, defended in Siegel's book *The Rationality of Perception*, bias affects the perceptual content of our experiences themselves. We literally have "biased experiences."[40] According to one weaker form of the thesis, bias affects what we attend to in our visual field, and hence what information we receive from perception. According to another, bias affects the beliefs we form on the basis of our perceptual experience. We know that at least the weaker forms of this thesis are true. It is not important for our purposes to decide between the stronger and the weaker forms of the thesis that bias affects perceptual belief. In either case, there is an epistemological problem facing the attempt to adopt an objective epistemic standpoint.

It is psychologically hard if not impossible to avoid regarding our ordinary perceptual beliefs as yielding an objective picture of the world. Since what we attend to in perception is affected by our background beliefs, perception in fact does not give us an objective picture of the world. So we are left, perhaps unavoidably in a society with group hierarchies and large inequities, with beliefs that seem to be objectively grounded, but are in fact biased.

Even ground-level processes such as perception can be less reliable sources of perceptual belief because of structural facts about society, such as hierarchical structures between groups that violate different kinds of equality. There is reason to believe that this is the normal working of perception.[41] If we live in a society with an unequal hierarchical structure, that will create stereotypes that influence perception. It is not the mechanisms that are functioning incorrectly; these same mechanisms would provide stereotypes not susceptible to those errors in societies with a different structure. It is part of ordinary epistemic functioning in societies with flawed social structures to have beliefs based on perceptual mechanisms that mislead us in characteristic ways. If knowledge required a perceptual faculty that did not mislead us in these ways, we would not know anything. We cannot idealize our perceptual faculties on pain of becoming skeptics.

Our particular interest here is not with flawed ideology generally, but with the flawed ideologies that are most democratically problematic. Some flawed ideologies will be democratically problematic, because they lead to widespread theoretical irrationality, which typically results in failure to track one's own interests, for example. The defense of equality in this book rests upon the claim that the ideologies that tend emerge in societies with substantive material, social, and economic inequalities will also tend to be democratically problematic. Here is the structure of the argument, the details of which are defended in the next chapter.

Democratic society requires a culture of political equality. In the next chapter, I argue that inequalities, even material inequalities, give rise to flawed ideological beliefs.[42] In a society that is meritocratic, those who fail to possess resources will tend to possess the flawed ideological belief that their failure to acquire resources is a social injustice. In a society that is not meritocratic, those who possess an unjustly high position in the hierarchy, perhaps one not justified by "merit," will have the flawed ideology that their position in the hierarchy is justified, for example, by individual merit in a society that is meritocratic. Both of these flawed ideologies are democratically problematic: the flawed ideology of the resource-poor in societies in which resources are divided by merit, and the flawed ideology of the resource-wealthy in societies in which resources are unjustly divided.

Because of my own view of political reality, that is, my view of which kind of situation is more likely to be politically relevant, I will focus on explaining why, in societies with unjust inequality, the belief that society is meritocratic will be part of a democratically problematic flawed ideology. In short, I think that it is much more important to explain what is happening in this kind of case than in the flawed ideology of a resentful and undeserving poor. In fact, I suspect that there is no coherent metaphysics of merit that could support the claim that some citizens deserve a significantly better overall proportion of society's resources. And even if there were such a metaphysics, if it were normative in any way, the description of a meritocratic society would be so distinct from any existing human society that it would be revealed to be fantasy. For example, I believe that there is no defensible normative notion of merit that grants more merit to the baby of a wealthy family than to the baby of a poor family.

Given the examples of democratically problematic flawed ideological beliefs I focus on explaining, one might worry that my project is itself ideological. I am only discussing the belief that society is a meritocracy in the context of situations in which it is a false ideological belief, part of the legitimation myth of the elite. I am only discussing these societies, rather than societies in which the larger problem is the flawed ideological beliefs of the undeserving poor. Perhaps my skepticism about the metaphysics of meritocracy is itself the product of my own ideological stance.

Let's suppose that this is correct, and that my skepticism about meritocracy is the product of my own ideological viewpoint. We may even suppose that my skepticism about meritocracy is part of a *flawed* ideology. It is irrelevant. Even supposing that I am suffering from a flawed leftist ideology, this in no way compromises the objectivity of my arguments. At best, it explains *only my choice of examples*. These are the examples my ideology leads me to think it is most important to understand. I may be wrong that these examples are the most important. But this by itself in no way impugns the objectivity of my description of the cases.

If the kind of examples I choose to analyze are not only unimportant but also *nonexistent*, then my project of understanding them would be fruitless. But it is beyond serious doubt that there are actual societies in which some people have more resources than they deserve, on any defensible normative notion of merit. The young child of a multimillionaire has not herself "earned" the wealth to which she is privileged. Though I may be wrong that even democratic states today involve a great deal of unacknowledged unjust inequality, it is undeniable that there are many cases of societies with large amounts of unacknowledged, clearly unjust inequalities, today and in the past. My description of how these unjust inequalities remain unacknowledged remains relevant to our understanding of such societies. If I am suffering from a flawed ideology that leads me to see injustice where it is not, it at most undermines the number of societies to which I believe my analysis applies. Throughout the book, when I give actual examples of injustice, I provide evidence that they are examples of injustice. But even if I am wrong about all the actual examples I discuss, it does not impugn my theoretical project of understanding examples of that kind. Empirical claims about actual examples are not part of my central theoretical goals in this book.

One might worry, however, that my ideology does not just influence my choice of examples to discuss. One might worry that it also biases the *tools* I use in their analysis. However, the tools I use were developed in areas of philosophy that are overtly nonpolitical. In chapter 4, in the analysis of one mechanism employed in propaganda, I used tools from formal semantics and pragmatics. These tools are required in the analysis of run-of-the-mill nonpolitical speech. In this chapter and the next, I employ tools from analytic epistemology, the characteristic puzzles of which lack any political content. So it is hard to see a case for the thesis that the tools I employ in chapters 4, 5, and 6 carry with them a political bias.

I also make heavy use of social psychology. Many of the theorists I discuss share my concern with the mechanisms that enable illegitimate authority. Because of the overlap, social psychology is an extraordinarily rich source of empirical insight into the questions of this book. But one might have the same sources of worry about the social psychology to which I appeal. Perhaps, because many central results of social psychology have been in the service of explaining the mechanisms by which illegitimate authority is exercised and maintained, these theorists suffer from a flawed ideology that undermines the objectivity of their work.

Again, I have a difficult time seeing how the objectivity of work that explains how illegitimate authority is exercised and maintained is a fortiori impugned even by false beliefs about the prevalence and threat of illegitimate authority. What false beliefs about the prevalence and threat of illegitimate authority may do is influence which phenomena will be most discussed. False beliefs about the prevalence and threat of illegitimate authority may also impugn the use of these results in politics. But one would have to see a completely different argument to give any credence to the thought that the objectivity of the results themselves is tainted. One would have to provide evidence that the tools of social psychology are themselves biased. And because the tools of social psychology are the same across ideologies, this would be a bias that would undermine the practice of social psychology *itself*. This would undermine the use of these tools even when directed to the understanding of very different examples.

I am only interested in explaining why the flawed ideologies that naturally emerge in societies with substantive unjust inequality are democratically problematic. I am skeptical of the real-world relevance of explaining the flawed ideology of the undeserving poor. But this does not compromise the objectivity of my analysis. I suspect that there would be no avoiding the resources I develop in any investigation of ideology, even if it were directed at my own.

This chapter has been in the service of explaining what Tamar Gendler calls the "unavoidable cognitive consequences" of being a member of a society that "violates one's normative ideals."[43] She marshals psychological evidence in favor of the claim that "either you will need to deliberately restrict your attention or experience so as not to encode certain sorts of genuine regularities . . . [o]r you will need to engage in . . . rationalization, changing your normative ideals to accord with the relevant sorts of experienced regularity (for example, by coming to endorse the legitimacy of these stereotypical associations)." I have sketched in some detail the processes by which this occurs. My focus in the next chapter is to complete the book's argument for equality. It is worthwhile to be clear about its structure.

We began this book with Martin Delany's argument that failures of equality of attainment lead to failures of equal respect by causing the false belief that those who control less of the resources are inferior (as well as loss of self-respect by the negatively privileged groups).[44] But the book's argument against inequality is not that failures of equal respect and the undermining of the self-respect are a moral harm (which they no doubt are). It is rather that the beliefs that enable these moral harms are particularly democratically problematic, because such beliefs make antidemocratic demagoguery effective.

The beliefs that tend to arise in conditions of stark inequality, such as belief in the inferiority of other groups, or one's own, tend to undermine democratic ideals, such as reasonableness. It is natural to think that the perspectives of inferior beings, or those less worthy of equality, are not reasonable perspectives. But this too is not the book's argument against inequality, or not exactly. The argument is rather that such ideological beliefs occlude the unreasonable nature of certain claims, institutions, and policies. If there are social injustices, a policy seeking to address them is reasonable. But it will be treated as unreasonable, in a society committed to an ideology that there are no social injustices. Claims that contribute to injustice will fail to be recognized as such. In short, demagoguery will be effective.

My goal is to develop the best version of this argument. I am less concerned with defending a reaction to its conclusion. I have argued that this argument has a lengthy philosophical tradition as an objection to democracy. Given the inevitability of certain kinds of inequality, say, due to the fact of disability or differences in natural capacities, one can understand its lengthy philosophical history as an antidemocratic argument. But it also can be taken as an argument that democracy should seek to minimize even material inequalities.

We have looked at various ways in which beliefs can arise that are resistant in distinctive ways to revision (where a belief's resistance to revision may be due to structural features of a society, rather than an intrinsic feature of that belief). Possession of such beliefs can be a consequence of the normal functioning of epistemic mechanisms in societies with structural features that prevent acquiring evidence against them or discounting counterevidence. We have also seen how ordinary mechanisms of acquiring knowledge may, as part of their ordinary functioning, lead to biased beliefs that *seem* to be objectively grounded. I now turn to the mechanisms at work in the ideologies discussed by philosophers from Aristotle to Marx: why do highly privileged groups believe the ideology of their own superiority, and why do oppressed groups accept the ideology of their own inferiority? I will argue that inequalities lead to the promulgation of these ideologies, and I will show that Aristotle was right to think that these ideologies are democratically problematic. Thus, the next chapter completes the book's argument for equality.

POLITICAL IDEOLOGIES

I have argued in the previous chapter that ideologies can be flawed in a certain sense. They are flawed, in the relevant sense, when they function as persistent barriers to the acquisition of knowledge. There can be flawed ideologies about many subject matters. Some are not particularly democratically worrying. A flawed ideology that systematically prevents an agent from realizing that the Syracuse Orange basketball team will not win the National Championship every year is not democratically worrying. But certain flawed ideologies are democratically worrying. These are the flawed ideologies that affect the central topics of contestation in liberal democracies, for example, the distribution of the goods of society. In this chapter, I consider some specific flawed ideologies, which, I will argue, using tools from social psychology, characteristically arise under certain social conditions. The second task of the chapter is to explain why these ideologies are democratically problematic. Here, I will use the tools of analytic epistemology.

There are two different kinds of flawed ideologies that have been at the center of political philosophy since at least the time of Aristotle. These are the flawed ideological beliefs *those with control of resources* tend to develop, and the flawed ideological beliefs *those without control of resources* tend to develop. The subject of my chapter is the flawed ideological beliefs that arise in societies with an unjust distribution of resources. I will not follow Aristotle in discussing the flawed ideologies that arise in societies with a just but unequal distribution of resources.

I will be discussing the notion of merit, in a claim, for example, like "the wealthy in Germany have gained their fortunes by merit." I myself am suspicious of the notion of pure merit. And even if we suppose that there is some natural kind in the world that we are measuring when we make judgments of merit, my own view is that there will still be many obvious cases in which inequalities are not justified by such judgments. The fact of inherited wealth shows that two citizens can be born, before either has been meritorious at all, with substantial inequality between them. Even if we take judgments of merit at face-value, as measuring something *real*, every actual human society has countless examples of vast inequalities due simply to birth position. Inherited wealth is just one such example. I therefore focus my discussion on hierarchies of status and power in conditions of natural equality, rather than hierarchies of status and power in conditions of natural superiority and inferiority. But nothing in my central argument depends upon my view that there is much actual injustice. The argument concerns substantial inequalities, no matter what their source.

In other words, in discussing the effects of substantial inequality, it will not matter for my central purposes whether or not the substantial inequalities are justified or unjustified. In other words, it will not matter whether those with control of the resources *deserve* control of the resources. And it will not matter whether those without control of the resources do not deserve control of the resources. My argument shows that substantial inequalities are democratically problematic, whether or not these inequalities are justified by differences in merit.

The sociologist Max Weber argues that members of privileged groups, by something like sociological necessity, develop flawed ideological beliefs:

The fates of human beings are not equal. Men differ in their states of health and wealth or social status or what not. Simple observation shows that in every such situation he who is more favored feels the never ceasing need to look upon his position as in some way "legitimate," upon his advantage being "deserved," and the other's disadvantage as being brought about by the latter's "fault." That the purely accidental causes of the difference may be ever so obvious makes no difference.[1]

Weber adds, "[T]he continued exercise of every domination ... always has the strongest need of self-justification through appealing to the principles of its legitimation."[2] Weber describes this as a "need" that also "makes itself felt in the relation between positively and negatively privileged groups of human beings."[3] If so, it is natural to expect that those who are born into a privileged group will have flawed ideological beliefs concerning the privileges they have. In particular, they will believe they deserve the privileges they obtain as a result of accidental forces, such as birth position. These beliefs will be flawed ideological beliefs.

Weber's hypothesis that those who dominate others will develop what Lebron calls a "legitimizing myth" is an empirical claim about processes of belief formation. Is there scientific evidence of this sort of belief formation occurring? Or does the claim that flawed belief can arise in this deviant fashion seem like an unjustified empirical claim. What is the scientific evidence that the psychology of humans works this way?

The scientific evidence for a transition of the sort required by the account of ideology I have sketched is *self-affirmation theory*, a view in social psychology deriving from a famous paper by the Stanford psychologist Claude Steele published in 1988. According to self-affirmation theory, individuals are motivated to maintain a self-conception as a "good and appropriate person."[4] There is a substantial body of results within this literature suggesting that "self-threatening feedback can exacerbate outgroup derogation and use of stereotypes."[5] In other words, the large body of results that constitutes the self-affirmation theory literature in social psychology is evidence that the possibility of having to confront one's own (for example) racist behavior leads to false stereotypes that serve as self-justifications of one's attitudes. The self-affirmation theory literature is the empirical body of literature that provides evidence that everyone has a strong need for self-justification. It is not implausible to suppose that self-affirmation, in those who control societies' resources, manifests in a narrative that legitimates oppressive domination of others.[6]

Self-affirmation theory is a mechanism that very plausibly underlies Weber's description of the legitimation myth of the elites. There is also additional empirical data in support of the formation of the specific kind of legitimation myth described by Weber.

There is a broad correlation across countries between wealth and support for the right-wing party. The correlation is small yet steady. But the problem with studying changes in political affiliation that co-occur with changes in self-interest is that very few if any political parties in countries are natural groupings. They tend to form in response to contingent events. The fact that political parties are in the main groupings of very different interest groups makes Weber's claim difficult to test.[7] Furthermore, "It is extremely difficult to identify and interview a representative sample of wealthy Americans."[8]

Page et al. set out to investigate the policy preferences of high-wealth individuals; the average annual income of their respondents, who lived in Chicago, exceeded $1,000,000, and the median wealth of their sample was well over $7,000,000.[9] They discovered that this group of high-wealth individuals is very involved in politics: 68 percent of them had contributed to political campaigns, and 21 percent had bundled contributions for politicians. Unsurprisingly, they had remarkable access to politicians: 40 percent had contacted their senator, and a not insignificant number were on a first-name basis with

national politicians of great power. Finally, their policy preferences on economic issues strongly reflected their self-interest:
44 percent acknowledged that their political activities were focused on narrow self-interest, mostly banking policy, ensuring
that federal funds would flow to their financial service institutions of choice, and that regulation was minimized. Ironically,
their chief concern was federal deficits, presumably because of
the fear of increased taxation on their wealth.

A study in 2014 by two economists, Nattavudh Powdthavee,
of the London School of Economics, and Andrew J. Oswald,
of the University of Warwick, took the form of a longitudinal
study of lottery winners, looking at changes in their political
beliefs.[10] The hypothesis that they set out to test was whether
"voting choices are made out of self-interest and then come to
be embroidered in the mind with a form of moral rhetoric."
This is a perfect description of flawed ideological belief, as we
have been describing it. The nature of the study helps focus on
the isolated effect of acquiring more wealth suddenly, since the
individuals who won large lotteries were not statistically more
likely to undergo other personal changes that would lead to
shifts in political views.

The data set they used was from the British Household
Panel survey, a "representative random sample of households,
containing over 25,000 unique adult individuals, conducted
between September and Christmas of each year from 1991."
Data on political preferences has been collected since 1991, and
data on lottery winners has been gathered since 1997. The data
set contains almost 100,000 observations on political party
preferences, and reveals, perhaps unsurprisingly, that "there is
much stability" year to year in a person's political views. There
were 541 large lottery wins of over 500 pounds. They discovered a small but clearly statistically significant shift to the right
after winning a sizeable sum in the lottery. They also found
"that an increase in a person's overall household income in
year t is associated with a rise in their belief in the justice of
the current wealth distribution in society." More evidence

is of course required; if British society is in fact thoroughly meritocratic, perhaps the accumulation of wealth caused by a winning lottery ticket frees the winner from a flawed ideological belief about unjust distribution of wealth. But if British society is not meritocratic, then the results speak in favor of Weber's claim.[11]

A significantly unequal distribution of the goods of society leads to expectations on behalf of those who benefit that they will receive more of the goods of society than they in fact deserve. Failure to receive the goods one is accustomed to receiving will be a disruption of one's expectations that is prone to be mistaken as a violation of justice. There will be a motive from self-interest not to correct the resulting "moral error." That is another way of saying that large and unjust distributions of goods will lead those that are its beneficiaries to adopt a flawed ideology. The existence of flawed ideologies explains the efficacy of demagoguery, the kind of propaganda that undermines democratic deliberation. The notion of equality at the basis of democracy is political, not material. However, because large material inequalities lead to the formation of flawed ideologies that undermine democracy, some kind of general material equality is quite likely a *prerequisite* for states to be capable of following democratic ideals.

There are causes of flawed ideological belief other than failures of equality in various senses. Societies in which uniformity of ideology is encouraged will give rise to expectations that one will encounter only others who share that ideology.[12] If one is used to discussions and friendships only with those with the same ideology, encountering someone whose ideology differs may violate one's expectations. Of course, certain kinds of violations of expectations are welcome, rather than disturbing. A violation of the expectation of catching a cold from a plane trip is welcome, rather than disturbing.[13] But if one is raised to think of certain expectations as moral norms, violations of the conventions to which one has grown accustomed will again characteristically seem like a disruption of normal expectations of the sort that is easily mistaken for an encounter with someone who should be morally condemned. That is why those who are brought up in communities with a uniform ideology tend to experience those who fail to share that ideology as morally deviant. Therefore, societies that encourage uniformity of ideology will often result in flawed ideologies, ideologies that contain or produce moral error, that is, false moral beliefs.

Those who are raised in communities with a uniform ideology will identify themselves with that ideology. And there are now decades of evidence in social psychology supporting the view that group identification generally has a distinctive nonrational effect on belief formation. Albert Hastorf and Hadley Cantril discovered that students from two different Ivy League universities who watched a football game between their schools came to very different conclusions about the controversial refereeing calls during the game.[14] Their university affiliation predicted the different conclusions. So students at the two universities arrived at different beliefs on the basis of the same evidence, because of differing group loyalties. This is a phenomenon that the psychologist Ziva Kunda calls *motivated reasoning*.[15]

There is now a long history of the psychological study of motivated reasoning. In a recent study, the legal theorist Dan Kahan and his colleagues presented 202 experimental subjects with a three-and-a-half-minute film of a protest outside a building, after testing them for their cultural and political worldviews.[16] The subjects were asked to imagine themselves as members of a jury, deciding whether the police had violated the protestor's constitutional right to free speech in intervening. Half the subjects were told that the film was of protesters outside an abortion clinic protesting legalized abortion, and the other half were told that the film was of protestors outside a military recruitment center objecting to the military's ban on openly gay and lesbian members of the military. Kahan and colleagues discovered that political orientation strongly affected subjects' legal judgments. Subjects with diametrically opposed political views reacted in "strong and opposite ways to the experimental manipulation":[17] 70 percent of the political conservatives judged that the police had violated the demonstrators' rights in the abortion clinic case, but only 16 percent of political conservatives who saw the same video presented as a protest against the military judged that the police had violated the demonstrators' rights; strong political progressives had precisely the opposite reaction. Kahan's research shows that the effects of motivated reasoning are not limited to watching sports.

Dan Kahan usefully defines motivated reasoning as "the tendency of people to unconsciously process information . . . to promote goals or interests extrinsic to the decision making task at hand."[18] According to Kahan, a goal motivates cognition when it affects the assessment of evidence, for example, the evidence of one's senses (as in when rooting for a team, one sees a controversial referee call), or scientific evidence (as I think of certain kinds of theists confronted with the evidence for evolution, and they no doubt think of me).[19]

Kahan identifies one overall source of motivated reasoning in the political domain, what he calls "identity protective cognition." Identity protective cognition is motivated reasoning with the goal of "affirming one's membership in an important reference group."[20] Kahan suggests that all cases of motivated political reasoning can be explained by identity protective cognition (though I do not need to be committed to the bold claim that *all* ideological belief comes from identity protective cognition).

Rawls argues that "a permanent feature of the public culture of democracy" is a "diversity of reasonable comprehensive religious, philosophical, and moral doctrines."[21] In other words, the public culture of democracy requires distinct ideologies (this is what Rawls calls "the fact of reasonable pluralism"). Given identity protective cognition, members of a society with a uniform ideology will adopt flawed ideological moral beliefs when confronted with novel ideologies. I will argue that the presence of flawed ideological beliefs is what allows for effective demagoguery, of the sort that undermines democratic deliberation. Without the existence of reasonable pluralism, there is too much latitude for effective demagoguery to allow for democracy.

We have seen now in detail two structural societal sources of flawed ideological belief in a society. The first is substantive failures of equality of different sorts. The second is ideological uniformity. In arguing that substantive failures of equality will tend to lead those who control the resources to develop a characteristic kind of legitimation myth, I have justified Weber's view. One task of this chapter has been completed.

What about the flawed ideology of those who do not control society's resources? As we have seen, in a society that is in fact meritocratic, the flawed ideology will take one form. But consider instead the flawed ideology of those who do not control society's resources in societies in which there is an unjust distribution of resources. Since members of these groups are *in fact* oppressed, a flawed ideology could *prevent them from recognizing their own oppression*, or, with less commitment, *prevent them from acting so as to alleviate their oppression*. What reason is there to think that those who suffer from unjust inequalities will tend to develop a flawed ideology that prevents them from recognizing the injustice?

In *Of the First Principles of Government* (1.4.1), David Hume writes:

> NOTHING appears more surprizing to those, who consider human affairs with a philosophical eye, than the easiness with which the many are governed by the few; and the implicit submission, with which men resign their own sentiments and passions to those of their rulers. When we enquire by what means this wonder is effected, we shall find, that, as FORCE is always on the side of the governed, the governors have nothing to support them but opinion. It is

therefore, on opinion only that government is founded; and this maxim extends to the most despotic and most military governments, as well as to the most free and most popular. The soldan of EGYPT, or the emperor of ROME, might drive his harmless subjects, like brute beasts, against their sentiments and inclination: But he must, at least, have led his *mamalukes*, or *prætorian bands*, like men, by their opinion.

The puzzle Hume here raises is as follows. Why are subjects whose interests are not furthered by the agenda of the elite nevertheless guided by the opinions the elite wish them to have? Max Weber later writes:

> Every highly privileged group develops the myth of its natural, especially its blood, superiority. Under conditions of stable distribution of power and, consequently, of an estatist order, that myth is accepted by the negatively privileged group.[22]

It is natural to think that the elite maintain power by promulgating the flawed ideology that their interests are the interests of the society at large. Weber's point concerns the *mechanism* by which they do so, namely, by promulgating the ideology of elite superiority and the belief that the society is a meritocracy. Many other thinkers have made similar points.[23] In trying to make the point plausible, I will delve into some detail about the mechanisms in question. But first, I want to free the project of describing this kind of mechanism of oppression from two commitments it lacks.

First, Weber mentions "blood superiority." Since Weber's time, a powerful societal sanction has arisen against claims of blood superiority. The narrative of highly privileged groups, at least in Western societies, is no longer one of the *genetic* inferiority of the negatively privileged groups. Even the most virulently racist groups have replaced claims of genetic inferiority with claims of *cultural* inferiority. The virulently racist and anti-Semitic Hungarian political party Jobbik is clear that

it regards the Roma as criminal because of their *culture*, not because of their *genetics*. In the West, therefore, Weber's "myth of
natural and blood superiority" has been everywhere replaced
by a myth of *cultural* superiority.

Second, one might misunderstand Weber, as well as what
follows, as an attempt at a *complete* explanation of the failures
of negatively privileged groups to act politically in their own
interests. But this is not correct about Weber, and not correct
about my project. Weber has many other criticisms of democracy. For example, Weber has concerns about the undemocratic nature of bureaucracies. Weber's claim is a partial, not
total, explanation of the failures of democracy.

In any case, the notion of "negative privilege" has potentially
many interpretations. Suppose that we take "negative privilege"
to be measured in terms of relative ownership of goods. In this
case, many people may be negatively privileged toward those
they never encounter, but not negatively privileged relative to
those they encounter. This will hinder political action to correct
unjust distributions with respect to the former group. Moreover, negative privilege comes in degrees. If so, perhaps the expected utility of acting alone is not sufficiently great. There are
many other potential explanations of the failure of negatively
privileged groups to act other than Weber's claim. It is no part
of my project to attribute to Weber's claim all the failure of negatively privileged groups to act. Weber's claim helps us to understand how one kind of propaganda exploits the presence of
the elite ideology in the negatively privileged groups to further
some goal of the elite group. For example, if one can get negatively privileged groups to accept that the system is basically fair
and meritocratic, then one can lead them to oppose attempts to
reform corruption. It just makes sound economic sense for the
positively privileged groups to get members of negatively privileged groups to accept that the system is fair and meritocratic.
That is the only use to which I put Weber's claim.

I am not defending the view that Weber's claim is a complete explanation of the facts of injustice. Nevertheless, despite

my modest claims for it, the view that negatively privileged groups acquire flawed ideologies that prevent them from recognizing their own oppression faces understandable skepticism. Here is what I think are the two most plausible sources of skepticism about the view.

The first source of skepticism is natural befuddlement at why someone should willingly adopt a belief to the effect that a group to which she belongs is culturally inferior, in those cases in which that belief runs obviously contrary to self-interest. The second source of skepticism about Weber's view, which is more difficult to dispel, is that negatively privileged groups have a great deal of evidence of the flaws in the ideology of the highly privileged group. I don't consciously register that virtually every homeless person I see on the streets of America is one color, and it is not my skin color. But these facts are painfully obvious to those on the street, who no doubt find it deeply humiliating to have to beg for food from members of a privileged class who, from their perspective at least, can be reasonably taken to have that privilege because of accidental factors of birth. Why, given what seems to be an undeniable point about the experiences of members of negatively privileged groups, should they nevertheless have the tendency to adopt the ideology of the highly privileged group? I will respond to these objections to Weber in order.

It is indeed implausible in the extreme that someone would *willingly* adopt a belief that entails the inferiority of her own group. However, this kind of skepticism about the view relies on a false picture of how beliefs are formed. It relies on the false premise that, in Bernard Williams's evocative phrase, one can *decide to believe*.[24] Since it is evident that one would not rationally decide to adopt a belief that presents one's own group in a negative light, someone gripped by this model of belief formation will be skeptical of the claim.

However, we cannot simply decide to believe something. It is not up to me to decide whether or not I am on Mars now. It is similarly not up to me to decide about the direct evidence of my senses. But testimony from authoritative sources is a primary source of evidence. This is why the school system of a state is the paradigm example of an *ideological state apparatus*, in Althusser's sense.[25]

Colonialism in Africa brought with it schools, but the schools were generally Christian schools. Belgian schools in the Congo for the natives began in 1906: "Until 1955, schools listed in government statistics were, in the majority of cases, mission-operated schools. From the viewpoint of the government, Catholic mission schools were government schools."[26] The situation was no different in British colonies. Renouncing one's native faith and adopting the faith of the oppressor were often a requirement for economic advancement under British rule. Adults who retained their native tribal faith were excluded from the economic system.

For example, the first school to offer Western secondary education in Africa was Alliance High School in Kenya, founded in 1926 by the Alliance of Protestant Churches, The Church of Scotland Mission. Alliance High School graduates form much of Kenya's ruling intellectual elite, from chief justices of Kenya, to attorney generals, presidential candidates, and various high-ranking government ministers. Even the great Kenyan author Ngugi wa Thiong'o is an Alliance High School graduate. As Ernest Stabler writes, "[B]ehind the emphasis on scholarship, and the development of character through games, and the training in leadership offered to prefects, there lay a central core of Christian faith."[27] Christian education was given the same attention in terms of the curriculum as physics.[28] When Laurence Campbell became headmaster after the legendary Carey Francis retired in 1962, he wrote in the Headmaster's Notes to New Members of Staff:

> From the first Alliance has set out to be a Christian family of boys and masters. The heart of everything is our primary loyalty to Jesus Christ. This does not just mean that we have Chapel services and R. K. lessons and other "pious"

activities, though these exist and are important. It means that all we do—class work, games, school life, personal relationships, as well as Chapel and the rest—should be seen as service we offer to our Master. Through all these we seek to serve Him and to help our boys to become strong, intelligent, Christian men.[29]

Alliance High School has long been Kenya's most prominent high school. Admission to Alliance is a ticket to success in the future. Yet attending Alliance High School involved being told that the dire circumstances in which one was raised were due to one's parents' failure to abandon their "primitive faith."[30] To deny the success of these efforts, to deny the sincerity of Christians in Kenya who denounce *their very own ancestors* as primitive infidels, is simply not plausible. History testifies to the difficulty of rejecting a broad and consistent tapestry of testimonial evidence from apparently authoritative information providers, especially when it begins at an early age.

Bernard Williams has argued, granting that belief is not under direct voluntary control, that belief is nevertheless under *indirect* voluntary control.[31] I can voluntarily join communities that doubt the sources of evidence I have and, after long exposure, learn to reject such sources of evidence. Perhaps I have been raised in a religious cult. I can choose to go to a university and take courses in other cultures that force me to confront the contingencies of my upbringing. But *spontaneous* belief formation is in general an involuntary process. We acquire beliefs spontaneously from the testimony of authority figures, from the lack of reliable sources that contradict them, and so on. Even to begin the process of indirect voluntary control over belief is clearly an arduous, often life-changing task, one that often involves separation from family and community.

There is a simple argument from the premise that belief is not under our direct voluntary control to the conclusion that "negatively privileged groups" will acquire the flawed ideological beliefs of the "positively privileged group." The positively privileged group will control the dominant narrative. If the positively privileged group controls the dominant narrative, then the testimonial evidence of authorities will be the ideology of the positively privileged group. That is the mechanism by which the flawed ideology of the positively privileged group comes to be held by the negatively privileged groups. The negatively privileged groups are not exposed to an alternative ideology.

If the argument is plausible, it raises even more serious concerns in a liberal democratic state. A liberal democratic state requires provision of schooling for all, as well as a news media. The concern is that the education system as well as the news media will become an organ for the propagation of the ideology of the positively privileged group. This is why what is taught in public schools is invariably, in states that self-identify as liberal democracies, a matter of great political contestation. Control of what is taught in the public schools amounts to control of the basic political dialectic. It seems implausible to deny that members of the highly privileged group will win such battles of control.

Weber's view is consistent with the possibility of occasional resistance to the highly privileged group's ideology. But this will be possible only by individuals with great force of will, by the individual effort involved in exercising the kind of "indirect voluntary control" discussed above. Resistance to the adoption of the ideology of the highly privileged group will often involve what Kristie Dotson has called "third order changes."[32] A third-order change "requires perceivers to be aware of a range of differing sets of hermeneutical resources in order to be capable of shifting resources appropriately." This requires "fluency in differing hermeneutical resources." Yet structural features of society often prevent third-order changes, for example, because of the control of the public dialectic by a dominant group. This is what Dotson calls *contributory injustice*.

It may seem easy to adopt such changes in societies characterized by a combination of easy access to alternative information sources and a sufficiently diverse local community that supports entertaining and debating alternative viewpoints. But even when both of these factors are in place, there appears to be no softening of ideological positions, and if anything, the reverse is the case. As the sociologist C. Wright Mills noted, "People, we know, tend to select those formal media which confirm what they already believe and enjoy. In a parallel way, they tend in the metropolitan segregation to come into live touch with those whose opinions are similar to theirs. Others they tend to treat unseriously. . . . They do not, accordingly, experience genuine clashes of view-point, about genuine issues. And when they do, they tend to consider it mere rudeness."[33] Dotson is surely correct to say that third-order changes "are not easy," even in societies that appear to be superficially open.[34]

Unjust societies often involve structural conditions that impose contributory injustice. In part 1, "Southern Night," of his book *Black Boy*, published in 1944, the American writer Richard Wright provides vivid testimony of the role played by public schools in preventing the negatively privileged group from entertaining and accessing alternative narratives of itself:

> I dreamed of going north and writing books, novels. . . . But where had I got this notion of doing something in the future, of going away from home and accomplishing something that would be recognized by others? . . . I knew that I lived in a country in which the aspirations of black people were limited, marked-off. Yet I felt that I had to go somewhere and do something to redeem my being alive. I was building up in me a dream which the entire educational system of the South had been rigged to stifle. I was feeling the very thing that the state of Mississippi had spent millions of dollars to make sure that I would never feel; I was becoming aware of the thing that the Jim Crow laws had been drafted and passed to keep out of my consciousness; I was acting on impulses that southern senators in the nation's capital had striven to keep out of Negro life; I was

beginning to dream the dreams that the state had said were wrong, that the schools said were taboo. . . . My classmates felt that I was doing something that was vaguely wrong, but they did not know how to express it. As the outside world grew more meaningful, I became more concerned, tense; and my classmates and my teachers would say: "Why do you ask so many questions?" Or "Keep quiet." . . . In me was shaping a yearning for a kind of consciousness, a mode of being that the way of life about me had said could not be, must not be, and upon which the penalty of death had been placed. Somewhere in the dead of the southern night my life had switched onto the wrong track and, without my knowing it, the locomotive of my heart was rushing down a dangerously steep slope heading for a collision, heedless of the warning red lights that blinked all about me, the sirens and the bells and the screams that filled the air.[35]

Wright's description of the American South of his youth is one in which the education system and media are permeated with the myth of Black inferiority, which is largely accepted by the negatively privileged population of southern Blacks. There are structural barriers to accessing alternative conceptualizations. Dotson's notion of contributory injustice is a perfect description of the kind of injustice involved when a highly privileged group uses the school systems to promulgate the ideology of their own superiority to members of the negatively privileged group, and to prevent the possibility of adopting new ones.

There is a substantial body of evidence of a more systematic sort for Weber's claim that members of negatively privileged groups tend to adopt the flawed ideology of the elites. Again, the Stanford psychologist Claude Steele has provided it, in a set of experiments that has given rise to a massive empirical literature. This is the literature on *stereotype threat*, which has been shown to be a significant impediment to achievement by negatively privileged groups. The literature on stereotype threat is a distinct literature from the literature on self-affirmation

theory. But taken together, they comprise the scientific explanation of the flawed ideologies of highly privileged and negatively privileged groups.

Claude Steele and Joshua Aronson describe the phenomenon of stereotype threat as "the immediate situational threat
that derives from the broad dissemination of negative stereotypes about one's group—the threat of possibly being judged
and treated stereotypically, or of possibly self-fulfilling such
a stereotype."[36] Steele hypothesized that when members of
groups that are negatively stereotyped as poor at a certain task
face frustratingly difficult challenges in that task, and their
stereotype is highlighted, they more readily adopt the negative
stereotype in that situation. In a paper from 1995, Steele and Aronson give difficult GRE verbal questions to college students,
in two separate conditions. In the "diagnostic" condition, students are told that it is a test of their "reading and verbal reasoning abilities." In the "nondiagnostic" condition, students are
told that the purpose of the research is just to examine "psychological factors involved in solving verbal problems." In the
diagnostic condition, Black students performed significantly
worse relative to whites than in the nondiagnostic condition.

Steele and Aronson write that because stereotype "threat
persists over time, it may have the further effect of pressuring
these students to protectively disidentify with achievement in
school and related intellectual domains. That is, it may pressure the person to define or redefine the self-concept such that
school achievement is neither a basis of self-evaluation nor a
personal identity."[37] In short, the undeniably real psychological phenomenon of stereotype threat is the naturalistic basis
for the adoption of the flawed ideology of the elite group by
the negatively privileged group. Black Americans were stigma-
tized as less intelligent to justify restricting their life prospects.
But the very prejudices that operate to oppress them work, via
the mechanism Steele and Aronson describe, to lead them to
adopt those prejudices as beliefs, in a form of identity protective cognition.

I have argued for the plausibility of Weber's claim that negatively privileged groups tend to adopt the elite ideology of their own inferiority. But this tells us nothing about the *mechanisms* by which this occurs. Two explanations are required. First, we need an explanation of the mechanisms by which highly privileged groups win control of the media and public education. Second, we need an explanation of why the negatively privileged groups adopt the dominant narrative as it is presented in the media and public schools.

A number of theorists have laid out the mechanisms by which highly privileged groups win control over the media and public education. Consider first the media. Noam Chomsky and Edward Herman seek to explain how, without postulating a conspiracy theory, the mass media can end up producing "news" from the perspective of the flawed ideology of powerful interest groups.[38] The explanation is their so-called propaganda model. It explains how government restrictions on the media and private industry and oligarchic control of the media interact together to present selectively controlled information. The propaganda model explains how each node in the transfer of information from world to audience via the media must be cleared through a kind of checkpoint: federal government acceptance, local government acceptance, corporate ownership acceptance, corporate sponsor acceptance (the last is to assure corporate profits). Given the interdependence of the nodes, these pressures tend to lend themselves to coalescing around a rough pattern of uniform interests (just think of the role of advertising in every show one watches on television). The interdependence also allows the whole media system to be rapidly deployed in the service of propaganda in times of supposed emergency.

It is possible to see Chomsky and Herman's propaganda model at work, even in the recent past, in apparently robust liberal democratic states. In the aftermath of the Al Qaeda terrorist attacks of September 11, 2001, on the United States, the administration of the United States undertook a massive propaganda campaign to legitimate the invasion of Iraq, a country that was uninvolved in the terrorist attack. Lee Artz summarizes a widely held consensus about the US media during this time:

> [T]he U.S. corporate media deemed the administration's rhetorical appeals newsworthy and legitimate, accordingly giving them favorable consideration and promotion, and often dramatizing the same copy points emphasized by government speakers.[39]

CBS news is the most watched and influential network news. During the run-up to the Iraq War, its prominent anchor, Dan Rather, was as explicit as possible about the media role in the push to war. Shortly after the terrorist attack, in a CNN To-night interview with Howard Kurtz, Rather said:

> I want to fulfill my role as a decent human member of the community and a decent and patriotic American. And therefore, I am willing to give the government, the president, and the military the benefit of any doubt here in the beginning.

A year later, in an interview on *Larry King Live* on November 4, 2002, Rather said:

> And, you know, I'm of the belief that you can have only one commander-in-chief at a time, only one president at a time. President Bush is our president. Whatever he decides vis-à-vis war or peace in Iraq is what we will do as a country. And I for one will swing in behind him as a citizen ... and support whatever his decision is.[40]

Rather here endorses the view that the role of the media at times when the leader declares a crisis is not to investigate whether or not the leader is correct to declare a crisis, but rather to trust the leader's word and provide propaganda to unify the masses behind the decisions, whether motivated or not, of the "commander-in-chief."

Carl Schmitt argues that the liberal conception of laws that justify every foreseeable application must always give way to what he calls "the exception."[41] The exception "can at best be characterized as a case of extreme peril, a danger to the existence of the state, or the like. But it cannot be circumscribed factually and made to conform to a preformed law."[42] The decision that the situation is an exception cannot be made in a way that conforms to liberalism. Schmitt argues, in an admittedly somewhat quasi-mystical character, that the "decisionist character" of declaring an exception is a feature of absolute monarchy, and not of "the organic unity" of "what the people will."[43] In an exception, there is not enough time for an informed vote.

It is the primary role of the news media in a liberal democratic state to ensure that claims of state emergency, which by their nature lead to the suspension of liberal democratic principles, are very rare and always legitimate. Some political theorists maintain that even in a liberal democracy, it is acceptable for the news media to endorse obedience to authority in times of existential emergency (though even this is clearly undemocratic). But before even contemplating so doing, it is the primary responsibility of the media in a liberal democracy, in the face of *claims* of emergency by political or economic elites, to police those claims. It is hard to see that a venue is a liberal democratic news media at all if it does not fulfill this, its central function.

Wars and emergencies are clearly moments of exception. Because of this, there is a tendency in liberal democracies to adopt the language of emergency, especially when advancing policies that violate liberal democratic norms. In the introduction, we saw that Michigan's Public Act 4 of 2011, The Local Government and School District Financial Accountability Act is phrased in the language of emergency. It is rightly phrased in the language of emergency, since it violates liberal democratic principles. One might wonder whether there are in principle financial reasons to overturn democratic norms. However, many theorists do agree that in times of war, democratic norms may be set aside. For this reason, the vocabulary used in the United States of a "war on drugs" is a clear signal that liberal democratic norms will be violated to deal with an emergency situation.[44] In general, politicians are apt to appeal to the vocabulary of emergency in those situations in which they want to bypass democratic deliberation.

In a liberal democratic society, politicians will always make claims of exception for policies about which they care deeply. They will wrap these claims in the language of exception: "emergency manager," as if the majority Black cities in the state of Michigan underwent tornadoes and floods; the "war on drugs," as if drug use was an enemy outside. It is the job of the media in a democratic society to police politicians' appeal to exceptions in the language of emergency.[45]

At the time, Dan Rather was one of the most respected news anchors in the United States. His attitude was not exceptional. Bill Moyers's documentary *Buying the War* contains clips of Oprah Winfrey showing clear war propaganda about the Iraqi people's wish to be freed by the United States, and then replying to a respectful and deferential audience member's expression of befuddlement, "We're not trying to propagandize, show you propaganda. We're just showing you what is." She then silences the audience member, clearly communicating that any expression of doubt whatsoever that the Iraqi people were not eager for the United States to invade was beyond the bounds of reasonable discourse, to audience laughter. Such attitudes explain the prevalence of the widespread false beliefs intentionally promulgated by the administration of President George Bush, which led the US public to their strong support of the war. To take one example, a *Washington Post* poll in September 2003 found that almost 70 *percent* of Americans believed that Saddam Hussein was personally involved in the 9/11 attack, a view widely suggested by the Bush administration in the months following the attack.[46]

In an interview with the then secretary of defense Donald Rumsfeld in Errol Morris's documentary film *The Unknown*

Known, released in 2014, former Secretary Rumsfeld tells Morris, "It was very clear that the direct planning for 9/11 was done by Osama bin Laden's people, Al Qaeda, and in Afghanistan. I don't think the American people were confused about that." When Morris presented Rumsfeld with the aforementioned *Washington Post* poll, Rumsfeld replied, "I don't remember anyone in the Bush administration saying anything like that, nor do I recall anyone believing that." In reply, Morris played a press briefing of Secretary Rumsfeld himself from February 4, 2003, in the White House, in which Secretary Rumsfeld replied, when asked by a reporter about an explicit denial by Saddam Hussein of any relationship with Al Qaeda, "And Abraham Lincoln was short." When pressed to respond directly to Saddam Hussein's denial of any relationship with Al Qaeda, Secretary Rumsfeld replied, "How does one respond to that? It's just a continuous pattern. This is a case of the local liar coming up again and people repeating what he said and forgetting to say that he never, almost never, rarely tells the truth."[47]

The facts make it beyond reasonable doubt that even in liberal democracies political leaders and private industry conspire in some, perhaps occasionally unconscious, way with the media to deceive the public into acting on false beliefs. The mechanisms are furthermore not mysterious.

The case of the Iraq war in 2003 in the United States is an example in which political and economic elites exploited a free press to convince a large majority of American citizens of beliefs that lacked so much real world evidential support that those very elites later repudiated being associated with them. It is plausible to suppose that the multitrillion dollar cost of the Iraq War, not to mention the lives lost on both sides, was not in the interest of the nearly 70 percent of Americans convinced by the flawed ideology of patriotism and demonization used to motivate it. We thus have provided evidence that the highly privileged group will in fact be able to exploit the mechanisms of the media and public schools to produce beliefs that are contrary to the interests of the majority of people who are served by them.[48]

I must defer an explanation of the mechanisms by which the privileged group or groups control the media to their advantage to the by now large literature on government and corporate influence on the media. But there should be no doubt that the phenomenon is real.

That the groups that control the resources will control the dominant public narrative is not a surprising empirical claim. When the ideology of the groups that control the resources is one of their own superiority, which is a consequence of the claim that resource control is distributed by merit, this will be the dominant public narrative. And some of the iconic studies in social psychology are devoted to explaining why people tend to accept something presented by "expert" authority figures as the official narrative.

There are not many multiply replicable results in social psychology. But one result that stands out in terms of both its robustness and its bearing on the issue at hand shows that the psychology of persons is not naturally suited to pursue autonomy, either of belief or of action. These are the well-known results of the Yale social psychologist Stanley Milgram in the 1960s. Milgram's large body of experimental work on obedience to authority provides strong evidence that the assertions of authority figures are accepted even in the face of explicit counterevidence. We have argued that the highly privileged groups will present their ideology as the dominant narrative, presumably including "experts" who argue for it from positions of authority. Milgram's results give an evidential basis for the claim that such claims will be given special weight.

Here is the description Milgram provides of his experimental setup:

> The focus of the study concerns the amount of electric shock a subject is willing to administer to another person when ordered by an experiment to give the "victim"

increasingly more severe punishment. The act of administrating shock is set in the context of a learning experiment,
ostensibly designed to study the effect of punishment on
memory. Aside from the experimenter, one naïve subject
and one accomplice perform in each session. On arrival
each subject is paid $4.50. After a general talk by the exper-
imenter, telling how little scientists know about the effect
of punishment on memory, subjects are informed that one
member of the pair will serve as teacher and one as learner.
A rigged drawing is held so that the naïve subject is always
the teacher, and the accomplice becomes the learner. The
learner is taken to an adjacent room and strapped in an
"electric chair."

The naïve subject is told that it is his task to teach the
learner a list of paired associates, to test him on the list, and
to administer punishment whenever the learner errs in the
test. Punishment takes the form of electric shock, delivered
to the learner by means of a shock generator controlled
by the naïve subject. The teacher is instructed to increase
the intensity of electric shock one step on each error. The
learner, according to plan, provides many wrong answers, so
that before long the naïve subject must give him the strongest shock on the generator. Increases in shock level are met
by increasingly insistent demands from the learner that the
experiment be stopped because of the growing discomfort
from him. However, in clear terms the experimenter orders
the teacher to continue with the procedure in disregard of
the learner's protests. . . . The experimenter's authority operates not in a free field, but against ever-mounting coun-
terveiling pressure from the person being punished. . . .

For the purpose of delivering shock, a simulated shock
generator is used, with 30 clearly marked voltage levels that
range from 15 to 450 volts. . . . The naïve subject is given a
sample shock of 45 volts to convince him of the authenticity
of the instrument. The generator bears verbal designations
that range from "Slight Shock" to "Danger: Severe Shock."[49]

The original experiments were performed at Yale University. Milgram found that 65 percent of the subjects ended up administrating the maximum shock to the "learner." Throughout the 1960s, Milgram performed variants on the original experiment, with all kinds of different socioeconomic groups, only to find time and again shockingly high levels of obedience to authority:

> With numbing regularity good people were seen to knuckle under the demands of authority and perform actions that were callous and severe. Men who are in everyday life responsible and decent were seduced by the trappings of authority, by the control of their perceptions, and by the uncritical acceptance of the experimenter's definition of the situation, into performing harsh acts.[50]

The challenge in explaining why negatively privileged groups would accept the ideology of the highly privileged group is that negatively privileged groups have clear evidence that the ideology is false. They see around them instances of social injustice that are caused by that ideology. But we see in the Milgram experiments that the true experimental subjects, those administering the shocks, were *also* given ample evidence throughout that their actions were wrong. The fake subject in the electric chair complained repeatedly of pain, and noted the presence of a dangerous heart condition. But by a large majority, the real subjects nevertheless persisted in applying the electrical shocks. They did so because of their uncritical acceptance of the scientist in charge's claims of the moral acceptability of their actions, despite clear evidence to the contrary. Milgram's work thereby addresses perhaps the most puzzling aspect of the thesis that negatively privileged groups generally tend to accept the ideology of the highly privileged group. Milgram's work supports the view that "uncritical acceptance" of the claims of authority figures, especially when delivered in the language of pseudoscientific expertise, is the norm rather than the exception. Thus, Milgram's work provides some evidence of at least many groups susceptibility to a technicist ideology.

The Milgram experiments, and to a considerably more limited extent previous experiments in social psychology by Milgram's advisor, Solomon Asch, show that the ideological beliefs of authority figures, especially when presented as scientific "experts," are given great weight. But social hierarchies work in many less obvious ways to confer epistemic advantage on privileged groups. Susanna Siegel draws our attention, for example, to forthcoming work showing that members of in-groups follow the gaze of fellow in-group members more than they do the gaze of out-group members.[51] As Siegel points out, the unconscious perceptual habits associated with social hierarchy deliver an epistemic advantage to in-group members:

> Ingroup participants follow gaze more readily of ingroup members than outgroup members, whereas outgroup participants follow gaze of both ingroup and outgroup members. To the extent that gaze-following indicates confidence that the followed-person's object of attention or experience of it is epistemically valuable, it is reasonable to hypothesize that this result reflects an underlying pattern of social valuation. This kind of selection effect shapes our epistemic situation.

Yet another set of considerations bearing on the epistemic advantages of highly privileged groups comes from recent analytic epistemology.

The problem flawed ideological belief poses for negatively privileged groups is that it prevents them from acting to overcome the injustices they face. Max Weber points out that all highly privileged groups throughout history share one thing in common, the ideology that they have achieved their success through merit. Members of the highly privileged group, through control of the media and the education system, will make it part of the dominant narrative of the society that the goods of society are justly distributed, according to merit rather than accident of birth position (this will occur even in conditions in which there are obvious differences in equality from birth, due, for example, to inheritance). This is, as Weber argues, exactly what one should expect in any society with a highly privileged group that has an unjust accumulation of its goods. In fact, one would expect that the more unjust and more arbitrary the distribution of goods is in a society, the more intensely and more fervently the view that the distribution of goods is due to pure merit will be held, as the study of UK lottery winners suggests.

Suppose we accept that members of negatively privileged groups tend to adopt the dominant narrative. If so, they will be incapable of acting against the very system that oppresses them. Members of the negatively privileged group will fling themselves against the high barriers erected against them, only to blame themselves for their failure to scale them. The few who do manage the feat will be convinced that they did so out of their own individual merit. They then will be used as pawns in a propaganda game of legitimatization of the dominant ideology. The situation will seem deceitful to no one.

On the assumption that belief in the meritocratic nature of society is a flawed ideological belief, it will be held more firmly than rational beliefs. Because members of the highly privileged group accept this myth, they will be highly motivated to celebrate members of negatively privileged groups who succeed in surmounting the high barriers to success facing their group. They will accept them because they serve as a legitimation of the dominant narrative. And members of the highly privileged group will develop an ideology that explains the failures of most members of the negatively privileged groups to acquire the goods of society in terms of "cultural" flaws of that group.

Adoption of the flawed ideology of the highly privileged group clearly would handicap the negatively privileged group. To act against the structure that oppresses them, they need to know something about the way in which it holds them back from achievement. There are presumably no *particular* propositions the negatively privileged group needs to know in order to act against their oppression. They might not even have to know that they are oppressed. But if they blame their lack of advancement on themselves rather than on the special barriers they face, they will be prevented from acting against the forces that oppress them. The negatively privileged groups will be prevented from attaining the knowledge needed to act precisely by the flawed ideological beliefs they adopt from the dominant narrative. A primary nexus of democratic contestation is over the distribution of resources. Members of negatively privileged groups will be hindered in such contestation by acceptance of the dominant ideology, that society's resources are fairly divided by merit.

We have seen that in conditions of substantive unjust inequality, the belief that resources are fairly divided by merit will tend to be adopted as a dominant ideology. In societies in which there is substantive unjust inequality, the ideology is flawed. It is irrelevant whether or not we are realists about merit; in conditions of unjust distribution, it is not true that resources are divided by merit. That it is held as an ideology prevents its rational revision in the face of evidence. Members of society will be prevented from accessing social reality. Furthermore, the aspects of social reality that the ideology will prevent people from accessing are facts directly relevant for central issues of democratic contestation. Therefore, it is a flawed ideology that is democratically problematic. It is worthwhile pursuing in detail the effects of this flawed ideology on democratic contestation. By focusing on the exact role that this flawed ideology plays in democratic contestation, we can explain why it is such a democratically problematic ideology in conditions of unjust distribution of resources.

Langton draws our attention to the fact that *epistemic authority* and *practical authority* often interact.[52] To take an example from Joseph Raz, a doctor's practical authority to grant, for example, prescriptions depends upon her epistemic authority, or expertise. Langton emphasizes that a mixture between epistemic authority and practical authority is characteristic of hate speech by legal authorities. About the Nazi publications of Julius Streicher, Langton writes:

They possess, not the practical authority of law, whether slave law or apartheid law. They possess, in the first instance, a perceived *epistemic* authority, given the endorsement of the ruling Nazi party, whose imprimatur enables them to masquerade as expert knowledge of a Jewish menace. To say that Nazi propaganda has "perceived epistemic authority" amounts to saying it has the *credibility* component of epistemic authority, in this domain or jurisdiction. But this in turn enables its urgings and recommendations to be *practically* authoritative, for those in its jurisdiction who see it in these terms.

In a similar way, those who own the resources of society will tend to believe that they do so deservedly; they will appeal to a perceived epistemic authority to justify their practical authority in preventing those without resources from taking what is in fact rightfully theirs. Those without resources will be disadvantaged in such a situation, both practically and epistemically. Explaining why those who own the resources of society assume the kind of epistemic privilege that gives them practical authority is a task for epistemology. We can shed light upon the intertwining of epistemic and practical authority to which Langton draws our attention by reflection on the role knowledge plays in practical deliberation.

In a book I wrote and a paper I coauthored, a more precise version of the following claim about knowledge is defended.[53] The claim concerns the epistemic norms of action (so one may have satisfied the epistemic norms, without satisfying other norms on action):

> (Knowledge-Action) One can act on p if and only if one knows that p.[54]

Whether one can act on a proposition is a matter of how much is at stake. So the knowledge-action principle entails that whether or not someone knows that p at a certain time depends upon the practical decisions they face at that time. Let's call this consequence of (Knowledge-Action) the *interest-relativism* of knowledge (sometimes also called "pragmatic encroachment").

The philosopher Ángel Pinillos conducted the following experiment, which nicely motivates the thesis of the interest-relativism of knowledge.[55] The subjects were undergraduate students at Arizona State University: seventy-seven were presented with the first case below, (Typo-Low), and sixty-seven were presented with the second case below, (Typo-High):

(Typo-Low): Peter, a good college student, has just finished writing a two-page paper for an English class. The paper is due tomorrow. Even though Peter is a pretty good speller, he has a dictionary with him that he can use to check and make sure there are no typos. But very little is at stake. The teacher is just asking for a rough draft and it won't matter if there are a few typos. Nonetheless Peter would like to have no typos at all.

(Typo-High): John, a good college student, has just finished writing a two-page paper for an English class. The paper is due tomorrow. Even though John is a pretty good speller, he has a dictionary with him that he can use to check and make sure there are no typos. There is a lot at stake. The teacher is a stickler and guarantees that no one will get an A for the paper if it has a typo. He demands perfection. John, however, finds himself in an unusual circumstance. He needs an A for this paper to get an A in the class. And he needs an A in the class to keep his scholarship. Without the scholarship, he can't stay in school. Leaving college would be devastating for John and his family who have sacrificed a lot to help John through school. So it turns out that it is extremely important for John that there are no typos in this paper. And he is well aware of this.

Immediately after being presented with the vignette, students were asked the following question: "How many times do you think Peter [John] has to proofread his paper before he knows that there are no typos? ____ times." Subjects were told to insert an appropriate number in the blank space. Pinillos found a highly statistically significant distinction between the two cases. The median answer for (Typo-Low) was that Peter has to proofread his paper twice before he knows that there are no typos. The median answer for (Typo-High) was that John has to proofread his paper five times before he knows that there are no typos. Mayseless and Kruglanski already provided strong evidence from social psychology that we expect that people facing a high-stakes decision must gather more evidence in order to act on a belief than if that decision were low-stakes.[56] If knowledge is the norm of action, it is unsurprising that we expect that those facing a high-stakes decision must gather more evidence in order to know something that is the basis for their decision.

The interest-relativism of knowledge has direct consequences for political action. Consider an employee of a business who believes that its workers are being exploited. She is wondering about whether or not to act on her belief by organizing a union. Let's suppose that if the business owners are taking advantage of the workers, she will be successful in convincing her fellow workers to join the union. And let's suppose that if the owners are not taking advantage of the workers, she will be unsuccessful in convincing her fellow workers to join the union. She faces a substantial risk of losing her job for attempting to organize a union. In this case, it will be much harder for her to know that the owners are taking advantage of the workers. The interest-relative nature of knowledge places obstacles in the way of oppressed groups trying to act to ameliorate their oppression.

Given interest-relativism about knowledge, here is the precise role the ideology that the society is meritocratic plays, in a society with unjust inequalities, in democratic contestation. Because of adherence to this ideology, members of highly privileged groups will believe that they deserve their position in the status hierarchy. Possession of the ideology makes them unable to recognize the presence of social injustice (since it is an ideology, that is, resistant to rational revision). They will assume that they are not at risk of doing something that violates their system of values. Their practical authority will give them at the very least a *presumed* epistemic authority. The presumed epistemic authority thus attained can be used to strengthen their practical authority, the very practical authority that gives the higher epistemic standing that comes with having less at stake.

Kristie Dotson defines *epistemic oppression* as "epistemic exclusions afforded positions and communities that produce deficiencies in social knowledge," where an *epistemic exclusion* "is an infringement on the epistemic agency of knowers that reduces her or his ability to participate in a given epistemic community."[57] If knowledge is interest-relative, then those who society regularly places in high-stakes positions when deliberating for its goods are epistemically oppressed, in Dotson's sense. The interest-relativism of knowledge explains why those without resources face epistemic oppression. It is at least one part of an explanation of the self-reinforcing mechanism at work in control of both the mechanisms of retribution and the delivery of information, as they play out in the consolidation of oppressive power and domination.

Is knowledge interest-relative? As it turns out, it is not relevant to these consequences. Every competing explanation also results in a very similar and equally destructive form of epistemic debilitation.[58] Controversy remains over (a) its extent and (b) its source.

What is the extent of the dependence of knowledge on interests? Empirical surveys of judgments have divided into two groups. One kind of result, due to Ángel Pinillos, has revealed strong effects of practical stakes on judgments about knowledge. The second kind of result reveals clear statistically significant results of stakes on judgments of knowledge, but only in high-stakes cases, where matters of great significance are at issue.

My aim here is to establish that negatively privileged groups are epistemologically disadvantaged in debates about the justifiability of distribution of fundamental goods in a society. These are very high-stakes situations for negatively privileged groups. What is at issue in the political case are very high-stakes situations. So we may set aside debates about the scope of the phenomenon as irrelevant to our purposes. After a decade of discussion, almost everyone agrees that the phenomenon is real in deciding about what to do in matters of great import, such as those at issue in political dispute about the distribution of societal goods.

There are different alternative accounts of the phenomenon of judgments of knowledge being sensitive to what one ought to act upon. I will focus on three, and show that all three of them also have the same consequence, that those who are placed by structural features of society in high-stakes situations in competing for its goods are at an epistemic disadvantage, and hence are epistemically oppressed, in Dotson's sense.

Here is one account of the phenomenon, due to the philosopher Brian Weatherson.[59] On Weatherson's account, those in high-stakes situations still have the same level of justified credence as those not in lower-stakes situations who have the same evidence. However, when a great deal is at stake, we have higher standards for full belief. But it is full belief that is required for action, and full belief that is required for knowledge. In that paper, Weatherson seeks to explain the phenomena that lead to pragmatic encroachment, without impugning the purity of the nature of knowledge. Those whom society places in high-stakes situations have a higher standard of evidence to reach in order to fully believe. And knowledge, as well as the norms of action, presupposes full belief.[60]

If we set aside other worries with this as an alternative to the interest-relativity of knowledge, it should be clear that it too results in epistemic oppression. Those who are in high-stakes situations when vying for the goods of society will have to meet higher standards for full belief. This is an epistemic harm. Since it is reasonable to hold, just as above, that negatively privileged groups will have more at stake in disputes over society's goods, they will be epistemically disadvantaged in just the ways described above, with the interest-relativity of knowledge.

Here is a second alternative to explain the data motivating the interest-relativity of knowledge, without endorsing it. It is an alternative explanation that I have previously called *confidence shaking*.[61] Someone placed in a high-stakes situation has their confidence sufficiently shaken by stress that it reduces their degree of belief "below the threshold required for knowledge."[62] Since, as before, knowledge requires full belief, the confidence-shaking account also predicts that those whom society places in high-stakes situations in negotiations over its goods will be epistemically disadvantaged. I have argued that this is not a complete explanation of the phenomena that motivate the interest-relativity of knowledge. Be that as it may, it too clearly results in certain kinds of systematic epistemic oppression.

Here is a third alternative to explain the data motivating the interest-relativity of knowledge, without endorsing it; it is a kind of error theory.[63] It is natural to assume that those facing high-stakes decisions are prone to wishful thinking. For example, both sides of opposing armies facing off in battle tend to be imbued with a belief that they will gain the victory. It's natural to react to someone who makes an important decision based on a "gut reaction," rather than by gathering more information, that this person has based the decision on wishful thinking. They should have acquired more information. Perhaps what is happening in the cases that motivate the interest-relativity of knowledge is that we falsely think that those facing high-stakes decisions are engaged in wishful thinking, and on this basis we refuse to attribute knowledge to them.

There is evidence; for example, the political theorist Archon Fung and the epistemologist Jennifer Nagel have argued that there are good effects of what Fung calls "hot deliberation."[64] Fung rightly points out that "hot deliberation—discussions in which participants have high stakes and affect the exercise of public power—tends to increase the rationality of processes."[65] But this does not show that the resource poor, for example, have a deliberative advantage. First, as Fung recognizes, "information is costly."[66] The resource poor will not have the same access to information, for many reasons. It is hard to see that the high-stakes effect on increased rationality will make up for this. Secondly, the key interest-relative examples of importance to democratic deliberation and civic action will be ones in which the resource-poor group is in a high-stakes position and the resource-rich group is not. It would be natural for the resource-rich group, as we just discussed, to view the resource-poor group as engaged in wishful thinking, even if the resource-poor group was more rational.[67] Third, and most importantly, the view that hot deliberation spurs more careful thinking presupposes that those in high-stakes situations do have a higher epistemic bar to reach. As Jennifer Nagel argues, this shows that, given the same evidence available, those in high-stakes situations will face barriers to knowledge that those in low-stakes situations do not.[68] Asymmetries between those in high-stakes situations and those in less-high-stake situations will accentuate the cost of the greater cognitive demand.[69]

In the previous chapter, we discussed one kind of "epistemic injustice" introduced by Fricker, namely, *hermeneutical injustice*.[70] Hermeneutical injustice is when a group is systematically denied access to the resources to conceptualize their social world correctly. The other kind of epistemic injustice Fricker describes is what she calls *testimonial injustice*, which is "when prejudice causes a hearer to give a deflated level of credibility to a speaker's word."[71] In documenting the harms of persisting testimonial injustice, Fricker singles out its effects on any condition of knowledge that involves an "epistemic confidence" condition, "whether it comes in as part of the belief condition or as a part of a justification condition."[72] She emphasizes in stark terms the cost that someone in this situation faces, that a person in this condition "literally *loses knowledge*."

She explores various consequences of persistent loss in epistemic confidence. For example, if I persistently lose knowledge through underconfidence, then I will come to doubt (perhaps rightly) my own capacities. This process may reasonably be expected to lead to damage to my self-worth.[73]

Neither the interest-relativity of knowledge nor any of the alternative explanations I have discussed straightforwardly involves prejudice. So they are not themselves forms of epistemic injustice. But they do entail that those whom society places in high-stakes positions when negotiating over its goods tend to "literally lose knowledge" in political contexts. These are therefore all ways in which negative privilege results in epistemic harm. All of the alternative accounts of the phenomena motivating pragmatic encroachment, including the various contextualist accounts, entail that negative privilege leads to epistemic harm, even when the source is not group prejudice. Even an error-theoretic account, where those in high-stakes situations *retain* knowledge but are treated as if they *lack* knowledge, entails that those whom society places in high-stakes situations when bargaining for its goods are at an epistemological disadvantage.

The perceived epistemic challenge facing groups that lack society's resources will prevent them from acting. In schools, they will hear that the society in which they live is a meritocracy. They will encounter confident elites who seem, because they are more confident, more deserving of the goods of society. If the dominant ideology involves a belief that the rich have the goods they do because of hard work alone, members of negatively privileged groups will be especially hindered in democratic contestation. The self-serving ideology of the elites will make sense out of the injustice that members of the negatively privileged groups will encounter. And since knowledge is required to act, if any of the accounts that explain the phenomenon in terms of failure to know are correct (whatever the source), negatively privileged groups will be prevented from acting to alleviate their negatively privileged status. They will not be able to act on the basis of knowledge of injustice, because their negatively privileged status may, in the presence of the alternative explanation provided by the ideology of elite superiority, as well as the prospect of retribution by those controlling the prisons and the police, prevent them from acquiring knowledge.

The interest-relativity of knowledge, as well as any of the alternatives that explain the phenomena it addresses, also explains an important feature of epistemic oppression: its *relativity*. Subordinate groups do not just face higher standards for knowledge *generally*. They still know ordinary propositions about their location, their households, and so on. It is just that with respect to their knowledge of *certain propositions* in *certain situations* they face epistemic obstacles that members of privileged groups do not face in those very situations. The interest-relativity of knowledge predicts this. Members of underprivileged groups will have to meet higher standards for knowledge of propositions that are, for them, "serious practical questions," in the sense I have elaborated.[74] They will face higher standards for knowing facts in situations in which those facts bear on important decisions they have to make. Epistemic oppression is about epistemic difficulties that arise in *certain* situations with regard to *certain* facts.[75]

Though the framework I sketch elsewhere is well suited to account for the relative nature of epistemic oppression, the kinds of facts about power, subordination, and interests that have an effect on knowledge are not adequately captured by simple appeal to the "practical interests" of an agent in a situation, of the sort found there.[76] For example, a woman who faces the threat of being beaten for not cooking dinner in a certain way faces a high-stakes decision with respect to the proposition that that is a way to cook dinner. Nevertheless, it doesn't seem that this is an ideal example of a case in which subordinate status leads to higher epistemic standards.[77] The framework of interest-relativity gives one a schema to see how power and interests can raise obstacles to knowledge of facts in situations in which they have a certain kind of practical importance. The framework of interest-relativity accommodates the specificity of the loss of knowledge; it depends on practical features of the circumstance in which the putative knower is placed and the proposition in question. But there is much more work to be done to explain the *kind* of practical importance that is at issue.

The effects of interests on knowledge, whether direct or indirect, have further negative implications for members of oppressed groups, ones particularly relevant for democracy. If someone makes a claim in the form of an assertion, we expect her to know what she is saying. That is why utterances of so-called Moore's Paradoxical sentences like "Tyrone went to the party, but I do not know that Tyrone went to the party" are invariably odd. If one asserts something, one suggests that one knows what one asserts. This is due to the nature of the speech act of assertion. Thus, many philosophers accept:

(Knowledge Norm for Assertion) Assert that p only if you know that p.

The knowledge norm of assertion characterizes the speech act of assertion as guided by knowledge. If one asserts without knowing, one is subject to criticism. That is in the nature of assertion. It is why it is strange to assert, "Tyrone went to the party, but I do not know that Tyrone went to the party." One asserts something, but then denies explicitly that one is adhering to the norm that characterizes assertion.

The knowledge norm does not entail that assertions that are false, or unjustified, or are delivered insincerely fail to be assertions. One can be criticized for not adhering to the rules of the game while still playing the game.

The knowledge norm of assertion, together with the interest-relativity of knowledge, *or any of the suggested alternatives*, entails that negatively privileged groups will be severely hindered in democratic deliberation. The assertions of members of negatively privileged groups will be taken less seriously in the formation of policy that bears heavily on their interests. Their claims that they face social injustice will be regarded as wishful thinking that functions as a justification of character flaws. The widespread ideology that merit fully justifies the society's distribution of goods is part of the reinforcing mechanism by which this process works, as it prevents members of society from rationally evaluating specific claims of social injustice that challenge the ideology, and reinforces the sense that particular assertions of social injustice are wishful thinking.[78] It is a straightforward consequence of the discussions in much of recent epistemology that negatively privileged groups face significant additional disadvantages in the purely epistemic part of the democratic political process. *In conditions of injustice, joint deliberation about how to distribute the goods of society rarely takes place on an equal rational footing between all participants.*

José Medina has emphasized that hermeneutical injustice in Fricker's sense does not merely function to prevent negatively privileged groups from recognizing their own oppression. It also functions to prevent positively privileged groups from recognizing their moral complicity in oppression. For example, white Americans who lack the concept of white privilege are hindered in their ability to see the advantages they receive at the expense of nonwhite citizens. The kinds of epistemic injustice I have been discussing are not forms of epistemic injustice contemplated by Fricker. But an analogous point to Medina's is apt here as well: they do not merely pose worries for oppressed groups. In societies with group hierarchies, members of positively privileged groups will have interests at stake in political deliberation: they will not want to perform unjust acts, for example. But their ideology leads them to regard the system as meritocratic. Therefore, they will not be *aware* of the risks of performing unjust acts. If the risks of their actions are made salient to them, they will deny them. So they will not perceive themselves to face the same obstacles to knowledge as members of negatively privileged groups.

The oppressed will lack self-confidence, which will undermine knowledge. But members of the privileged group will characteristically have inappropriately high levels of confidence.[79]

In Plato's *Gorgias*, Socrates argues that tyrants do not have real power. One thing Socrates might mean here is that tyrants lack the capacity to realize their own ends. Socrates points out that we do not regard a fool who does what he thinks best as powerful, as having the capacity to pursue successfully his own deepest goals. Socrates is arguing that the case is similar with the tyrant. The tyrant does what she thinks is best. But precisely the lack of knowledge that makes her a tyrant in the first place prevents her from doing what is best. More generally, the flawed ideology that the elite use to justify their status leads to lack of knowledge. And this lack of knowledge prevents them from realizing their deepest goals.

In a series of papers, Kristie Dotson has argued that Black American feminists since the beginning of the twentieth century have been calling attention to the damaging epistemic effects of negative privilege. Dotson's specific example is the effects of negative privilege on epistemic confidence. She shows that the complaint of a failure to be regarded as a legitimate source of reasons, being "invisible," resulted in a loss of epistemic confidence, and a concomitant failure of knowledge, in the ways we have canvassed above, in the discussion of "confidence shaking." She also clearly documents the recognition among Black feminists throughout the twentieth century of the paralyzing consequences on action. Dotson's work shows that one of the major topics of twenty-first-century analytic epistemology was also one of the major topics in Black feminist philosophy for a century.

The connections between knowledge, action, and assertion have mainly been explored separately from their political implications. But these connections show why certain ideologies can be democratically problematic. An exploration of the connections between knowledge, action, and assertion is thus crucial to the theory of ideology. It is in the investigation of these connections that we find an important way of elucidating the thought that knowledge is power.

Analytic epistemology is supposed to possess rigor but lack importance. The theory of ideology is supposed to lack rigor but have importance. It is possible to see some portion, indeed a large portion, of analytic epistemology as the testing ground for the theory of ideology, with fictional, depoliticized examples to focus on the abstract structure of epistemic normativity (and, as we have seen, feminist epistemology explores the same problem space, but uses actual examples as sources of insight). Given that epistemology is the discipline that explains when a belief is correctly formed, it is no surprise that it is epistemology that ultimately lies at the center of the theory of ideology.

Our focus has been on the development of flawed ideologies. I have argued that they arise from certain kinds of group identities, ones that emerge from conditions of stark inequality, and are kept in place by the education system, the media, and, as I will argue in the next chapter, the elite's sincere belief in their own superiority and the justice of the system that rewards it. But group identity must not of necessity lead to flawed ideology. A group identity that results from a social script that is in some sense *democratic* will not eventuate in a flawed ideology.

Stephen Darwall draws a distinction between "recognition respect" and "honor respect." Recognition respect of someone as an equal moral person involves "a second-personal acknowledgment of the authority of the other's point of view."[80] A democratic identity is one that allows for democratic deliberation; it must be one that is sensitive to the reasons others give, which is tantamount to giving sufficient weight to their point of view. A democratic identity is consistent with religious and cultural diversity. It is, however, *not* consistent with viewing religious and cultural diversity as laid out in an evaluable hierarchy, with thinking that being Jewish is better than being Catholic. Such hierarchies are the source of flawed ideology.

In Jean-Jacques Rousseau's *Confessions*, he records his recognition of the striking fact that "we were unconsciously affected in our thoughts, our feelings, and even our actions by the impact of . . . slight changes upon us." He reports that he intended to write a book about how to "prevent, change, or modify" the unconscious desires that cause "errors" in "reason."[81] It is reasonable to conclude from these remarks that Rousseau intended to write a book on the way in which we are "unconsciously affected" by our surroundings, and form a web of expectation about the world that characteristically leads to moral error, errors that are the result of reason led astray. His hope was to give advice that would lead us to adopt a social script that would not lead to moral errors. Though Rousseau did not complete this work, we can complete at least one large part of it. If one's identity is based on a life involving a social script that allows one to expect as a matter of course a rationally unjustifiable amount of society's goods, given one's choices, then one's social script will typically involve unreasonable expectations. So one should construct one's identity in a way that avoids hierarchies that would justify unreasonable expectations. That is the best way to avoid the formation of false beliefs that lead to moral error.[82]

In this book, I argue that minimizing stark material inequalities is a precondition for democracy. In such conditions, for example, members of highly privileged groups will acquire a false ideology of their own superiority. It is easy to see the challenge as just a challenge for democratic *deliberation*. But the challenge in fact is far more general. It challenges any form of democracy.

We have seen that flawed ideologies aid the material interests of the highly privileged group, the elites. But false ideologies harm the elites in ways that cut deeper than material interest. The reason that members of unjustly privileged groups are led to adopt legitimizing myths is that they cannot confront the possibility that their actions are unjust. False ideologies blind even those they seem to help, by making them "untrue to themselves." The flawed ideology of the elites leads members of the elite to support policies that they would not accept if they knew what the real source of their support is. Flawed ideologies threaten the *autonomy* of members of highly privileged groups.[83]

On one classic view of autonomy, credited often to Kant, someone's action is autonomous only if that person, the *agent* of that action, would upon rational reflection endorse her reason for doing it. I must act *by my own will* in order for it to be autonomous, via a reason I would reflectively endorse. If this conception of autonomy is correct, then the ideology of the elites leads to the loss of autonomy by members of the elite. If elites generally acquire false ideologies, then members of highly privileged groups regularly act from motives that they would, upon rational reflection, reject. They do not recognize that they are acting from ill-conceived motives. Therefore, their actions are not autonomous, in the sense that the agents would not *reflectively endorse* their actual reasons for acting.[84] So false ideologies are a barrier to autonomous action, even for elites. The ideology of the elites leads to the loss of material freedoms by negatively privileged groups. But it also leads to the loss of freedoms that are equally essential by the elites.

Even absent appeal to a Kantian conception of autonomy, one can see how false ideologies can be democratically problematic in ways that have nothing to do with deliberation. If our interests include doing the right thing, which they often do, then false ideologies prevent members of highly privileged groups from fulfilling some of their central goals. Acceptance of the false ideology of the elite group does lead negatively privileged groups to act against their own material interests. But the false ideology of the elite group leads to members of the elite group acting against their own *ethical* interests. Inequality is epistemologically problematic for everyone.

Gross inequalities of whatever kind are not the same as ethnic differences. Ethnic differences can coexist without gross inequalities, as long as the cultures of the different ethnicities are sufficiently democratic. We tend to think of a democratic identity as one that involves the presupposition of universal ideals.[85] But it is an open question whether or not an Enlightenment model is a necessary companion to a democratic identity. For some reason, historically, the assumption of universal moral norms seems to be accompanied by the exclusion of those who fail to share those norms.

The eighteenth-century German philosopher Johann Gottfried von Herder was a critic of the Enlightenment. Isaiah Berlin argues in his essay "Herder and the Enlightenment" that Herder thought human identity came through culture, language, and practice. Herder's well-known belief in the connection between language and thought led him to the view that the death of a language was the demise of a unique perspective on the world. Identities arising from different languages and cultures were fundamentally different identities. Yet Herder's anti-Enlightenment sentiment led him to a deep commitment to a "belief not merely in the multiplicity, but in the incommensurability, of the values of different cultures and societies."[86] Herder held that the incommensurability of value entailed that different identities do not stand in a hierarchical structure with one another. As a result, Herder held a deep antipathy for colonialism.[87] Herder absolutely rejected the idea of imposing the culture and religion of one group on another.[88] Herder's values appear to be democratic values, and they can coexist with the celebration of particularity. The great question of how difference can coexist with tolerance is, however, beyond the scope of this book.

In the past two chapters, we have laid out the basic notions of the epistemology of political ideologies. Here is the solution I have suggested to what we may call, following Etienne de la Boétie, "the problem of voluntary servitude."[89] In conditions of significant inequality, such as large differences in the distribution of society's resources, those who benefit, the elites, will have certain perceived epistemic advantages over the negatively privileged group, an advantage that will manifest, as we have seen from Langton, in practical terms. They will employ their epistemic and practical advantage to claim expertise over issues of *value*, which are in fact beyond the domain of expertise. They will use their presumed expertise and control of the resources to set the agenda for the media and the schools as methods of applying and conveying their own ideology. Looking at an actual historical example in detail will help us to understand how this characteristically occurs.

THE IDEOLOGY OF ELITES:
A CASE STUDY

In the previous chapters, I laid out the concept of ideology I favor. Using Max Weber, I argued that elites in civil society invariably acquire a flawed ideology to explain their possession of an unjust amount of the goods of society. The purpose of the flawed ideology is to provide an apparently factual (in the best case, apparently scientific) justification for the otherwise manifestly unjust distribution of society's goods. I then argued that, as a mechanism of social control, the elite seek to instill the ideology in the negatively privileged groups. By this route, the negatively privileged groups acquire the beliefs that justify the very structural features of their society that cause their oppression. I then laid out some very general psychological and epistemological facts that make it plausible that such efforts will be successful.

The ideology of the elites is the flawed ideology that those who possess more than they deserve tell themselves to justify their excessive control over the goods of the society into which they are born. My aim in this chapter is twofold. First, I will describe some basic elements of the ideology of elites. My second aim is to elucidate its function in the retention of power by means of a particular historical example, the reorganization of the secondary school system in the United States in the second decade of the twentieth century.

In contemporary societies, one basis of the ideology of elites is the belief that the society into which they are born is *meritocratic*; this is a belief held particularly strongly by those born into wealth and privilege. But since it is quite obvious that in most societies the goods are divided unequally and not according to merit, a much more detailed structure of flawed ideological belief is required to explain how manifest injustices in the pattern of distribution of the goods of society can be present in the environment of someone who firmly believes in the meritocratic nature of the very system that quite obviously leads to the existence of those very injustices.

As we have seen from the discussion of the Antebellum South, the flawed belief in the case of American racism is that Blacks are lazy. The fact that wealthy white Southerners in the Antebellum South could believe that the system in which they lived was meritocratic, despite the obvious existence of slavery, is explained by their possession of beliefs about their own superiority over those who were enslaved. This is an instance of a more general phenomenon:

> People with advantages are loath to believe that they just happen to be people with advantages. They come readily to define themselves as inherently worthy of what they possess; they come to believe themselves "naturally" elite; and, in fact, to imagine their possessions and their privileges as natural extensions of their own elite selves. In this sense, the idea of the elite as composed of men and women having a finer moral character is an ideology of the elite as a privileged ruling stratum, and this is true whether the ideology is elite-made or made up for it by others.[1]

In book 1, chapter 7, of *The Politics*, Aristotle argues that the *master* and the *slave* engage in two quite distinct kinds of activities. The "science" of the slave, the activities suited to the slave, include "cookery and similar menial arts." More generally, the slave is naturally born to know how to perform servile activities. In contrast, those in the household who are "above toil" have others attend to their household while they "occupy themselves with philosophy or with politics." Aristotle here sketches a second characteristic flawed belief of the ideology of elites, one that has always undergirded the division of society into classes, a division that knows no national boundaries.

The Ancient Greeks recognized that practical skill revealed intelligence. But the discussion of slaves in Aristotle's *Politics* reveals that they did have a category for a kind of labor that was not intelligent in nature. Let us call this *manual labor* or *menial labor*.[2] Aristotle thus provides a natural basis for a division of society into groups, one of which will serve as the source of the leaders, and one of which is thought of specifically as the source of manual labor.

The characteristic defense of class distinctions is an ideologically flawed belief in a distinction between theory and practice, or between *mere practical skill* and the exercise of theoretical knowledge. The ideology of class elitism rests upon a belief, already clearly articulated in Plato and Aristotle, that at least one group in society is not capable of theoretical activity, but only of manual labor. The form in which the ideology of elites is transmitted to the negatively privileged group is as a focus on the teaching of manual and vocational skills in the school system to negatively privileged groups, together with indoctrination into the ideology of elites.[3]

In "Hegemony, Intellectuals, and the State," the Italian philosopher Antonio Gramsci writes:

What are the maximum limits of acceptance of the term "intellectual"? Can one find a unitary criterion to characterize equally all the diverse and disparate activities of intellectuals and to distinguish these at the same time and in an essential way from the activities of other social groupings? The most widespread error of method seems to me that of having looked for this criterion of distinction in the intrinsic nature of intellectual activities, rather than in the ensemble of the system of relations in which these activities (and therefore the intellectual groups who personify them) have their place within the general complex of social relations. Indeed, the worker or proletariat, for example, is not specifically characterized by his manual or instrumental work, but by performing this work in specific conditions and in specific social relations. Apart from the consideration that purely physical labour does not exist. In any physical work, even the most degraded and mechanical, there exists a minimum of technical qualification, that is, a minimum of creative intellectual activity.... All men are intellectuals, one could therefore say, but not all men have the function of intellectuals.

When one distinguishes between intellectuals and non-intellectuals, one is referring in reality only to the immediate social function of the professional category of the intellectuals, that is, one has in mind the direction in which their specific professional activity is weighted, whether towards intellectual elaboration or towards muscular nervous effect. This means that although one can speak of intellectuals, one cannot speak of non-intellectuals, because non-intellectuals do not exist. But even the relationship between efforts of intellectual-cerebral elaboration and muscular-nervous effort is not always the same, so that there are varying degrees of specific intellectual activity. There is no human activity from which every form of intellectual participation can be excluded: *Homo faber* cannot be separated from *Homo sapiens*.

Gramsci's point here is that the distinction that is drawn between practical skill and intellectual reflection cannot be drawn. There are no laborers, no wage earners, no people whose activity is *solely* a matter of physical strength.

Gramsci argues that "purely physical labor" does not exist, and so the category of a manual laborer is a sociological one, not based on any fundamental naturalistic distinction of the sort Aristotle tries to draw. Throughout Gramsci's famous *Prison Notebooks*, he subjects the notion of an "intellectual" to a similar critical deconstruction. Gramsci is clear that there is no naturalistic grounding for a division of society into intellectuals and others, only their "social function," which is that of "organizing social hegemony and state domination."[4] Gramsci admits that "the concept of intellectuals is broadened extensively" here, and this is reflected in his work on the wide diversity of social roles of the so-called intellectual, which break into "grades" and status hierarchies (from elementary school teacher to university professor). And as we have seen, in the sense of "intellectual" in which it means someone whose work prevents them from using their knowledge to make intelligent decisions, "there are no non-intellectuals."

In Patricia Hill Collins's discussion of Sojourner Truth's "Ain't I a Woman?" speech, she draws our attention to our conception of an intellectual as someone with a great deal of literary knowledge, accreditation from universities perhaps, and fluency in writing. Sojourner Truth could neither read nor write. Yet, as we saw in chapter 5, Sojourner Truth was "exposing a concept as ideological or culturally constructed rather than as natural or a simple reflection of reality."[5] Sojourner Truth's speech has lasted the test of time as an ideological critique of the concept of *woman*, of its connection to weakness and femininity. It is intellectuals who provide critiques of this kind; and Sojourner Truth's analysis of the contradictions in the concept of *woman* is one of the most important analyses of its kind. If we are to retain a view of intellectuals that requires literacy, we must admit that it is a quasi-incoherent social construct whose incoherence often masks the problematic ideological work the concept is used to perform.

When commonsense reflection reveals the vacuity of a distinction crucial for separating society on an unjust basis into those who receive most of its resources and those who do not, there is a need for a legitimation narrative for the flawed ideology, which is often provided by science. For example, Khalil Muhammad tells the story of the nineteenth- and early-twentieth-century efforts of social scientists to provide a scientific justification of the stereotype of American Blacks as prone toward violence and criminality.[6] Unlike particular American stereotypes about race, the division of labor into those capable of creative intellectual innovation (for example, "entrepreneurs") and laborers transcends all societies and times. So there is naturally an especially pressing human inclination to seek a scientific basis for it. Arguably, the distinction between "procedural" and "declarative" knowledge in cognitive neuroscience is one such example.

The following description of how neuroscientists presented the distinction between procedural and declarative knowledge comes from a recent *New York Times* piece, "Is the 'Dumb Jock' Really a Nerd?," which I coauthored with the Johns Hopkins neuroscientist John Krakauer. H. M. was a patient who suffered a temporal medial lobe lesion that caused him to forget very rapidly every piece of information he learned. In a groundbreaking experiment published in 1962, the psychologist Brenda Milner had H. M. perform a mirror-drawing task. The task required H. M. to trace the outline of a star with a pencil, using a mirror to guide him, with vision of his arm obscured. Over the course of three days, H. M. improved his performance of this task, even though he had no explicit memory of having encountered it on previous days. This is an admittedly fascinating and important result. But what exactly is its significance?

The standard interpretation is that H. M. was able to *acquire and improve motor skills*, even though he could not retain *knowledge of facts*. As a recent newspaper article explains in the context of an interview with the distinguished neuroscientist Suzanne Corkin:

Henry was not capable of learning new information, though his knowledge of past events—the Wall Street Crash, Pearl Harbor and so on—was clear. Only a very few tiny details of TV programmes he watched repetitively ever stuck. He could, however, learn and retain new motor skills, which led to important understanding of the difference between conscious memory and unconscious. The latter category would include learning how to play tennis or ride a bicycle, or even play the piano—things that the brain encodes and transmits to the muscles through conditioning, memories which we come to think of as intuitive.

According to this article, H. M. was able to "learn and retain new motor skills" (and even improve). Examples of such learning are "how to play tennis or ride a bicycle." H. M. is therefore taken to show that motor skills, a paradigm example of which is *tennis*, are not the employment of knowledge.

One can see from this description of the distinction between procedural and declarative knowledge, drawn from our *New York Times* piece, that a part of its seductiveness is due to its promise in supplying the human need for a naturalistic basis by which to divide thinkers from laborers. In our paper from 2013, "Motor Skill Depends upon Knowledge of Facts," in *Frontiers of Human Neuroscience*, Krakauer and I argue that the distinction does not in any sense correspond to that between intellectual reflection and manual labor. H. M., we show, cannot acquire anything like a skill required for manual labor. As we there write:

To understand what the original results do or do not mean, it is useful to consider more recent experiments conducted in patients with similar medial temporal lobe lesions to HM since the 1960s. The general approach in follow-up studies in patients with medial temporal lobe lesions, as in the original Milner experiment, is to demonstrate dissociation between improvement in motor performance variables, usually time to completion and error/accuracy measures, and ability to explicitly recall aspects of the task. What becomes apparent when considering this literature is that the amnestic patients could not perform any of the tasks *unless instruction was provided on each day.*

Roy and Park find that medial temporal lobe patients are unable to acquire the skill of using simple novel tools without constant reinstruction.[7] Part of the account of the uncritical acceptance of a flawed understanding of the distinction may be a desire for a naturalistic explanation of the division of society into thinkers and doers that is a central component of the ideology of elites. It is this, after all, that draws research funding.

As in Ancient Greece, in twentieth-century Western democracies such as the United States, the system of education has been informed by the flawed ideological belief of the ideology of elites that education should fit each person to the task for which they are suited, along a continuum determined by the flawed distinction between intellectual and nonintellectual activity. In his paper "Labor and Leisure," John Dewey bemoans that "[p]robably the most deep-seated antithesis which has shown itself in educational history is that between education in preparation for useful labor and education for a life of leisure." Dewey continues:

> The separation of liberal education from professional and industrial education goes back to the time of the Greeks, and was formulated expressly on the basis of a division of classes into those who had to labor for a living and those who were relieved of this necessity. The conception that liberal education, adapted to men in the latter class, is intrinsically higher than the servile training given to the former class reflected the fact that one class was free and the other servile in its social status.

Dewey argues that the division is based upon a confusion, but nevertheless "[t]he idea still prevails that a truly cultural or liberal education cannot have anything in common, directly at least, with industrial affairs, and that the education which is fit for the masses must be a useful or practical education in a sense which opposes useful and practical to nurture of appreciation and liberation of thought."[8] Dewey was writing at the time of a complete restructuring of the US secondary school system. He was not making an abstract point, but rather commenting on how the concurrently occurring restructuring of the secondary school system was guided by a flawed ideological belief of the ideology of elites, namely, the view that one class, the labor class, was fit only for menial labor and destined for servility.

The Stanford sociology professor Edward Alsworth Ross's book *Social Control*, published in 1901, is an extended argument for the use of the educational system as the ideal mechanism of elite social control. Ross argues that "[t]he Elite, or those distinguished by ideas and talent, are the natural leaders of society," and when "populations thicken, interests clash, and the difficult problems of mutual adjustment become pressing, it is foolish and dangerous not to follow the lead of superior men."[9] Ross stresses throughout the importance of an elite to "spread its desires, tastes, and moral opinions."[10]

Ross's book contains a series of chapters on different mechanisms by which the elite can attain social control over the masses in a democracy. In chapter 14, Ross settles on education, noting "the time-honored policy of founding social order on a system of education."[11] Ross writes of fixing "in the plastic child mind principles upon which, later, may be built a huge structure of practical consequence." Education, for Ross, is a means of "'breaking in' the colt to the harness."[12] Ross argues that the most effective method of social control is a "school education that is provided gratuitously for all children by some great social organ."[13]

The theme of Ross's book is elite domination by control of societal norms, with education as the main mechanism of social control. These have been persisting themes in liberal democratic states throughout the twentieth century. Whatever skepticism is brought to the claim that elites can instill their ideology in negatively privileged groups, it is clearly not a skepticism shared by those who self-identify as elites in liberal democracies. Ross was not a crank working on the fringes of

educational theory at the time. His views had a deep and last-
ing influence on American educational policy.

In 1909, in an address titled "The Meaning of Liberal Education," delivered to the High School Teachers Association,
Woodrow Wilson, later to become the twenty-eighth president of the United States, articulated a view of the purpose of
education that reflected the influence of Ross's work and those
of his cohort:

> Let us go back and distinguish between the two things that
> we want to do; for we want to do two things in modern
> society. We want one class of persons to have a liberal edu-
> cation, and we want another class of persons, a very much
> larger class, of necessity, in every society, to forego the priv-
> ileges of a liberal education and fit themselves to perform
> specific difficult manual tasks.

At the basis of both Ross's and Wilson's separation of American society into elites and followers is the very distinction between *theoretical reflection* and *practical skill* that we have seen
to have no naturalistic basis. Only a small minority of Americans is suited for theoretical reflection, the basis of "a liberal
education." Most Americans are fit for acquiring practical skills
instead. As Wilson writes:

> [W]hat is technical education? It is one which condemns
> all but the extraordinary individual to a minor part in life,
> to a part not of command or direction but of specific per-
> formance, to the difficult manual tasks of the world which
> require skill, a perfect command of the muscles, a trained
> eye, a definite knowledge of physical relations and of com-
> plex machinery; its pupils are men schooled precisely in
> the particular processes which they are to apply. One of the
> drawbacks to American industry is that we do not make
> such men because we overshoot the mark and try to make
> them something else besides. The consequence is that nei-
> ther side of the task is completed or perfected, and we make

neither liberally-educated men nor serviceable experts. It is not that we should not wish to do it, it is that no matter how hard we wish we cannot do it. It is absolutely an unpatriotic thing to waste the money devoted to education by trying to do a thing which we know is impossible. The majority of men have to be drawers of water and hewers of wood. The mechanical tasks of the world are infinite, and they must be performed; and that nation which does not perform them with skill, which has not a great body of trained mechanics, is going to fall behind in the race of modern civilization. America has not been so thoughtful to train men to know how to make things. We have the stuff with which to make them, but we do not give our men the skill to make them. We try to do everything at once, and do nothing well enough.

Wilson's views of a "liberal education" are part of the "education as social control" movement explicitly stated and defended by Ross in *Social Control*. At its base is an ideology of elite superiority, including white male elite superiority.[14] And as we have seen, the self-justification of American antiliberal ideology is a presumed natural distinction between the exercise of intelligence and the exercise of mere practical skill. There are a select few capable of intelligent decision making. All others must be trained in manual skills, together with a uniform story of American history.

One of Edward Ross's students was David Snedden. Snedden's immense impact on the formation of twentieth-century American educational policy is nicely encapsulated in a paper by the Stanford professor David Labaree, who reports that Snedden's "strongest connection" at Stanford was with Ross.[15] In an address to alumni of Stanford in 1900, Snedden gave voice to the doctrine of education as social efficiency and control that became the guiding principal of American mass education. Here are two quotations, both repeated from Labaree's paper:

I want especially to consider that education as it effects that rank and file of society; for if we are right in thinking that training for leadership will largely become the function of the university, it still remains true that the most careful consideration must be given who will do duty in the ranks, who will follow, not lead.

In the nature of our civilization today there are the strongest reasons why the system of public education should increasingly continue to absorb, not only training for culture's sake, but that utilitarian training that looks to individual efficiency in the world of work.

Snedden's vision of education, clearly reflected in Wilson's speech in 1909, was as a system that divided society into groups, the most basic of which was the division into a small group of elites and a large group of followers.[16] The elites were the ones capable of creative and intelligent decision making based on theoretical knowledge. The mass of followers would be equipped for what Snedden regarded as unintelligent practical tasks. This speech immediately made Snedden a celebrity in educational reform.[17]

Snedden's view of the purpose of education as a means of social efficiency and social control was widely shared at the time. Irving King, a distinguished professor of education at the University of Iowa, published in 1913 a book called *Education for Social Efficiency*. In the first chapter, "The Social Origin and Function of Education," in a section titled "Schools as a Social Division of Labor," King writes, "The development of formal agencies of instruction . . . may be regarded as one of the many divisions of labor which become needful as society develops from the primitive to the civilized level. The school, as an institution, and teaching, as a profession, are but phases of the inevitable growth in complexity of a progressive social organism."[18] King rejects a conception of education that has as a method "the giving to each child, as far as possible, the experience of adult society" and emphasizes that education has "always attempted also to *train*, to *discipline* the child."[19] He notes optimistically that we "are only beginning to appreciate the possibilities of education if it may but enlarge the scope of its efforts and put the development of efficiency in the child upon a scientific basis." King rejects "old individualistic conceptions of education" as relics of an outmoded preindustrial society.[20]

King advocated a new model of education, based upon what Joel Spring calls "socialized classroom work."[21] King advocated the view that "society functioned most efficiently when organized into corporate groups." This is not the view of King's teacher, John Dewey. Spring aptly summarizes the differences between the views of teacher and student as follows:

> Socialized education as it spread through the American schools continued to be viewed as a method by which unity and a sense of community could be instilled in future American citizens. But there was one important qualitative difference between Dewey's original work and later statements on social unity. Dewey had wanted to replace the mechanical atmosphere of the classroom with social activity so that social unity would be the result of social understanding. Later methods of organizing group projects and creating a spirit of cooperative endeavor in the schoolroom tried to achieve unity through reliance on the social pressure of the group. Essentially what was to happen was that the individual was to lose his own personal identity to the group.[22]

Dewey was a deliberative democrat. The aim of socialized classroom work, for him, was to train in the culture of democracy, equal respect, and mutual decision making. King's aim was to instill obedience to authority and the recognition that the whole had dominance over the parts. The latter is Plato's conception of the ideal state; the former is one classical conception of democracy.

As we saw in chapter 1, Benjamin Constant criticized Rousseau's conception of freedom for lending itself too easily to authoritarian abuse. In his essay from 1819, "The Liberty of Ancients and the Liberty of the Moderns," Constant writes of Rousseau, "[B]y transposing into our modern age an extent of social power, of collective sovereignty, which belonged to other centuries, this sublime genius, animated by the purest love of liberty, has nevertheless furnished deadly pretexts for more than one kind of tyranny."[23] Benjamin Constant worried that Rousseau's conception of liberty as obedience to self-imposed law could be used by a despot as an instrument of coercion:

> The action carried out in the name of all, being necessarily willy-nilly in the hands of one individual or a few people, it follows that in handing yourself over to everyone else, it is certainly not true that you are giving yourself to no one. On the contrary, it is to surrender yourself to those who act in the name of all. It follows that in handing yourself over entirely, you do not enter a universally equal condition, since some people profit exclusively from the sacrifice of the rest.

Constant's description of the potential misuse of Rousseau is a perfect description of King's and Snedden's use of the language of democracy for the purpose of social control.

Like Rousseau, Dewey clearly had a "positive" conception of liberty, one that, unlike Rousseau's, is connected with collective deliberation. Dewey argued that a democratic ethos and sense of community could be created by collective deliberation in the service of a mutual community goal. We can see the depth of the worry raised by Constant and Berlin here for such rich conceptions of liberty. Even a democratic theorist as profound as Dewey, perhaps by deception, was led to confuse his notion of liberty with an authoritarian conception that has no place for individual liberty.[24]

After completing his dissertation at Teacher's College and serving on the faculty there, Snedden went on to become the first state commissioner for education in Massachusetts in 1909. As commissioner, Snedden appointed in 1912 Clarence Darwin

Kingsley to be the agent for the board to high schools.[25] Kingsley was to become the national voice for Snedden's educational theory, views that he brought to his subsequent appointment as chairman of the powerful National Education Association's Commission on the Reorganization of Secondary Education. The commission was tasked with reorganizing the secondary education system in the United States. The Commission on the Reorganization of Secondary Education set up sixteen committees for various disciplines. But the most important task the commission undertook was a blueprint for American secondary education in the twentieth century, which is entirely based on Snedden's views. It is one of the most important and influential documents in twentieth-century American educational history, setting out what Labaree rightly describes as "the defining principles" for all subsequent secondary education in the United States.[26]

The report, titled "The Cardinal Principles of Secondary Education," took three years to draft by a committee consisting of some of the most prominent figures in education. The document was a clear reflection of Ross's acceptance of Plato's notion that there is a natural division of labor between the rulers and the ruled.[27] In fact, the reference to *The Republic* is not subtle. Plato rejected democracy, and the "Cardinal Principles" document is entirely framed in the language of democracy. But closer inspection reveals great oddity. Section 2 of "The Cardinal Principles of Secondary Education" is titled "The Goal of Education in a Democracy." It begins: "Education in the United States should be guided by a clear conception of the meaning of democracy." Accordingly, the "Cardinal Principles" document provides a precise meaning of democracy. Democracy is a system whose "purpose is to organize society that each member may develop his personality primarily through activities designed for the well-being of his fellow members and of society as a whole."

After insisting on the importance of a clear conception of democracy, and defining the concept of democracy, the authors of "The Cardinal Principles of Secondary Education" draw some conclusions from it. The document argues that the ideal of democracy entails that "human activity be placed at a high level of efficiency; and to that efficiency be added an appreciation of its level of the significance of these activities ... and that the individual choose that vocation and those forms of social service in which his personality may most develop and become most effective."

There is something decidedly odd about this stretch of "The Cardinal Principles of Secondary Education." A democracy is defined as a state in which the education system leads each person to choose that vocation to which they are naturally suited. The immediate consequence of the definition of democracy is that *efficiency* is the goal of society. But this does not sound like a description of democracy. A democracy is meant to preserve individual liberty. Though there are different definitions of "liberty," none involves submerging one's will to the needs of the community for the sake of efficiency.[28] No democratic political philosopher in history has argued that democracy requires an individual to choose a vocation *because it is the one in which that individual will be the most effective for society*. As we saw in the introduction, the point of democracy is precisely to emphasize values *other* than efficiency.

In *The Republic*, Plato rejected democracy as a system in part because, by concentrating on liberty, it failed to maximize efficiency. But "The Cardinal Principles of Secondary Education" describes democracy not as a system that maximizes *liberty*, but rather as a system that maximizes *efficiency*. "The Cardinal Principles of Secondary Education" presents the antidemocratic system of book 2 of *The Republic* as democracy.

Political philosophers have proffered many conflicting versions of democracy over the centuries. Democratic political theory embraces a wide band of political systems. But there are some ground rules. No doubt the most basic ground rule of political philosophy is that democracy is *not the view that social efficiency is the sole value of society*. We philosophers grant to Plato that the system he advocates is not democracy. But the system described in "The Cardinal Principles of Secondary Education" describes the system of book 2 of *The Republic*, introduced as democracy. In short, it is the description of the education system of an undemocratic, illiberal state, framed in the language of democracy.

The redefinition of "democracy" as social control by elites for the purposes of social efficiency is reflected throughout American discourse in the twentieth century. In H. H. Goddard's paper from 1922, "The Levels of Intelligence," he writes:

> The number of people of relatively low intelligence is vastly greater than is generally appreciated and . . . this mass of low-level intelligence is an enormous menace to democracy unless it is recognized and properly treated. . . .
>
> The intelligent group must do the planning and organizing for the mass, . . . our whole attitude toward lower grades of intelligence must be . . . based upon an intelligent understanding of the mental capacity of each individual.[29]

Democracy is a system in which the chief values are autonomy and equality. A system in which one group of people makes choices for the majority of the population is the opposite of democracy. It is, as we have seen, Plato's vision of society in book 2 of *The Republic*, which in political philosophy is the classic opposition to democracy. Goddard simply assumes that "democracy" refers to an antidemocratic system, rule by elites, and he calls for limiting the autonomy of the masses to preserve it.

Elizabeth Cady Stanton stood before the Judiciary Committee of the US House of Representatives and said:

> The chief reason for opening to every soul the doors to the whole round of humans duties and pleasures is the individual development thus attained, the resources thus provided under all circumstances to mitigate the solitude that at times must come to everyone. I once asked Prince

Kropotkin, the Russian nihilist, how he endured his long years in prison, deprived of books, pen, ink, and paper. "Ah," he said, "I thought out many questions on which I had a deep interest. In the pursuit of an idea I took no note of time. When tired of solving knotty problems I recited all the beautiful passages in prose or verse I had ever learned. I became acquainted with my self and my own resources. I had a world of my own, a vast empire, that no Russian jailor or Czar could invade." Such is the value of liberal thought and broad culture when shut from all human companionship, bringing comfort and sunshine within even the four walls of a prison cell. As women ofttimes share a similar fate, should they not have all the consolation that the most liberal education can give?

The speech she gave that day in 1892 was called "The Solitude of Self." The words she delivered in the service of a liberal education for all also heralded the dawn of modernity, and its consequences for women:

> Is it, then, consistent to hold the developed woman of this day within the narrow political limits as the dame with the spinning wheel and knitting needle occupied in the past? No! No! Machinery has taken the labors of women as well as man on its tireless shoulders: the loom and the spinning wheel are but dreams of the past; the pen, the brush, the easel, the chisel, have taken their places, while the hopes and ambitions of women are essentially changed.

The authors of "The Cardinal Principles of Secondary Education" took themselves to represent the highest ideals of the new age, the first to apply scientific methods and reasoning to pedagogy. After three years of work, this is what these arbiters of modernity concluded about the education of women:

> In the education of every high-school girl, the household arts should have a prominent place because of their importance to the girl herself and to others whose welfare will be

directly in her keeping. The attention now devoted to this phase of education is inadequate, and especially so for girls preparing for occupations not related to the household arts and for girls planning for higher institutions. The majority of girls who enter wage-earning occupations directly from the high school remain in them for only a few years, after which home making becomes their lifelong occupation. For them the high-school period offers the only assured opportunity to prepare for that lifelong occupation, and it is during this period that they are most likely to form their ideals of life's duties and responsibilities.

The educational curricula of American high schools in the twentieth century was dominated by a patriarchal ideology no different than the one churches promulgated in the Middle Ages. Yet it was advanced by academics who took themselves to be guided by a new objective science of pedagogy, one that advanced the ideal of efficiency as a form of social control.

In 1916, The National Education Association's Committee on Social Studies in Secondary Education issued a report that was the result of a conflict between the teaching of history and the teaching of what was regarded as a more socially useful discipline, social studies. The legacy of the report of 1916 is complex. But understanding its complexity is important to seeing the different elements affecting the US public system down to the present time.

The National Education Association's Social Studies report reflects warring views on the nature and purpose of civics education in the public schools. John Dewey argued that a democratic society is one whose members should always be seeking to realize its ideals. A necessary part of this process is reflection on the failure of those ideals. Dewey's influence can be seen, for example, in the recommended course for the twelfth grade, "Problems of Democracy." The "Problems of Democracy" course that is outlined in the National Education Association's report turned out to be quite radical. Harold Rugg's popular textbook for that course, *An Introduction to Problems of American Culture*, contains a unit called "Public Opinion and American Life," which is devoted to explaining how people come to have the ideologies they do.[30] It includes an explanation, for example, of why the son of a factory owner would be raised to be against unions. It is considerably more political than standard textbooks of later eras.

Nevertheless, advocates of social control as a means to social efficiency also had a substantial effect on the report. In fact, the report is largely written in the language of social efficiency, and it has the goal of inculcating a single ideology in students, evident in the planning for the community civics course. It emphasizes the importance of "the average citizen in a democracy to think in terms of national interest" as a means of promoting "national efficiency," for which "national solidarity" was vital. It warned about the dangers of "internationalism" and of "humanity as greater than its divisions" and of talk of a "world community." According to Evans, its goals could be summarized as the establishment of social studies as a means to instill "reverence for American and Eurocentric ideals and traditions through history courses, social training for social efficiency and conformity through Community civics, and an attitude favoring progressive social betterment through the fledgling and experimental Problems of Democracy."[31]

The struggle between a conception of social studies as fostering, on the one hand, reflection on obstacles to societal improvement and, on the other, a uniform ideology that allows for efficient social control of the masses, via nationalist appeals to American exceptionalism, continued throughout the twentieth century and on to the present day. However, the role of educational theorists who masked an explicit aim of social control in the language of scientific efficiency in advocating the latter conception is rarely acknowledged.[32]

With scarcely concealed excitement, the website of The Eagle Forum, an organization formed by Phyllis Schlafly in 1975 in the fight against the Equal Rights Amendment, reviews *The*

American Citizens Handbook, the National Education Association's handbook for social studies teachers, published in 1951:

> Originally intended to promote citizenship among young people reaching voting age, this NEA handbook is a sort of civics almanac. It includes essays on citizenship, brief biographies of "heroes and heroines of American democracy," reprints of historical documents that are the "great charters of American democracy," and a description of our legal system.
>
> A section entitled "A Golden Treasury for the Citizen" offers passages suitable for memorization by children with the preface, "It is important that people who are to live and work together shall have a common mind—a like heritage of purpose, religious ideals, love of country, beauty, and wisdom to guide and inspire them." Numerous Old and New Testament selections are included, including the Ten Commandments, the Lord's Prayer and the Golden Rule.
>
> The book unabashedly celebrates old-fashioned virtue and patriotism. The Boy Scout's oath, national songs and uplifting poems appear alongside geography facts, a household budget form, and a chart of compound interest figures.[33]

There is no recognition of the fact that this aspect of the social studies curriculum was the creation of antidemocratic authoritarians whose central interest was social control of the masses in the service of efficiency. Whether the omission of this information was due to complicity or naiveté is the kind of question that presumably will remain forever unanswered.[34]

More recently, the battle over the nature of the social studies curriculum emerged in the debate in 1994 over the National Standards for United States History, paid for by the federal government of the United States and carried out by historians at UCLA. Lynne Cheney was head of the National Endowment for the Humanities from 1986 until 1993, and the wife of the politician Richard Cheney. Her fiery denunciation of the voluntary benchmarks suggested in the National Standards for United States History was published in a *Wall Street Journal* op-ed on October 20, 1994, under the title "The End of History." Cheney contrasted the National Standards with a previous document, called "Lessons from History," which was also produced at UCLA. About "Lessons," she writes:

> "Lessons" conveys the notion that wealth has sometimes had positive cultural consequences in this country, as elsewhere. For the period between 1815 and 1850, students are asked to consider how "the rise of the cities and the accumulation of wealth by industrial capitalists brought an efflorescence of culture—classical revival architecture; the rise of the theater and the establishment of academies of art and music; the first lyceums and historical societies; and a 'communication revolution' in which book and newspaper publishing accelerated and urban dwellers came into much closer contact with the outside world." . . . "Lessons" emphasizes the individual greatness that has flourished within our political system and in our representative institutions.

Cheney denounces the National Standards for concentrating on "multiple perspectives," and being overly influenced by "various political groups," of which she cites two, "African-American groups" and "Native-American groups." As a consequence of Cheney's criticisms, the National Standards were completely revised.[35]

Presumably, there are in fact multiple perspectives on US history, each of which does have a great deal of validity. African Americans and Native Americans (and women) have had a very different experience than white men. But Cheney's *Wall Street Journal* article is clear that she thinks that the purpose of mass education in American public schools is entirely different than accurately reporting the truth. She clearly regards the purpose of American history to be conveying a *single unified perspective*, rather than "multiple perspectives." The single unified perspective is supposed to convey a capitalist value system and reflect the perspective of the *highly privileged group*, and not negatively privileged groups, such as women, African Americans, and Native Americans. As we have seen, historically, Lynne Cheney is quite correct that this was the purpose of mass education in the United States.

We have now looked at some features of the ideology of elites. By investigating a particular example, I have aimed to make plausible Weber's claim that in societies with, for example, large and unequal distribution of goods, the elite are able to transmit their flawed ideological beliefs to the negatively privileged groups as a mechanism of social control.

The history of the education system in the United States is a morality tale of the consequences of allowing elites to use epistemic and practical advantage to claim expertise over judgments of value. C.L.R. James reminds us that the citizens of the Athenian democratic state were well aware of the dangers of granting expertise status.[36] It is to avoid these dangers that "[t]he essence of the Greek method, here as elsewhere, was the refusal to hand over these things to experts, but to trust to the intelligence and sense of justice of the population at large, which meant of course a majority of the common people."

Of course, experts are needed in a democracy; the debate over climate change shows as much. However, we cannot let experts dictate matters of value. There is no easy solution to the problem. How to follow or implement this task is well beyond the scope of this book.

CONCLUSION

This book has been in the service of warning of false hope of realized ideals. Large inequalities in society tend to lead to epistemic practices that are obstacles to the realization of liberal democratic ideals. I have argued that, by the nature of things, we will be prevented from perceiving these obstacles. Those who benefit from such inequalities will tend to believe that the ideals have nevertheless been realized, even in the face of clear evidence that they have not. They will use their privileged status to erect vehicles of propaganda devoted to obstructing investigation into the gaps between ideal and reality. The resulting school systems and media outlets will prevent even members of dispossessed groups from recognizing the existence of such gaps. When philosophy is taught in a way that does not include the intractability of these gaps as one of its central problems, it is rightly regarded as contributing to them.

But there is a danger that this book will be taken, incorrectly, to dismiss or ignore the importance of social movements in articulating and acting against inequalities and injustices of various sorts. This would be a drastic misinterpretation of my aims. Indeed, I hope to have made clear why those movements are all the more to be respected. No one familiar with American history can ignore how difficult it has been to bend the arc of history toward justice. Given the empirical evidence of the dire status of American citizens of African descent, it could be claimed that the bend in the arc is almost indiscernible.

Nor can the process of trying to achieve justice be viewed as simply the unfolding of democratic concepts into law and practice over time. Human agency, carefully crafted appeals, consciousness-raising of various sorts and at differing levels (individual, group, society-wide), cultural and artistic innovations and aesthetic challenges, years of human labor, blood, death, suffering, dreams, direct collective action, all and more were and are essential.

And still we must account for the aforementioned evidence of how little has been the progress of equality for some groups. Community organizers, agitators, rebels, activists, revolutionaries throughout the history of the American polity from Patrick Henry to Martin Luther King have known that challenging the flawed ideologies that dominate discourse, legitimate public practice, and shape the norms of civil society must be confronted sooner rather than later.

Radical social movements in their time are always viewed as disturbances of the moral order. It is only retrospectively that social movements are viewed as speaking truth to power in ways that make moral sense. In the United States, for example, Reverend Martin Luther King Jr. is universally celebrated, including by citizens who share the ideology of those who despised him in his lifetime. This may be used as evidence of their success. But given persisting failures of equality in the United States, a more plausible explanation is that they have been assimilated into a rhetoric that views the polity as ever more just, the society progressively more fair and decent. The fact that social movements make retrospective moral sense does not mean that the practices that accompany them change in materially significant ways.

One must be constantly vigilant of the tendency for the supposed success of social movements to be used to mask their failure. Embracing the moral sense of a social movement is an effective method to justify the end of critical scrutiny into the contradictions and tensions between professed political ideals and the actual circumstances of citizens. The success of the Civil Rights Movement seemed to invite a retreat from the type of critical inquiry I am engaged in here. There is a case to be made that the nobility and courage of those who participated in the Civil Rights Movement were used to mask continuing inequality.[1] Claims of persisting inequality could be dismissed as attempts to diminish the heroic efforts of those who participated in the Civil Rights Movement, who sought a "colorblind" society. An analysis of propaganda and its relationship to flawed ideology helps us understand this danger. As Vesla Weaver and Michelle Alexander have argued with respect to the American Civil Rights Movement in the 1960s, a social movement based on compelling the polity to recognize the role of race in inequality could be utilized to mask continued racial inequality. The heroic narrative of social movements faces the ever-present risk of being co-opted in the service of the message that the problems they addressed are now solved.

All social and political movements have struggled to create cognitive space for ideological moves, assumptions, and alternative narratives. Perhaps chief among these is the democratic revolution against monarchy. I have tried to explain why even its successes will characteristically be distorted, to explain why even liberal democratic ideals relatively quickly become assimilated to the ideology of the privileged that they were intended to supplant. Alongside this, I have sketched the mechanism by which the subversion of democratic ideals occurs. It is my hope, which by no means rises to the arrogance of expectation, that this book will play some positive role in its prevention.

ACKNOWLEDGMENTS

My mother, Sara Stanley, was for decades a court reporter in criminal court. I owe to her my lifelong sensitivity to the injustice and racial bias of the American judicial system. On a personal level, she has always "had my back," even, and maybe especially, when I am dealing with problems caused by me acting in ways that she thinks are unwise. I owe a great many of the strengths of my character to her; knowing that I share those strengths helps me immensely when times get hard.

I here continue the project of Manfred Stanley and Mary Stanley. It would just be wrong not to acknowledge Mary Stanley's huge intellectual impact not only on me, but on this book. By selecting books she knew would guide me, she silently helped plan it. She spent several weekends talking intensively with me about drafts, and helped me write some crucial paragraphs. She has been a huge influence.

My brother Marcus Stanley has been the most brilliant and perceptive interlocutor and commentator throughout the whole process. He also read and commented upon the most number of versions of this book. His constant critical feedback has forced me to explain my claims in ever greater clarity and detail (though not yet to his satisfaction). My wife Njeri Thande has also read and commented on many drafts. Her comments have made it a much better book. If I managed to remain grounded at any time during the writing of this book, I have to thank my son Emile for it.

I owe an immense debt of gratitude to the feminist philosophers and philosophers of race who have worked tirelessly over the past few decades laying the theoretical foundations that allowed me to write this book, while enduring ceaseless abuse for not pursuing "real" philosophy. For me personally, the work of Rae Langton was very important to conceptualizing a bridge between my work in philosophy of language and epistemology and social and political philosophy.

Noam Chomsky and Edward Herman do not think of propaganda exactly as I do. Nevertheless, it will be clear that their work and many of Chomsky's writings are an inspiration for this project, and in particular Chomsky's conception of the sphere of political philosophy. I am grateful not just for his insights into this topic in his many writings that have influenced me, but for the model he provides to younger scholars.

I have been planning to write this book for many years. What helped me to begin was writing for the *New York Times* blog *The Stone*. My first contribution, "The Ways of Silencing," was published in June 2011. It was on the topic of propaganda, as were three of my subsequent four contributions. I did not start physically writing this book until October 2013. The process of writing has taken exactly a year, of the hardest work I remember. My editors for *The Stone*, Peter Catapano and Simon Critchley, deserve thanks for helping me work out my ideas with precision over the last four years. I owe particular thanks to Catapano. Our sometimes intense interchanges over pieces during the last four years forced me to clarify my thoughts on the subject of this book, and made me a better writer. Of the Rutgers graduate students during that time who helped me think through these issues, I owe particular thanks to Gabriel Greenberg. Joshua Armstrong, Karen Lewis, and Carlotta Pavese were also willing to drop everything and help me work through ideas. Carlotta also read an early draft of several chapters.

This book was written entirely at Yale University, exploiting the rich intellectual resources of my home institution. My Yale colleagues have been incredibly helpful. Despite chairing the department, Stephen Darwall has read and commented on at least a dozen drafts of various stages of this book. From my very first day at Yale, he has provided a nonstop education in democratic political philosophy, and the moral philosophy that undergirds it. He encouraged the project from the very beginning, and without his unwavering support, I would not have finished it. Chief among my Yale colleagues, I must thank him.

I have been in a twenty-five-year-long discussion about philosophy with Tamar Szabo Gendler and Zoltan Gendler Szabo. Gendler's work on alief is a deeply important contribution to the theory of ideology. I have learned much engaging with it, and in discussion with her about it over many years. I was looking forward to continuing those discussions at length. However, Gendler became deputy provost of my institution upon my arrival, and is now dean of arts and sciences. Reflection upon and engagement with her philosophical work over the last decade, both in print and in person, has been crucial for my project in this book; and now she has enabled it in another way, by creating an ideal institutional atmosphere to pursue these questions. Szabo's office is next door to mine, and too many points along the way result from our corridor discussions.

My law school colleague Dan Kahan has read and commented on two complete drafts of the book. As in the case of Darwall, his intellectual influence on the book is obvious. Another Yale colleague to whom I owe a large debt is Christopher Lebron. Chris has been simply invaluable in my transition to social and political philosophy. While coparenting with our similarly aged sons, I always ran my latest ideas by Chris. I had to stop adding footnotes to our discussions, because his contributions to the everyday construction of my arguments were simply too numerous. Dan Greco is every philosopher's dream colleague; helpful suggestions from him that substantially improved the book continued until the very last moment before I had to submit it. Hélène Landemore provided me with amazing detailed and helpful commentary on an early draft of the manuscript. One of the reasons I was excited about moving to Yale was to be colleagues with Vesla Weaver, whose paper from 2007, "Frontlash," was the catalyst for so much of my political thinking about ideology and propaganda. My high expectations about being her colleague have been met and exceeded. Casiano Hacker-Cordón also was a tremendous resource, in providing me with both readings and needed discussion. Steven Smith provided very helpful comments on an early draft. Discussion with other Yale colleagues helped, including Seyla Benhabib, Bryan Garston, Verity Harte, Jonathan Kramnick, Daniel Lanpher, and Tracey Meares. Last but not least, the contributions of Yale's wonderful graduate students and post-docs have been crucial. Daniel Putnam worked closely with me throughout, reading draft after draft. Yuan Yuan read several late drafts of the book and held my hand to the fire about certain crucial mistakes, until I repaired them. Matthew Lindauer and Sam Schpall also provided extremely helpful comments on full drafts of the manuscript. Jessie Munton has helped me immeasurably with the issues in chapter 5, reading draft after draft. She too is working on the perceptual effects of stereotypes, and my own thinking about these issues has been hammered out in lengthy conversations with her about the overlaps between her project and mine. Emily Kress was an absolutely invaluable source of information on the material on ancient philosophy. Jessica Keiser helped a great deal with the philosophy of language material, as a sounding board. Jiewuh Song helped me situate one of my central arguments in the landscape of contemporary political philosophy. All in all, I am thrilled to be part of Yale's fantastic intellectual community.

Outside of my Yale colleagues, there are some people I relied heavily upon in writing this book. They have inexplicably provided invaluable written comments, despite no professional attachment to me, and large burdens elsewhere in their lives. My childhood friend, the political philosopher Peter Levine, was present at a talk I gave at the Kennedy School in 2012, and since then has been a crucial interlocutor. He read and commented in detail upon many early versions of the first few chapters, and provided invaluable guidance at the initial stages of the project. Kristie Dotson and Kathryn Pogin both went through multiple drafts of chapters with a fine-tooth comb and were always available for sometimes multihour consultations. Dotson has just been extraordinarily generous with her time. Her work, as is clear, has made a large impact on my own, particularly on the two chapters on ideology. I have also just been greatly affected by engagement with her work. We are fortunate to have someone so smart in our discipline. Astonishingly, Pogin is just a first-year graduate student. I am looking forward to her finishing her dissertation and getting a job so that it's less embarrassing when she points out mistakes and repairs obvious unclear arguments. Sally Haslanger, Bryce Huebner, Alex Guerrero, Jennifer Saul, and Susanna Siegel all provided invaluable written comments on various chapters, inexplicably taking breaks from their absurdly busy schedules to aid this project. Intense interchanges with Haslanger since I spoke at MIT in 2012 have made the chapters on ideology incomparably better; the last year has been a gradual process of coming to see that her critiques of an individualist account of ideology are correct. Saul has read many versions of chapter 4, and because of her critiques, it too is much better than it would have been. I am stunned by their intellectual generosity.

Michael Morris, the Columbia social psychologist, has been a consistently essential source of relevant work in social psychology, and discussion about it. Having a brilliant cultural and social psychologist as one's good friend has been immensely useful. Gilah Kletenik has been an extraordinarily useful sounding board for my ideas, dating back several years; everybody's rabbi should be so philosophically gifted. Kate Manne, Lynne Tirrell, David Livingstone Smith, and Rebecca

Kukla also provided incredibly helpful written comments and support.

In graduate school, I took one class in political philosophy, with Joshua Cohen. I began writing about social and political philosophy not for academic journals, but for the *New York Times*. I sent him a draft of my first piece, and he was very encouraging. Since then, he has been inexplicably generous with his time. He also invited me to give a talk at Stanford Political Theory, where I presented chapter 4, with Ken Taylor responding. I am grateful to Ken's comments, and also those of the audience.

I was an assistant professor at Cornell from 1995 to 2000. There was a remarkable group of graduate students there at the time. I was fortunate enough to serve on Chris Sturr's dissertation committee. Chris's dissertation was about ideology; Allen Wood and Karen Jones were his other committee members. Susanna Siegel and Lisa Rivera were also constant discussion partners. We had a remarkable multiyear discussion about ideology, and I have been thinking about the topic ever since. It is for this reason that I went into epistemology in the first place. I owe Chris a large debt of gratitude, and also Wood and Jones.

Michael Rosen, whose book *On Voluntary Servitude* helped structure my thoughts about the topic of ideology, has been very intellectually generous. He organized a last-minute workshop with several graduate students in political theory—Emma Saunders-Hastings, Tae-Yeoun Keum, Bernardo Zacka, and Jacob Roundtree—on an early draft of the manuscript. This was an extraordinarily helpful event. I have been moved by how my peers in political philosophy have been in helping me with the field. Alex Guerrero particularly helped me navigate the shoals of my new field. Melvin Rogers and Tamsin Shaw were often available on Facebook chat to answer a novice's desperate pleas for help with the literature and the concepts of political philosophy. Rogers's work was an invaluable guide to Du Bois and, more generally, has had a major impact on this book. Late in the writing of this book, I met Robert Gooding-Williams, and had a lengthy invaluable discussion with him about Du Bois, in which he made me defend my interpretations and gave me other passages to discuss. David Goldberg has been very helpful, since he came to my Gail Stine Lecture at Wayne State, with advice and sources in American political theory. The Rutgers educational historian Ben Justice provided invaluable help with the final chapter. Discussions with Khalil Muhammad about the topic of technicist ideology were extraordinarily helpful.

Lori Gruen has encouraged me throughout, and has provided feedback on many drafts and regular conversation about political philosophy. She has helped in countless ways, substantively, with the content, and personally, with encouragement about the direction of my research. She also arranged two seminars with a group of prison scholars that she has taught in many political philosophy classes at Cheshire Correctional Institution, a maximum-security men's prison in Connecticut. The second of these was an "author meets critics" session on the draft that went to readers. Craig Gore, James Davis, David Haywood, Clyde Meikle, John Moye, Andre Pierce, and Jason Torello gave very useful short responses to the book. The responses and the ensuing discussion made a large impact on the final version of the book. Discussion with them about schools and the similarity of schools, from their perspective, to the prison system convinced me to conclude the book with a chapter on the US educational system.

I have given this material at many places, including the University of Maryland, Humboldt University, Berlin, Freie Universität, Semantics in Europe, Wayne State University, and Southern Illinois University. I am grateful to the many comments I received on those occasions. I owe particular thanks to one audience member. My first talk on this material was as a keynote speaker at the University of Maryland's PHLINC conference, in January 2014. I presented an incorrect definition of propaganda in my paper. Georges Rey, whom I had never before met, would not let his objections go during the question session. Rey was right. But he was also kind of annoying, so I have not yet told him that. Perhaps he will discover it here.

In January 2014, Vesla Weaver and I published a *New York Times* piece on mass incarceration. My contribution included using philosophy to explain the antidemocratic consequences of the racial nature of mass incarceration. However, the philosophers I cited in that piece were uniformly *white* philosophers. In a remarkable short essay, "Race, Racism, and Thinking with Philosophy," the philosophers Tommy Curry and John Drabinski write about our essay that "[i]t is disconcerting because the essay wants, at bottom, to elevate the visibility of the Black experience, to make suffering under institutional racism identifiable and to hear the voices of the victims. But at the very moment in which that voice could be most bold, the philosophical moment, the authors turn to a very different set of thinkers. They turn to white thinkers." I am profoundly grateful to Curry and Drabinski for this exchange. It caused me, at a time at which I was learning the so-called canon in political philosophy, to turn to the social and political philosophy tradition that has been produced by Black authors, one that I was not unfamiliar with from my youth. As a result, I was able to see how rich this tradition is, and how much is reproduced in later works by white authors, without recognition. I have tried in this book to rectify the imbalance. I have learned political philosophy not just from Rawls, but also from Du Bois. I promised that I wouldn't make the same mistake again. I hope I have kept that promise in this book.

The readers for Princeton University Press were Rae Langton and Tommie Shelby. Both devoted what must have been large portions of the summer to detailed comments on my manuscript. Princeton simply could not have acquired better readers. I am very fortunate to have had their input. It is a vastly better book because of it.

Robert Demke was a first-rate copy editor, both in his care in reading the manuscript and in his patience with my revisions.

My editor, Rob Tempio, has been remarkable. Without his constant encouragement, I would not have had the courage to write this book.

While writing these acknowledgments, I am acutely conscious of the fact that there are many authors whose work I should have read, but have not, authors whose voices should be heard in a book on this topic. I apologize in advance for these omissions. On the topics of this book, there are simply too many brilliant voices that are not heard.

NOTES

PREFACE

1. Stanley, *The Technological Conscience*.
2. Kenyatta, *Facing Mt. Kenya*, p. 22.
3. Stanley, *The Technological Conscience*, p. 98.
4. My father was also writing in the wake of the Milgram Experiments, conducted at Yale University in the 1960s, and discussed in chapter 6.
5. Muhammad, *The Condemnation of Blackness*.
6. Collins, *Black Feminist Thought*, p. 255.
7. Wynter, "No Humans Involved."
8. https://www.youtube.com/watch?v=vbhAllAdmzE.
9. Hart, *High Price*.
10. Philosophy's racial problem is so extreme that I am hesitant to discuss it in the same paragraph as its misogyny problem, because of the risk that addressing one of the problems will seem to be addressing the other as well.
11. Williamson, *Knowledge and Its Limits*.
12. Stanley, *Knowledge and Practical Interests*.
13. Largely, but not entirely: Russell and Doris do notice the clear political consequences of the view I argued for in my book (which I called "IRI," for "Interest-Relative Invariantism"). They write, "On accounts like IRI, the rich apparently know a great deal more about mundane matters—such as whether the bank is open on Saturdays—simply

because such matters are not as crucial to their practical interests,," and they note somewhat sarcastically that colleagues who live in nicer but more expensive areas of the country are at least, according to IRI, epistemologically disadvantaged by their situation. Understandably, they present this as an objection, but to me it is a welcome consequence of the view, one that does needed explanatory work in the political realm. Russell and Doris, "Knowledge by Indifference," p. 434.

14. Gendler, "Alief in Action (and Reaction)."

15. Rae Langton also discusses the specific application of this work to the topic of my book, namely, the effects of propaganda on liberal democracy. In her letter to the UK Leveson Inquiry commission of July 19, 2012, she explains that speech that undermines political equality is democratically problematic.

INTRODUCTION: THE PROBLEM OF PROPAGANDA

1. Klemperer, *Language of the Third Reich*.

2. Ibid., p. 2.

3. Scanlon, "The Diversity of Objections to Inequality."

4. Joshua Cohen and Joel Rogers consider it in fact to be the most serious objection to deliberative democracy, and complain that it is rarely isolated from less serious objections and addressed. As they write, the worry is that "deliberation is a ruse unless substantial background equality of position is already assured. Or, conversely: under conditions of substantial inequality of power, a requirement of presenting reasons is unlikely to limit or neutralize power." Cohen and Rogers, "Power and Reason."

5. As Madison writes, "A zeal for different opinions concerning religion, concerning government, and many other points, as well of speculation as of practice; an attachment to different leaders ambitiously contending for pre-eminence and power; or to persons of other descriptions whose fortunes have been interesting to the human passions, have, in turn, divided mankind into parties, inflamed them with mutual animosity, and rendered them much more disposed to vex and oppress each other than to co-operate for their common good. So strong is this propensity of mankind to fall into mutual animosities, that where no substantial occasion presents itself, the most frivolous and fanciful distinctions have been sufficient to kindle their unfriendly passions and excite their most violent conflicts. But the most common and durable source of factions has been the various and unequal distribution of property." Madison, "Federalist 10."

6. Bernard Williams argues that Plato assumes that a city has a property F (just, oligarchic, or democratic) if and only if its people have property F. Williams argues that this is generally incorrect, but is especially incoherent in the case of democracy, as Plato is clear that a democratic character is ever shifting and a democracy is characterized by "all sorts of character." Williams, "The Analogy of City and Soul." Ferrari convincingly argues that Plato was not committed to what he calls "the predominance rule." Ferrari, *City and Soul in Plato's Republic*, chap. 2. I do not make the assumption in what follows that, for Plato, a democratic culture must be filled with citizens of democratic character.

7. All quotations from Plato are from Cooper, *Plato*. Citations are hereafter given parenthetically in the text.

8. Anderson, "Outlaws," pp. 108–9.

9. Again, I do not assume that a city has a democratic culture in virtue of having citizens with the properties of a city with a democratic culture, and thus do not fall afoul of Bernard Williams's criticism of this principle.

10. The economic theory of democracy is championed in Downs, *An Economic Theory of Democracy*.

11. See, for example, Frank, *What's the Matter with Kansas?*; Graetz and Shapiro, *Death by a Thousand Cuts*.

12. Hayek, "Individualism," p. 15.

13. Estlund, *Democratic Authority*; Landemore, *Democratic Reason*.

14. I will use "collective deliberation" as a synonym for joint deliberation. This means that when I use "collective deliberation," I am not using it in a sense that implicates an ontology involving a collective agent. Thanks to Daniel Putnam for discussion.

15. Delany writes that they are "[s]ensible of the high-handed injustice done to the colored people in the United States" and that "[t]hey earnestly contended, and doubtless honestly meaning what they said, that . . . as they had oppressed and trampled down the colored people, they would now elevate them." Delany, *The Condition, Elevation, Emigration, and Destiny*, p. 24.

16. Ibid., p. 26.

17. Ibid., p. 29.

18. Ibid., p. 43.

19. Ibid., p. 42. He hastens to add, "By this, we do not wish to be understood as advocating the actual equal attainments of every individual; but we do mean to say, that if these attainments be necessary for the elevation of the white man, they are necessary for the elevation of the colored man."

20. Central to Delany's argument is a lengthy case of the virtues of individual Black citizens, which he supports by providing many examples of impressive Black attainment in the face of large structural obstacles.

21. Delany, *The Condition, Elevation, Emigration, and Destiny*, p. 87.

22. http://www.blackyouthproject.com/2014/03/conversations-we-are-not-having-a-black-youth-project-economic-justice-series-a-social-movement-not-self-improvement/.

23. Just from 1980 to 2006, the rate of incarceration of the former group (jail and prison) increased four times as much as the increase in the white rate (Tonry and Melewski, "The Malign Effects of Drug and Crime Control.

24. http://www.gallup.com/poll/1687/race-relations.aspx#3.

25. http://publicreligion.org/newsroom/2012/04/millennial-values-survey-2012/.

26. Callahan, *Education and the Cult of Efficiency*, p. 2.

27. Burnham, *The Managerial Revolution*.

28. Ibid., 169–70.

29. In Burnham's time, there was good evidence that the United States was a managerial society, rather than a democracy. Joel Spring writes, "The philosophy of the corporate state upon which modern institutions were built was formed during a transitional period in history in the late nineteenth and early twentieth centuries. Americans living in the changing urban and industrial world of this period were convinced that their era was a bridge between a traditional agrarian America of independent yeoman and a future dependent on cooperative activities in large-scale industries and vast urban areas. . . . The vision of America as a land of independent yeoman had to be replaced with a corporate image of society where social relationships were to center around large-scale organizations. Within the corporate organization of society each man was to do a specialized task in cooperation with the entire social system." Spring, *Education and the Rise of the Corporate State*, p. 2.

30. http://billmoyers.com/2014/04/25/lawrence-lessig-has-a-moon shot-plan-to-halt-our-slide-toward-plutocracy/. A 2014 Reason-Rupe poll found that 75 percent of Americans agree that "politicians are corrupted by campaign donations." http://reason.com/poll/2014/04/03 /americans-say-75-percent-of-politicians.

31. http://clarusrg.com/content/july-27–2012.

32. Hoggan, *Climate Cover-Up*, p. 186.

33. One may continue to maintain that propaganda is not a fundamental problem for democracy, in electoral democracies such as the United States. The congressional districts in the US state of North Carolina were strategically mapped by a Republican state legislature in 2011 (one can admit this while recognizing that people on the same political "team" seem to cluster together). In the 2012 congressional elections in that state, 51 percent of North Carolina residents voted for Democrats, and 49 percent voted for Republicans. Nevertheless, in that year, three Republicans won Democratic seats and Democrats added no seats. The Hungarian right-wing party Fidesz also engaged in strategic redistricting. Strategic redistricting does not have anything to do with propaganda. However, the general popularity of Fidesz and their far-right partner Jobbik, who won 20 percent of the 2014 Hungarian vote, is not due to redistricting. It has to do with an antidemocratic ideology that stresses ethnic and religious purity, an ideology that perhaps is due to its populace's greater familiarity with authoritarian norms. It has, that is, to do with the acceptance of an antidemocratic ideology that makes them susceptible to antidemocratic propaganda in the guise of democracy.

34. Plato only sets out a curriculum for the rulers and the members of the military. It is unclear what his view is for the other members of society. Thanks to Verity Harte for discussion.

35. Irwin, *Classical Thought*, p. 110.

36. http://www.demos.org/publication/detroit-bankruptcy.

37. http://www.theguardian.com/environment/true-north/2014/jun /25/detroits-water-war-a-tap-shut-off-that-could-impact-300000-people.

38. Streeck, "The Crises of Democratic Capitalism."

39. In *Debtocracy*, a massively popular documentary film released in 2011, Katerina Kitidi and Aris Hatzistefanou portray the European Union as having replaced democracy with "debtocracy," a system that is designed to maximize the overall economic health of European elites by using some countries as mechanisms to pay the banks.

40. Gilens and Page, "Testing Theories of American Politics."

41. It is legitimate to worry that the survey evidence upon which for example his 2014 paper relies does not provide enough fine-grained data to warrant his conclusions.

CHAPTER 1. PROPAGANDA IN THE HISTORY OF POLITICAL THOUGHT

1. Rousseau, *The Social Contract*, bk. 4, chap. 1.

2. It is not implausible to take the worry that free speech allows demagoguery to be behind David Hume's description of press freedom as an "evil," in his concluding comment in 1.2 in *Of the First Principles of Government*: "It must however be allowed, that the unbounded liberty of the press, though it be difficult, perhaps impossible, to propose a suitable remedy for it, is one of the evils, attending those mixt forms of government."

3. There are some democracies that legislate this issue. In India, the world's most populous democracy, the first amendment to the constitution seeks to limit "abuse of the freedom of speech," that is, demagogic use of language.

4. Mills, "Ideal Theory as Ideology."

5. Mills, *The Racial Contract*, p. 123.

6. John Rawls, who is widely (though not correctly) regarded as the exemplar of the ideal theoretic correct, is of course acutely aware that stability is an ideal of a political system, in addition to justice. In the four-page discussion in his major work on liberal democracy, he notes that "the problem of stability has been on our minds from the outset." Rawls, *Political Liberalism*, pp. 140–44, quotation at p. 141.

7. Pareto, *The Rise and Fall of the Elites*, pp. 86–87.

8. Schmitt, *The Concept of the Political*, p. 30.

9. Rousseau, *The Social Contract*, bk. 1, chap. 7.

10. Ibid., bk. 1, chap. 8.

11. Ibid., bk. 4, chap. 1.

12. Ibid.

13. Ibid., bk. 4, chap. 2.

14. Ibid.

15. Perhaps somewhat similarly, Sharon Krause regularly contrasts deliberation as "will formation" with deliberation as "opinion formation," where only the former is sufficient for the genuine democratic legitimacy of a policy. Krause, *Civil Passions*.

16. The link between equal respect and conversation (rather than oratory) is at least as old as Cicero, and is the topic of chapters 37 and 38 of book 1 of Cicero's *On Duties*. As Cicero writes in 1.38, "We must also take special care to preserve the bearing of respect and esteem for those with whom we converse."

17. Darwall, *Honor, History & Relationship*, p. 17.

18. Ibid., p. 15.

19. Constant, *Principles of Politics*, p. 180.

20. For a subtle and incisive discussion of the possibilities of such a defense, in the context of the conception of freedom of expression articulated in Alexander Meiklejohn's *Political Freedom*, see Scanlon, "Freedom of Expression and Categories of Expression."

21. Thanks to Vanessa Wills for the reference.

CHAPTER 2. PROPAGANDA DEFINED

1. http://www.trilateral.org/download/doc/crisis_of_democracy.pdf.

2. Ibid., p. 34. Crozier includes under the essential liberal democratic norms that are potentially under threat "the Christian Ethos" (p. 47).

3. Ibid., pp. 63–64.

4. Ibid., p. 75.

5. Huntington fails to note that obedience to authority is the political ideal of a monarchy or of dictatorial rule.

6. Ibid., p. 98.

7. Ibid., p. 113. Huntington also warns that "[m]arginal social groups, as in the case of the blacks, are now becoming full political participants," which carries with it the danger of "overloading the political system with demands" (p. 114).

8. I will argue in the beginning of chapter 3 that Ben Bernanke's use of the expression "fiscal cliff" was one such case.

9. One might think that this is not enough to defeat the spirit of the falsity condition on propaganda. The philosopher Jennifer Saul has recently argued convincingly that misleading is at least as morally problematic as lying. Saul, *Lying, Misleading, and What Is Said*, chap. 4. One could imagine replacing the falsity condition on demagoguery with a "misleading" condition on propaganda. But in fact this would be to replace the falsity condition with something like the insincerity condition, which is disputed in what follows.

10. See chapter 4 on the "expressive model" of propaganda.

11. Klemperer, *Language of the Third Reich*, p. 38.

12. Ibid., p. 162.

13. This is the characterization of "propaganda" offered by Rosen, *On Voluntary Servitude*, p. 52.

14. Klemperer, *Language of the Third Reich*, p. 163.

15. Rosen, *On Voluntary Servitude*, p. 78.

16. In any case, the sincerity of the speaker is often irrelevant in effective cases of propaganda. In his famous diaries, Klemperer quotes a friend as saying that though the National Socialist government is aware that war is not directly in its interests, "they have over-cultivated national rhetoric [and] will *have* to undertake something." Propaganda even in the narrow sense of language consciously used to deceive will, if effective, end up legitimizing actions it supports, even if the original call to action was insincere.

17. "In countries where the levers of power are in the hands of a state bureaucracy, the monopolistic control over the media, often supplemented by official censorship, makes it clear that the media serve the ends of a dominant elite. It is much more difficult to see a propaganda system at work where the media are private and formal censorship is absent. This is especially true where the media actively compete, periodically attack and expose corporate and governmental malfeasance, and aggressively portray themselves as spokesmen for free speech and the general community interest." Chomsky and Herman, *Manufacturing Consent*, p. 1.

18. Dan Greco has suggested to me that propaganda in a totalitarian society works like advertising does in a democratic society. People don't take the claims made in advertising seriously. Nevertheless, advertising works. It affects our behavior even though we do not take it seriously.

19. Lippmann, *The Phantom Public*, pp. 37–38.

20. Klemperer, *Language of the Third Reich*, p. 210.

21. Ibid., p. 211.

22. Randal Marlin articulates something like Lippmann and Klemperer's proposal. See Marlin, *Propaganda and the Ethics of Persuasion*, p. 22. Marlin's view is this:

> PROPAGANDA = (def.) The organized attempt through communication to affect belief or action or inculcate attitudes in a large audience in ways that circumvent or suppress an individual's adequately informed, rational, reflective judgment.

In her paper, "Understanding Propaganda: The Epistemic Merit Model and Its Application to Art," Sheryl Tuttle Ross proposes a novel account of propaganda. According to Tuttle, propaganda must be delivered intentionally with a certain kind of purpose, but can be true.

23. Chomsky and Herman, *Manufacturing Consent*.

24. Thanks to Stephen Darwall for crucial initial help with this characterization; he recommended this more specific definition over my initial characterization.

25. "Die Wille wird als ein Vermögen gedacht, der Vorstellung gewisser Gesetze gemäß sich selbst zum Handeln zu bestimmen." Immanuel Kant, *Metaphysik der Sitten*, BA64.

26. Thanks to Kate Manne for emphasizing to me that propaganda can be the result of silence as well as speech.

27. Kant, *The Metaphysics of Morals*, part 2, chap. 2, sec. 1.

28. The best overall sketch of the issues in the morality of propaganda that I know of is Marlin, *Propaganda and the Ethics of Persuasion*, chap. 4.

29. There is another way of thinking of the case surrounding cigarette warning labels, suggested to me by Mattias Kumm. The urge to reach for a cigarette is paradigmatically a sign of addiction, and not the expression of rational will. Perhaps the point of frightening cigarette labels is to cause people to pause to check their reflexive bad habit and give them time to make an autonomous decision. Thus, on this account, harsh cigarette warning labels actually aid the deliberative process by disturbing reflex. Regardless, there will be certain practices of the sort I describe with cigarette warning labels that are democratically acceptable: where we in effect cede our autonomy to someone else to control it, when we deem them to be reliable. These are democratically acceptable.

30. Hart, *High Price*, chap. 12.

31. Hoggan, *Climate Cover-Up*, p. 42.

32. Ibid., p. 156.

33. Here is another example, along the same lines. Many governments, including Western democracies such as the United States, employ propaganda as political warfare. The false messages they deliver, for example, to undermine the reputation of an enemy leader, are often called "counter-information." But, as Susan Stebbing points out, "[t]he word 'counter-information' does not make sense." Calling statements that are known to be false "counter-information" is to wrap contributions that run counter to the norms of rational discourse in a veil that imitates the norms of rational discourse. Stebbing, *Thinking to Some Purpose*, p. 63.

34. This example was suggested to me by Andre Pierce, during a seminar I gave at Cheshire Correctional Institution in Connecticut, a maximum-security prison.

35. Thanks to Stephen Darwall for the example.

36. Du Bois, *Black Reconstruction in America: 1860–1880*, p. 714.

37. Du Bois, "Criteria of Negro Art."

38. Thanks to Daniel James for the reference.

39. Monson, *Saying Something*, pp. 116–77.

40. Justin Cober-Lake has argued that Coltrane demurred from taking this as his intention (http://www.popmatters.com/chapter/04Autumn /coberlake.html). But of course, given the characterization of propaganda I have given, it is irrelevant what Coltrane actually intended.

41. Shelby, "Justice, Deviance, and the Dark Ghetto," p. 128.

42. There remains a worry that Du Bois's method may backfire in contexts in which there is insufficient understanding of the problematic nature of the ideal (that is, the situation in America Du Bois describes). Embracing problematic ideals of (for example) obedience to authority is often the result of flawed ideological belief, for example, the flawed ideological belief that conditions are such that such authority is legitimate. The worry with Du Bois's proposal for targeting problematic ideals with the use of undermining propaganda is that it presupposes the ability to evaluate the ideal in a rational and impartial manner. Thanks to Kristie Dotson for discussion.

43. Rothschild, *Economic Sentiments*, chap. 1.

44. Coates, "The Case for Reparations."

45. http://votingrights.news21.com/article/election-fraud/.

46. Claudia Mills characterizes manipulation as an instance of communication that "purports to be offering good reasons, when in fact it does not." Mills, "Politics and Manipulation." This is close to my characterization of demagoguery, but it is not exactly the same. On the characterization I have given, the bad goal that the political communication urges is connected to the good reason it purports to represent, in that it runs directly counter to that very reason.

47. Thanks to Chris Lebron here, who suggested the "reinterpretation" idea as a characterization of propaganda. Lebron is clearly right that this is what is being attempted in many characteristic cases of propaganda. It presupposes, however, that the original meaning is not compatible with the goal. So the characterization I have given is conceptually prior.

48. Haslanger, "Oppressions."

49. Ibid., p. 334.

50. Ibid.

51. Thus, Mills characterizes a "manipulator" as someone who is aware that she is presenting a bad reason disguised as a good reason. Mill, "Politics and Manipulation."

52. For an extraordinary discussion of some of these points, see White, "You Just Believe That Because."

53. Tarski, "The Concept of Truth in Formalized Languages."

CHAPTER 3. PROPAGANDA IN LIBERAL DEMOCRACY

1. Some democratic political theorists are realists and reject all of the political ideals I discuss in this chapter as plausibly governing any state. It is irrelevant. Even if all candidate democratic ideals in normative political theory are hopelessly idealized, it is those ideals that will be characteristically used in propaganda.

2. The article was published on January 31, 2013, in the *New York Times* philosophy blog, *The Stone*. My brother was unable to put his name on it for professional reasons. http://opinionator.blogs.nytimes.com /2013/01/31/philosopher-kings-and-fiscal-cliffs/#more-139558.

3. This is all excerpted from the *New York Times* piece mentioned in note 2.

4. http://www.iie.com/publications/papers/20140205default-report .pdf.

5. Aristotle, *The Politics*, bk. 3, chap. 1.

6. Ibid., bk. 3, chap. 9.

7. Ibid., bk. 1, chap. 2.

8. Rawls, *Political Liberalism*, p. 443.

9. Estlund, *Democratic Authority*; and Landemore, *Democratic Reason*.

10. See Constant, *Principles of Politics*, pp. 310–11.

11. Du Bois, *The Souls of Black Folk*, p. 27.

12. More recently, in *A Theory of Justice*, John Rawls is clear about the special status of "political liberty," "the freedom to participate equally in political affairs" (p. 201). As we have seen at the beginning of the book, Rawls asserts that the principle of equal liberty takes the form of the principle of (equal) participation (p. 221). Rawls explicitly connects the principle of (equal) participation to Constant's "liberty of the ancients" (p. 222).

13. Darwall, *The Second Person Standpoint*, 56–57.

14. It is plausible to take the view of Bruce Ackerman of the ideals of public reason to be impartialist, but I will not argue the interpretive point here. Ackerman, *Social Justice in the Liberal State*.

15. http://www.nytimes.com/2014/04/07/us/politics/killing-on-bus -recalls-superpredator-threat-of-90s.html?_r=0.

16. In the next chapter, we look in more detail at the mechanism at the heart of this kind of case, namely, how an expression can evoke negative stereotypes, while nevertheless contributing to the expression of a truth.

17. Rawls certainly did not propose this as a norm of public reason. Public reason in Rawls is meant to occur in a society that has already agreed upon principles of justice. Thanks to Lori Watson for discussion. See Rawls, *Political Liberalism*.

18. See Mansbridge et al., "The Place of Self-Interest," esp. sec. 3. It is worth mentioning that Cohen and Rogers take Mansbridge to task for not recognizing this point. Mansbridge et al. (2010, p. 73, footnote 26) cite Cohen and Rogers approvingly on just this point, and argue that they are going further than the view in Cohen and Rogers in justifying statements of self-interest in public reason. Mansbridge et al., "The Place of Self-Interest," p. 73n26.

19. Du Bois, *The Souls of Black Folk*, p. 89.

20. Stebbing, *Thinking to Some Purpose*, p. 42.

21. Darwall, "Being With," p. 118.

22. See also Anderson, "What Is the Point of Equality?," p. 289.

23. Paul, *Transformative Experience*.

24. Krause, *Civil Passions*, pp. 162–65.

25. I will quote from the edition from 2005.

26. Rawls, *Political Liberalism*, p. 49.

27. Ibid., pp. 446–47.

28. http://opinionator.blogs.nytimes.com/2013/10/20/questions-for -free-market-moralists/?_r=0.

29. The central guiding ideal of public reason in Gutmann and Thompson, *Democracy and Disagreement*, "reciprocity," is essentially the notion of reasonableness as found in Du Bois and Rawls.

30. Darwall, "Accountability and the Second Person," pp. 71–72. Darwall argues that reasonableness is exemplified by the capacity to hold what Darwall calls *second-personal attitudes*. These attitudes are ones that are based on the notion of *reciprocity*, a form of what Stephen Darwall calls a *second person competence*. Darwall, *The Second Person Standpoint*, pp. 23–24. There are certain attitudes, on this view, that one can have only if one is capable of taking the perspective of the members of one's community.

31. Darwall, "The Second Personal Stance," p. 44.

32. Rawls, *Political Liberalism*, p. 243.

33. Garsten distinguishes a "motivational defense of rhetoric" from the project he defends in his book, which is to show that there is a kind of persuasive rhetoric that "engages our capacity for practical judgment." Garsten, *Saving Persuasion*, p. 174. Garsten is defending, for example, *anecdotal* reasons as legitimate contributions to public reason. Garston's defense is that this way of representing one's reasons is a constitutive part of what one might think of as bounded rationality, rationality given human limitations. Anecdotes and narratives can be reasons for creatures that "have a way of deciding what to do in particular situations that cannot be expressed in a set of rules." Ibid., p. 175. Defending anecdotes and narratives as characteristic expressions of human reason is obviously not defending propaganda in the sense I have characterized. Only a *motivational* defense of rhetoric is a defense of propaganda; it is a defense of rhetoric as cutting off rational debate to move immediately to action. Garsten is quite clear that he rejects this justification of rhetoric.

34. Rogers, "The People, Rhetoric, and Affect."

35. Also relevant in this regard is Rogers, "David Walker and the Political Power of the Appeal," which concerns David Walker's 1829 *Appeal to the Coloured Citizens of the World*. Rogers argues that "[t]he *Appeal* is a rhetorical performance—seeking to call out and honor the demotic capacity of his black fellows."

36. In responding to Christian List's account of the "discursive dilemma" in Joshua Cohen's contribution to Shawn Rosenberg's edited volume *Deliberation, Participation and Democracy*, he argues that it is not clear how deliberation can move from a less inclusive "we" to a more inclusive "we." This, I take it, is the assumption of Melvin Rogers's discussion. I explain the motivation for the assumption below.

37. Darwall, *The Second Person Standpoint*, p. 24.

38. Another way to improve the reasonableness of a debate is to increase everyone's reasonableness. For example, suppose everyone in the country was disregarding some other group's perspective. But there wasn't one group who was universally disregarded. An improvement of reasonableness could also take the form of a contribution that led people to disregard fewer people. Thanks to Daniel Putnam for discussion.

39. Williams, "The Woman's Part in a Man's Business," pp. 544–45.

40. See Darwall, "Being With," for a discussion of a richer Kantian notion of rational will and autonomy with which I am sympathetic.

41. Joshua Cohen makes this point in detail in his response from 2007 to Christian List's essay on the discursive dilemma. List argues that deliberation is required to expand recognition of group identification. Cohen develops the point in the body of the text in response to List.

42. Du Bois, *The Souls of Black Folk*, p. 3.

43. "There are 14 European countries where prisoners are allowed to vote, including Ireland, Spain, Sweden and Denmark; there are 16 where prisoners have limited voting rights, including France, Germany, Italy, Netherlands and Turkey. Prisoners are banned from voting in 6 countries including the UK, Bulgaria, Estonia, Hungary, Liechtenstein and Georgia." http://www.theguardian.com/society/2011/feb/10/prisoners -right-vote-european-court.

44. The worse the crime, the greater the desire for retribution; so sexual offenders, for example, are most often used as strategic political weapons, and so suffer the worst dehumanization of all.

45. Edelman speaks of "a small number of classic themes or myths [that] serve repeatedly as explanations of what is shaping the political scene." Edelman, *Politics of Symbolic Action*, p. 77. Edelman mentions two. The first is "the evocation of an outgroup, defined as 'different' and as plotting to commit harmful acts." The second is "the view that the political leader is benevolent and is effective in saving people from danger," in particular the danger posed by the members of the outgroup in the first myth.

46. As Stebbing notes, the demand of reasonableness should also hold between citizens of different nations, when the action considered action impinges on them. Stebbing, *Thinking to Some Purpose*, p. 41.

47. Gilens, *Why Americans Hate Welfare*, p. 95.

48. Ibid., pp. 97–98.

49. The study found that "[n]onblack respondents with the most negative views of black welfare recipients are 30 points higher in opposition to welfare than are those with the most positive views of black welfare mothers." Ibid., p. 99.

CHAPTER 4. LANGUAGE AS A MECHANISM OF CONTROL

1. Langton, "Speech Acts and Unspeakable Acts."

2. Langton, *Sexual Solipsism*, p. 105.

3. Stalnaker, "On the Representation of Context," p. 98.

4. Roberts, "Information Structure."

5. Earlier discussions of context added to the common ground "commitments slates," records of each individual's conversational commitments, which may or may not depart from the shared common ground. See Gazdar, *Pragmatics*.

6. Langton and West, "Scorekeeping."

7. Maitra, "Subordinating Speech," note 38.

8. More specifically, he wanted to model the semantics of words like "presumably" and "normally" in reasoning, as in the argument:

Normally, adults have a driver's license

John doesn't have a driver's license

Therefore, presumably John isn't an adult.

Worlds that are "normal" are the ones made closest by the ordering on worlds.

9. Potts, *The Logic of Conventional Implicatures*, p. 24.

10. Murray, "Varieties of Update."

11. Langton and West, "Scorekeeping."

12. Murray, "Varieties of Update."

13. Von Fintel and Gillies, "Must . . . Stay . . . Strong."

14. Leslie, "Generics: Cognition and Acquisition."

15. Leslie, "Carving Up the Social World with Generics."

16. Leslie, "The Original Sin of Cognition."

17. Langton, *Sexual Solipsism*, pp. 103–16. "An act of ranking is, in Austin's terms, a 'verdictive' illocution. It makes an authoritative claim about how the world is—it aims to fit the world. 'Guilty,' said by a jury, is verdictive. An important contrast would be with an illocution that is 'exercitive,' which says how the world is to be—it aims for the world to fit it." Ibid., p. 106.

18. Bourdieu and Passeron, *Reproduction in Education, Society and Culture*, p. 112. "The mere fact of transmitting a message within a relation of pedagogic communication implies and imposes a social definition . . . of what merits transmission, the code in which the message is to be transmitted, the persons entitled to transmit it or, better, impose its reception, the persons worthy of receiving it and consequently obliged to receive it. . . . Such a context governs teachers' and students' behavior so rigorously that efforts to set up a dialogue immediately turn into fiction or farce." Ibid., p. 109.

19. Thanks to Jennifer Saul for discussion.

20. Mary Kate McGowan, in her paper "Oppressive Speech," published in 2009, argues that there is a category of subordinating speech,

which she calls "covert excercitives," which do not require the speaker to have a position of authority. These are speech acts that have the effect of permitting oppressive speech in subsequent contexts, such as sexist speech among men that relaxes the norms of conversation to allow explicit speech. But even covert excercitives in McGowan's sense require "the speaker to have a certain status" (p. 402). In the case just mentioned, the speaker must be at minimum "one of the guys." (See also McGowan's earlier paper "Conversational Exercitives," published in 2004, which introduces the basic idea of a covert speech act that changes subject permissibility facts, but without the attendant defense of the lack of a need for the speaker to occupy a position of authority.)

21. Tirrell, "Genocidal Language Games"; and Camp, "Slurring Perspectives." Tirrell's analysis is of what she calls "deeply derogatory terms," which are a subclass of slurs. As Tirrell points out, there is a difference between a slur like "snob" and Goebbel's description of Jews as "vermin."

22. Camp, "Slurring Perspectives," p. 335.

23. Tirrell, "Genocidal Language Games," p. 190, 191. For Tirrell, deeply derogatory terms in addition mark the outsider group as having a "basic ontological status." "Jerk" is a slur, but not a deeply derogatory term.

24. Smith, *Less Than Human*.

25. Thanks to Zoltan Gendler Szabo for this point.

26. There are nonpolitical examples that pose similar problems for Anderson and Lepore's account. For example, as we have seen, Murray argues that evidentials always have the property of adding relevant information to the context-set, wherever they occur. So evidentials behave differently than presuppositions; their effect cannot be "cancelled." But evidentials, in languages in which they occur, are not on the list of "banned words." So Anderson and Lepore's analysis also presupposes a world in which evidentials do not exist (if Murray's analysis is correct).

27. Mendelberg, *The Race Card*, p. 32.

28. In 1798 New Jersey abolitionists declared their belief that free Blacks were "given to Idleness, Frolicking, Drunkenness, and in some few cases to Dishonesty." Ibid.

29. Ibid., p. 194.

30. Ibid., p. 193.

31. Ibid., chap. 7. Mendelberg summarizes her findings as follows: "[T]he implicitly racial message elicits a sizable effect from resentment on race policy views, and does so distinctively. With exposure to an implicitly racial message, a person sympathetic to blacks differs from a person who resents blacks by 57 points on a 100-point scale, a difference that places them at complete opposites on the issue of government intervention in racial matters. With counter-stereotypical and explicitly racial messages, however, resentment makes a much smaller difference. With a counter-stereotypical or an explicitly racial message, the same pair of people, one resentful and one not, only differs by 27 or 33 points on a 100 point scale.... A message about welfare that is not implicitly racial reduces the power of racial predispositions by nearly 50 percent." Ibid., p. 199.

32. http://www.nahj.org/nahjnews/articles/2006/March/immigra tioncoverage.shtml.

33. http://www.courts.ca.gov/opinions/documents/S202512.PDF.

34. In Jennifer Saul's, *Lying, Misleading, and What Is Said*, she argues that misleading is as morally problematic as lying. Gingrich's performance is evidence for her thesis.

35. Thanks to Calvin Miaw for alerting me to this exchange, after reading an earlier version of this chapter for the Stanford Political Theory workshop.

36. From Ralph Wedgwood's post on the *New York Times* blog, *The Stone*, "The Meaning of Same-Sex Marriage," http://opinionator.blogs. nytimes.com/2012/05/24/marriage-meaning-and-equality/?_php=true &_type=blogs&_r=0.

37. Dan Kahan, "Social Influence."

38. Walzer, *Spheres of Justice*, p. 9.

39. http://www.slate.com/articles/news_and_politics/history/2013 /12/linda_taylor_welfare_queen_ronald_reagan_made_her_a_notorious _american_villain.html.

40. See also Patricia Hill Collins's discussion of the images associated with "welfare mother" on pp. 78ff. of *Black Feminist Thought*.

41. Gilens, *Why Americans Hate Welfare*, p. 12.

42. Thanks to Daniel Putnam for discussion here.

43. Fricker, *Epistemic Injustice*.

44. Ibid., p. 45.

45. http://msnbcmedia.msn.com/i/msnbc/sections/news/snowden _cyber_offensive2_nbc_document.pdf.

46. https://firstlook.org/theintercept/document/2014/02/24/art -deception-training-new-generation-online-covert-operations/.

47. Anderson and Pildes, "Expressive Theories of Law."

48. Ibid., p. 1559.

49. This passage is from the handout to her APA Presidential Address of 2013: Haslanger, "Social Meaning and Philosophical Method."

50. Hayakawa, "General Semantics and Propaganda," p. 201.

51. Of course, even if discourse did work just by eliminating possible worlds from the context-set, this would not entail that any discourse with that structure is an instance of ideal communication. One can update the context-set with a set of possible worlds in which one group of society is inferior, and has a perspective not worthy of debate. Thanks to Ishani Maitra for discussion here.

52. Habermas, "What Is Universal Pragmatics?," pp. 84–85.

53. Ibid., p. 85.

54. Dewey, *The Public and Its Problems*, pp. 148–49.

55. Ibid., p. 146.

56. Christensen, *Putting Logic in Its Place*, pp. 145–46.

57. I am grateful to Kwame Anthony Appiah's American Philosophical Association Carus lectures in 2013, and discussion with him, as well as discussion with Daniel Greco.

CHAPTER 5. IDEOLOGY

1. Some critics of liberalism reject the personal-political distinction because "the personal is political" (or perhaps better understood, "the personal because political"). Political considerations of fairness are clearly relevant in family relations. This criticism of liberalism is perfectly consistent with everything I say in this book. I only assume right now for the sake of exposition that the family is a domain in which the political is not relevant. What I regard as essential in liberalism is the view that some kind of stance that is not partial in the sense of sports fandom (for example) is required in reasoning about what to do politically. I do not regard it as particularly plausible that there is a close analogy between sports fandom and family ties. Family structure is definitely a source of common concern, and hence an important political subject, in a quite uncontroversial way, a way in which sports fandom rarely is. Thanks to Linda Zerilli for discussion.

2. Rosen, *On Voluntary Servitude*, pp. 69–80, quotation at p. 73.

3. Ibid., p. 78.

4. Thanks to Jonathan Kramnick for discussion.

5. Tucker, *The Marx-Engels Reader*, p. 173.

6. As Tommie Shelby writes, ideological beliefs "influence the way agents understand their social life, and they often play a significant role in the construction of personal and social identities. . . . The relevant beliefs play a role in *mediating* social interaction; they are a part of the 'life-world' or 'common meanings' through which social actors live their lives and coordinate their actions." Shelby, "Ideology, Racism, and Critical Social Theory," pp. 159–60. Shelby takes ideology to be pejorative. Following Haslanger and others, I treat it instead as a neutral concept.

7. In particular, Gendler, "Alief in Action (and Reaction)."

8. Ibid., pp. 565–66.

9. Williamson, *Knowledge and Its Limits*.

10. It is tempting to formulate this normative ideal in terms of tracking, as in "belief tracks knowledge." The temptation should be resisted. There are counterexamples to the claim that the normative ideal of belief takes the form of a knowledge-tracking counterfactual.

11. Sosa, "How to Defeat Opposition to Moore"; Sosa, "How Must Knowledge Be Modally Related to What Is Known?"; and Williamson, *Knowledge and Its Limits*.

12. Williamson, *Knowledge and Its Limits*, p. 147.

13. See, for example, the discussion of "structures, schemas, and resources," in Haslanger, "Ideology, Generics, and Common Ground," pp. 461–65, and in general, all the essays in Haslanger, *Resisting Reality*.

14. Haslanger, "Oppressions."

15. Haslanger, "Mom, but Crop Tops Are Cute!," p. 411.

16. Lebron, *The Color of Our Shame*, p. 57. See also Gendler, "Alief in Action (and Reaction)," sec. 4, on "norm-discordance," what happens when social reality is not in accord with our ideals.

17. Fricker, *Epistemic Injustice*, p. 37, argues that we should construe social stereotypes as images, on pain of the postulation of "unconscious beliefs of considerable stealth." She establishes that images, or imagistic concepts perhaps, are implicated in ideologies (we have also seen this in Klemperer's description of "heroism"). But I prefer to interpret stereotypes as generic claims, as in Sarah-Jane Leslie's work, interpreted along the lines suggested by Veltman, as in the discussion in the previous chapter.

18. Stebbing, *Thinking to Some Purpose*, p. 33.

19. Fricker, *Epistemic Injustice*, p. 35, defines prejudice as "judgments, which may have a positive or a negative valence, and which display some (typically, epistemically culpable) resistance to counter-evidence owing to some affective investment on the part of the subject." Here is the relation of my discussion to her influential taxonomy. Roughly, what I am after is a description of something like *epistemic culpability* (though I'm not sure this deontological perspective is the right way to think about it; it may be problematically individualist). Fricker's "negative identity prejudices" are democratically problematic ideologies. But I also think that there are democratically problematic ideologies that are not negative identity prejudices (for example, the ones that explain the effectiveness of propaganda deployed by oil companies against political action addressing climate change). Finally (though this may not be a concern for Fricker's project), I worry that most beliefs, not just ideological beliefs, have at least some resistance to counterevidence. Peter Railton argues in forthcoming work that what in part explains what Fricker calls the "reasonable life expectancy" (p. 52) is in an affective attachment that makes one's commitment always somewhat disproportional to the evidence.

20. This quotation is from Ta-Nehisi Coates's article in *The Atlantic* from June 2014, "The Case for Reparations."

21. There are multiple ways in which structural features of society can inhibit rational revision of belief. First, they can make agents resistant to counterevidence. Secondly, as Maitra points out, they can discourage agents from seeking easily available counterevidence. Maitra, "Subordinating Speech," p. 206.

22. Murdoch, "The Idea of Perfection," pp. 16–17.

23. Ibid., p. 31.

24. Ibid., p. 32.

25. Ibid., p. 18.

26. Fricker, *Epistemic Injustice*, p. 151.

27. The philosopher José Medina has made this point of detail in his discussion of Fricker. Just as Murdoch calls our attention to the fact that M's jealousy leads her to retain her "old-fashioned" set of concepts, Medina emphasizes that it is often in the *interests* of privileged groups to lack concepts that would make clear the unjust nature of their privilege. It is in the interest of white Americans not to have the concept of white privilege. Medina, "Hermeneutical Injustice and Polyphonic Contextualism," p. 215.

28. I am here bypassing the thorny question of whether there could be unicorns. See Kripke, *Naming and Necessity*, p. 24.

29. Frege, *The Foundations of Arithmetic*, sec. 88.

30. For one excellent and informatively sympathetic discussion, see Tappenden, "Extending Knowledge and 'Fruitful Concepts.'"

31. Stanley, *The Technological Conscience*, p. 6.

32. Collins, *Black Feminist Thought*, pp. 253ff.

33. Senghor, *On African Socialism*, pp. 73–74.

34. See also Gendler "Alief in Action (and Reaction)."

35. Eberhardt et al., "Seeing Black," p. 877.

36. Goff et al., "Not Yet Human."

37. Ibid., p. 296.

38. Ibid., p. 304.

39. Siegel, "Epistemic Evaluability and Perceptual Farce."

40. See Siegel, *The Rationality of Perception*, for an argument for this thesis.

41. Jessie Munton persuasively argues for this in her forthcoming Yale dissertation.

42. Again, see the discussion of the third objection to deliberation, in Cohen and Rogers, "Power and Reason."

43. Gendler, "Alief in Action (and Reaction)," p. 578.

44. Martin Delany is sketching this argument in the passages I discussed in the introduction, which is why I began the book with it. Delany, *The Condition, Elevation, Emigration, and Destiny*. See also the discussion of the objection to inequality pertaining to "stigmatizing differences in status," where Scanlon echoes Delany. Scanlon, "The Diversity of Objections to Inequality."

CHAPTER 6. POLITICAL IDEOLOGIES

1. Weber, *On Law in Economy and Society*, p. 335.

2. Ibid., p. 336.

3. Ibid.

4. Sherman and Cohen, "The Psychology of Self-Defense," p. 186.

5. Ibid, p. 203.

6. Sherman and Cohen, in "The Psychology of Self-Defense," describe one's self-affirmation as *leading* to one's "political ideology," rather than as *mediating* between ideology and flawed ideological belief. But this is merely terminological. Sherman and Cohen use "political ideology" as an expression for the set of normative beliefs that, on my usage of "ideology," are the flawed ideological beliefs that are the consequences of a flawed ideology.

326 NOTES TO CHAPTER 6

7. The accidental groupings of US political parties explain the results of Gelman et al., "Rich State, Poor State, Red State, Blue State," which shows that the notion of "interest" is more complicated than material interests.

8. Page et al., "Democracy and the Policy Preferences."

9. Ibid.

10. Powdthavee and Oswald, "Does Money Make People Right-Wing and Inegalitarian?"

11. There is a tightly connected notion of political ideology as well. The psychologist Kent Tedin characterizes a political ideology as "an interrelated set of moral and political attitudes that possesses cognitive, affective, and motivational components. That is, ideology helps to explain why people do what they do; it organizes their values and beliefs and leads to political behavior." Tedin, "Political Ideology and the Vote."

12. As David Hume writes, "[S]uch is the nature of the human mind, that it always lays hold on every mind that approaches it; and as it is wonderfully fortified by an unanimity of sentiments, so is it shocked and disturbed by any contrariety. Hence the eagerness, which most people discover in a dispute; and hence their impatience of opposition, even in the most speculative and indifferent opinions." Hume, *Of the First Principles of Government*, 1.8.12.

13. Thanks to Stephen Darwall for the example.

14. Hastorf and Cantril, "They Saw a Game."

15. Kunda, "The Case for Motivated Reasoning."

16. Kahan et al., "They Saw a Protest."

17. Ibid., p. 27.

18. Kahan, "Neutral Principles, Motivated Cognition, and Some Problems."

19. Kahan also has a good summary of the dangers of motivated reasoning: "When subject to it, individuals can be unwittingly disabled from making dispassionate, open-minded, and fair judgments. Moreover, although people are poor at detecting motivated reasoning in themselves, they can readily discern its effect in others, in whom it is taken to manifest bias or bad faith. Accordingly, in collective deliberations, motivated cognition can trigger a self-reinforcing atmosphere of distrust and recrimination that prevents culturally diverse participants from converging on outcomes that suit their common ends."

20. "Individuals depend on select groups—from families to university faculties, from religious denominations to political parties—for

all manner of material and emotional support. Propositions that impugn the character or competence of such groups, or that contradict the groups' shared commitments, can thus jeopardize their individual members' well-being. Assenting to such a proposition him- or herself can sever an individual's bonds with such a group. The prospect that people outside the group might credit this proposition can also harm an individual by reducing the social standing or the self-esteem that person enjoys by virtue of his or her group's reputation." Kahan, "Neutral Principles, Motivated Cognition, and Some Problems," p. 20.

21. Rawls, *Political Liberalism*, p. 36.

22. Weber, *On Law in Economy and Society*, p. 336.

23. For example, "In a static society, which has reached a certain balance, there will always be some classes of leading groups (elites) the standards of which will become representative, and will be silently accepted even by those groups which are subjugated and essentially frustrated by these valuations." Mannheim, "A Few Concrete Examples."

24. See, for example, Williams, "Deciding to Believe."

25. Althusser, "Ideology and Ideological State Apparatus."

26. Cowan et al., *Education and Nation-Building in Africa*, p. 12.

27. Stabler, *The Schools of Kenya*, p. 104.

28. Ibid., p. 107.

29. Ibid., p. 112.

30. Part of my father Manfred Stanley's dissertation was on Alliance High School, where he spent several weeks. My father repeatedly told the story of Cary Francis, after drinking at night, slamming the table with his fist and saying, "By God, we are going to bring Christ to these savages."

31. Williams, "Deciding to Believe."

32. Dotson, "A Cautionary Tale," p. 34.

33. Mills, *The Power Elite*.

34. Dotson, "A Cautionary Tale," p. 35.

35. Wright, *Black Boy*, pp. 168–69.

36. Steele and Aronson, "Stereotype Threat and the Intellectual Test Performance."

37. See also the discussion of this point in Fricker, *Epistemic Injustice*, p. 54ff.

38. Chomsky and Herman, *Manufacturing Consent*.

39. Artz, "Political Legitimacy, Cultural Leadership, and Public Action."

40. These quotes are from Jenson, "The Problem with Patriotism."

41. Schmitt, *Political Theology*.

42. Ibid., p. 6.

43. Ibid., p. 49.

44. Thanks to Andre Pierce, a student in Lori Gruen's political philosophy seminar at Cheshire Maximum Correctional Facility, for the point that the language of the exception is often used in describing policies meant to deal with situations that do not in fact warrant appeal to the exception. Drug use, like alcohol use, does not, for example, warrant the national suspension of habeas corpus or of regular elections. So why, then, is battling addiction called a "war"? One does not wage war against one's own citizens in a liberal democracy.

45. What about the vocabulary, from the Johnson era, of the "war on poverty"? That language of emergency and exception is warranted when there is an existential threat to the polity. One of the arguments of this book is that large inequities of resources are an existential threat to liberal democracy. So, "war on poverty" does state the matter accurately, if my argument in this book is sound.

46. http://usatoday30.usatoday.com/news/washington/2003-09-06 -poll-iraq_x.htm.

47. http://www.thedailybeast.com/articles/2014/04/02/exclusive -watch-donald-rumsfeld-lie-about-saddam-hussein-s-9-11-involvement -in-the-unknown-known.html.

48. Another salient example is the so-called death tax in the United States, a relabeling of the inheritance tax. Abolishing the inheritance tax became a popular cause célèbre in the United States, though it affected only the top 2 percent of Americans. The story of how this occurred is told in detail in Graetz and Shapiro, *Death by a Thousand Cuts*.

49. Milgram, "Some Conditions of Obedience and Disobedience," pp. 103–4.

50. Ibid., p. 120.

51. Siegel, *The Rationality of Perception*.

52. Langton, "The Authority of Hate Speech."

53. Stanley, *Knowledge and Practical Interests*, and Hawthorne and Stanley, "Knowledge and Action."

54. For the more precise version of this principle, see Hawthorne and Stanley, "Knowledge and Action."

55. Pinillos, "Knowledge, Experiments, and Practical Interests."

56. Mayseless and Kruglanski, "What Makes You So Sure?"

57. Dotson, "A Cautionary Tale."

58. Some have denied the judgments upon which the connections have been based. But good empirical work has been done to vindicate them, as in Sripada and Stanley, "Empirical Tests of Interest-Relative Invariantism," and Pinillos, "Knowledge, Experiments, and Practical Interests."

59. Weatherson, "Can We Do without Pragmatic Encroachment?"

60. There is a serious worry that this view is a form of interest-relativity: *the interest-relativity of the norms of belief.* Weatherson, in "Knowledge, Bets, and Interests," later came to think this himself, and has developed some of the strongest arguments for the view.

61. Stanley, *Knowledge and Practical Interests*, pp. 6–7.

62. Ibid., p. 6.

63. This is similar in rough outlines to the account given in Nagel, "Epistemic Anxiety and Adaptive Invariantism."

64. Fung, "Recipes for Public Spheres," p. 345; Nagel, "Epistemic Anxiety and Adaptive Invariantism."

65. Fung, "Recipes for Public Spheres," p. 348.

66. Ibid., p. 340.

67. In Sripada and Stanley, "Empirical Tests of Interest-Relative Invariantism," we did not find evidence that subjects judged agents in "hot deliberation" as more rational. This is consistent with agents in hot deliberation being more rational. It may be that we regularly falsely regard such agents as engaged in wishful thinking.

68. Nagel, "Epistemic Anxiety and Adaptive Invariantism."

69. Fung does document that those in high-stakes situations are motivated to participate more. Therefore, even in asymmetrical cases, where only one group is in a high-stakes situation, there may be democratically beneficial effects that overcome asymmetry in resources. This is an empirical question. I am skeptical about the idealization away from the fact that the resource-rich groups tend to erect barriers to democratic participation by the resource-poorer groups. And even if it turns out to be confirmed that (for example) those upon whom a policy has a genuine effect do turn out more than others, this is not an *epistemic* benefit of being in a high-stakes situation. Fung, "Recipes for Public Spheres," p. 359.

70. Fricker, *Epistemic Injustice*.

71. Ibid., p. 1.

72. Ibid., p. 49.

73. Nagel's "Epistemic Anxiety and Adaptive Invariantism" is about the various effects of what she calls "epistemic anxiety," which is her "generic label for the inclination or desire for increased cognitive activity, and I will try to remain neutral about whether we should think of epistemic anxiety as setting a higher evidence threshold or selecting a more demanding strategy from the toolbox" (p. 414). Nagel points out that there are good effects of epistemic anxiety: people tend to use more reliable evidence-gathering methods. These good effects will have to be weighed against the bad ones (though the good effects will be mitigated by persistent hermeneutical injustice, which robs agents of the best tools to gather evidence).

74. Stanley, *Knowledge and Practical Interests*, chap. 5.

75. Thanks to Kate Manne for discussion.

76. Stanley, *Knowledge and Practical Interests*.

77. Thanks to Kate Manne for the example.

78. The ideology that society is a meritocracy, in a nonmeritocratic society, plays a similar "epistemically disabling" role as Anderson attributes to the ideal of color-blindness. Anderson, *The Imperative of Integration*.

79. Thanks to Kathryn Pogin for discussion.

80. Darwall, "Responsibility within Relations," p. 106.

81. Rousseau, *Confessions*, pp. 380–81. Thanks to Michael Rosen for bringing this passage to my attention.

82. Christopher Lebron argues that "the idea of character is fundamental to understanding and addressing racial inequality" in a democratic society. Lebron, *The Color of Our Shame*, p. 118. One way of viewing Lebron's work is as a demand for the recognition, in political philosophy, of the need to develop a notion of a distinctively democratic character, one that is incompatible with racial inequality. It is such a notion of democratic character that underlies the ideal of a democratic identity, the kind of attitude toward all of one's fellow citizens that underlies the possibility of democratic deliberation. It is the kind of identity that prevents deliberation from transforming into mere acclamation.

83. I learned this point from David Haywood, a prison scholar and student in Lori Gruen's political philosophy seminar in Cheshire Correctional Facility in Connecticut, who laid it out for me in detail.

84. There are autonomous actions done automatically, where we do not reflect upon our reasons for acting. And there are actions done autonomously where we would not recognize many descriptions of our reasons for acting. Stanley, *Know How*. Thus I endorse a non-Kantian view of autonomy. Whether there is a narrower range of actions, such as political ones, that require satisfying a Kantian view of autonomy is as yet unclear to me. Perhaps Darwall's "second-personal framework" requires the ability to defend one's actions to others, to answer their questions about why one did it, and I do think something like this applies in the political realm.

85. Stephen Darwall, for example, derives second-personal respect from an underlying Kantian basis; see Darwall, "Kant on Respect, Dignity, and the Duty of Respect."

86. Berlin, "Herder and the Enlightenment," p. 368.

87. See ibid., p. 375. In this passage, Berlin quotes Herder's *Auch eine Philosophie*, a work from 1774, as saying, "Foreign people were judged [by Rome] in terms of customs unknown to them."

88. Ibid., p. 376.

89. Etienne de la Boétie, *Discourse on Voluntary Servitude*.

CHAPTER 7. THE IDEOLOGY OF ELITES: A CASE STUDY

1. Mills, *The Power Elite*, p. 14.

2. Presumably the slave lacks *techne*, and so this is not skill in the more elevated sense that is admired by the Greeks.

3. Bernard Mandeville argues for the practical necessity of such inculcation in his essay from 1725, "An Essay on Charity and Charity Schools."

4. Gramsci, *Prison Notebooks*, vol. 4, sec. 49, p. 201.

5. Collins, *Black Feminist Thought*, p. 15.

6. Muhammad, *The Condemnation of Blackness*.

7. Roy and Park, "Dissociating the Memory Systems."

8. Dewey, "Labor and Leisure," p. 257.

9. Ross, *Social Control*, p. 83, 84.

10. Ibid., p. 328.

11. Ibid., p. 164.

12. Ibid., p. 166.

13. Ibid., 167.

14. Wilson also makes clear that he thinks that Black Americans are fit for only practical skill in his remarks about the Hampton Institute in Virginia, a historically Black college: "Of course, there ought to be combined with technical education just as much of the liberal education and of the book explanations of life as it is possible to combine with it without taking the efficiency out of the thing we are trying to do. I have in mind the Hampton Institute in Virginia, where the literary training is not neglected but subordinated. Where you are trying to give sufficient technical training you must subordinate the literary training, just as, when you are trying to give a liberal education, you must subordinate the technical training."

15. Labaree, "How Dewey Lost."

16. For a lengthy discussion of Snedden and his influence, see Krug, *The Shaping of the American High School*.

17. "Rejecting the idea of a uniform curriculum or uniform methods, Snedden proposed a conception of civilization as 'a thing of standardized parts'—preparation for which can be achieved by 'quality production.' To this end, Snedden employed the appealing metaphor of teamwork. Schools, he said, should 'be guided chiefly by the purpose of enabling each person, with his personal equipment and in the light of his probable part in the games of life, to make himself as a contributor to the success of the many teams—from family to nation—in which he must play his part.' The 'great community' as he liked to call it, could be achieved by 'division of function' and 'specialization of service.' The specialized skills that each worker brought to the process of production, the particular contributions that each player made to the success of the team, and the distinctive functions that each individual performed in the interest of a placid social order were all of one piece." Kliebard, *Schooled to Work*, p. 123.

18. King, *Education for Social Efficiency*, p. 7.

19. Ibid., pp. 9, 10.

20. Ibid., p. 14.

21. Spring, *Education and the Rise of the Corporate State*, p. 58.

22. Ibid., pp. 60–61.

23. In section 7 of his essay "Two Concepts of Liberty," Isaiah Berlin, citing Constant, makes the same criticism of Rousseau. Indeed, the point of Berlin's essay, that certain conceptions of liberty can be exploited for authoritarian abuse, is made very clearly by Constant (as Berlin acknowledges).

24. As we have seen, Rousseau was well aware of the danger of deliberation going awry in this way.

25. Labaree, "How Dewey Lost." p. 172.

26. Spring calls this "[t]he classic statement for the comprehensive high school." Spring, *Education and the Rise of the Corporate State*. Krug reports that in 1928, the Department of Superintendence "published an attempt to appraise its influence, based on replies from 1228 principals of high schools of various sizes throughout the United States. Of these, 689 said they had, within the preceding five years, undertaken reorganization of their programs in line with the cardinal principles." Krug, *The Shaping of the American High School*, p. 398.

27. As Diane Ravitch writes, "Progressive educators became accustomed to thinking of the schools in terms of their social function and to asserting that the work of the schools must meet the test of social efficiency. In education, social efficiency meant that every subject, every program, every study must be judged by whether it was socially useful. . . . What point was there teaching history, science, literature, mathematics, and foreign language to children who would never go to college? How was society served by wasting their time in such manifestly 'useless' and impractical studies?" Ravitch, "From History to Social Studies," pp. 125–26.

28. "The Cardinal Principles" does give some lip service to the language of individualism. Here, Friedrich Hayek's comment is worth bearing in mind: "No political term has suffered worse [from misuse] than 'individualism.' It not only has been distorted by its opponents into an unrecognizable caricature . . . [but also] has been used to describe several attitudes toward society which have as little in common among themselves as they have with those traditionally regarded as their opposites." Hayek, "Individualism," p. 3.

29. This quotation is from Bendix, *Work and Authority in Industry*, p. 305.

30. Rugg, *An Introduction to Problems of American Culture*.

31. Evans, *The Social Studies Wars*, p. 44.

32. Joel Spring summarizes the changes as follows. "The public schools of the twentieth century were organized to meet the needs of the corporate state and consequently, to protect the interests of the ruling elite and the technological machine." Spring, *Education and the Rise of the Corporate State*, p. 1.

33. http://www.eagleforum.org/educate/2005/aug05/book.html.

34. For an example of this tradition, see Adler, *The Paideia Proposal*.

35. Cheney's fury did not end there. In 2003, the Education Department printed up three hundred thousand copies of a seventy-three-page parent guide, "Helping Your Child Learn History." The pamphlets merely *mentioned* the National Standards. At the time, Lynne Cheney was not in government, though her husband was vice president of the United States. Nevertheless, her office contacted the Education Department, which then destroyed all three hundred thousand booklets to obliterate the evidence of the existence of National Standards.

　　36. James, "Every Cook Can Govern."

CONCLUSION

　　1. Weaver, "Frontlash."

BIBLIOGRAPHY

Ackerman, Bruce. *Social Justice in the Liberal State*. New Haven: Yale University Press, 1980.

Adler, Mortimer. *The Paideia Proposal: An Educational Manifesto*. New York: MacMillan, 1982.

Althusser, Louis. "Ideology and Ideological State Apparatus." Translated by Ben Brewster. In *Lenin and Philosophy, and Other Essays*, pp. 121–76. New York: Monthly Review Press, 1971.

Anderson, Elizabeth. *The Imperative of Integration*. Princeton: Princeton University Press, 2010.

———. "Outlaws." *Good Society* 23, no. 1 (2014): 103–13.

———. "What Is the Point of Equality?" *Ethics* 109, no. 2 (1999): 287–337.

Anderson, Elizabeth, and Richard Pildes. "Expressive Theories of Law: A General Restatement." *University of Pennsylvania Law Review* 148 (2000): 1503.

Anderson, Luvell, and Ernest Lepore. "Slurring Words." *Nous* 47, no. 1 (2013): 25–48.

Artz, Lee. "Political Legitimacy, Cultural Leadership, and Public Action." In Artz and Kamalipour, *Bring 'Em On*, pp. 7–21.

Artz, Lee, and Yahya Kamalipour, eds. *Bring 'Em On: Media and Politics in the Iraq War*. New York: Rowman and Littlefield, 2005.

Bendix, Reinhard. *Work and Authority in Industry*. New York: Harper and Row, 1956.

Berlin, Isaiah. "Herder and the Enlightenment." In *The Proper Study of Mankind*, pp. 359–435. New York: Farrar, Straus, and Giroux, 1997.

————. "Two Concepts of Liberty." In *The Proper Study of Mankind*. New York: Farrar, Straus, and Giroux, 1997.

Bourdieu, Pierre, and Jean-Claude Passeron. *Reproduction in Education, Society and Culture*. London: Sage, 1977.

Burnham, James. *The Managerial Revolution*. 4th ed. Bloomington: Indiana University Press, 1966.

Callahan, Raymond E. *Education and the Cult of Efficiency: A Study of the Social Forces That Have Shaped the Administration of the Public Schools*. Chicago: University of Chicago Press, 1962.

Camp, Elizabeth. "Slurring Perspectives." *Analytic Philosophy* 54, no. 3 (September 2013): 330–49.

Chomsky, Noam, and Edward Herman. *Manufacturing Consent: The Political Economy of the Mass Media*. New York: Pantheon, 1988.

Christensen, David. *Putting Logic in Its Place*. Oxford: Clarendon Press, 2004.

Cicero. *On Duties*. Translated by Andrew Peabody. Boston: Little, Brown, 1887.

Coates, Ta-nahesi. "The Case for Reparations." *Atlantic*, June 2014.

Cohen, Joshua, and Joel Rogers. "Power and Reason." In Fung and Wright, *Deepening Democracy*.

Collins, Patricia Hill. *Black Feminist Thought: Knowledge, Consciousness, and the Politics of Empowerment*. New York: Routledge, 2000.

Constant, Benjamin. *Principles of Politics Applicable to All Representative Governments*. In *Constant: Political Writings*, pp. 171–305. Cambridge: Cambridge University Press, 1988.

Cooper, John, ed. *Plato: Complete Works*. Indianapolis: Hackett, 1977.

Cowan, L. Gray, J. O'Connell, and D. Scanlon, eds. *Education and Nation-Building in Africa*. New York: Praeger, 1965.

Darwall, Stephen. "Accountability and the Second Person." In *The Second Person Standpoint*, pp. 65–90.

————. "Being With." In *Honor, History & Relationship*, pp. 110–30.

————. *Honor, History & Relationship: Essays in Second-Personal Ethics II*. Oxford: Oxford University Press, 2013.

————. "Kant on Respect, Dignity, and the Duty of Respect." In *Honor, History & Relationship*, pp. 247–70.

————. "Morality and Autonomy in Kant." In *The Second Person Standpoint*, pp. 213–42.

————. "Responsibility within Relations." In *Honor, History & Relationship*, pp. 91–109.

————. "The Second Personal Stance and Second Personal Reasons." In *The Second Person Standpoint*, pp. 39–61.

————. *The Second Person Standpoint: Morality, Respect, and Accountability*. Cambridge, Mass.: Harvard University Press, 2006.

Delany, Martin Robison Delany. *The Condition, Elevation, Emigration, and Destiny of the Colored People of the United States*. New York: Arno Press, 1968.

Dewey, John. "Labor and Leisure." In *Democracy and Education*, pp. 250–61. New York: MacMillan, 1916.

————. *The Public and Its Problems*. Athens: Swallow Press, 1954. First published in 1927.

Dotson, Kristie. "A Cautionary Tale: On Limiting Epistemic Oppression." *Frontiers* 33, no. 1 (2012): 24–47.

Downs, Anthony. *An Economic Theory of Democracy*. New York: Harper Press, 1957.

Du Bois, W.E.B. *Black Reconstruction in America: 1860–1880*. New York: Free Press, 1992. First published in 1935.

————. "Criteria of Negro Art" (1926).

————. *The Souls of Black Folk*. New York: Dover, 1994. First published in 1903.

Eberhardt, Jennifer, Philip Goff, Valarie Purdie, and Paul Davies. "Seeing Black: Race, Crime, and Visual Processing." *Journal of Personality and Social Psychology* 87, no. 6 (2004): 876–93.

Edelman, Murray. *Politics of Symbolic Action*. Chicago: Markham, 1971.

Estlund, David M. *Democratic Authority: A Philosophical Framework*. Princeton: Princeton University Press, 2008.

Evans, Ronald W. *The Social Studies Wars: What Should We Teach the Children?* New York: Teachers College Press, 2004.

Ferrari, G.R.F. *City and Soul in Plato's Republic*. Chicago: University of Chicago Press, 2005.

Fintel, Kai Von, and Thony Gillies. "Must . . . Stay . . . Strong." *Natural Language Semantics* 18, no. 4 (2010): 351–83.

Frank, Thomas. *What's the Matter with Kansas? How Conservatives Won the Heart of America*. New York: Henry Holt, 2004.

Frege, Gottlob. *The Foundations of Arithmetic*. 1884.

Fricker, Miranda. *Epistemic Injustice: Power & the Ethics of Knowing*. Oxford: Oxford University Press, 2007.

Fung, Archon. "Recipes for Public Spheres: Eight Institutional Design Choices and Their Consequences." *Journal of Political Philosophy* 11, no. 3 (2003): 338–67.

Fung, Archon, and Erik Olin Wright. *Deepening Democracy: Institutional Innovations in Empowered Participatory Government*. London: Verso, 2003.

Garsten, Bryan. *Saving Persuasion: A Defense of Rhetoric and Judgment.* Cambridge, Mass.: Harvard University Press, 2006.

Gazdar, Gerald. *Pragmatics: Implicature, Presupposition, and Logical Form.* New York: Academic Press, 1979.

Gelman, Andrew, Boris Shor, Joseph Bafumi, and David Park. "Rich State, Poor State, Red State, Blue State: What's the Matter with Connecticut?" *Quarterly Journal of Political Science* 2 (1987): 345–67.

Gendler, Tamar. "Alief and Belief." *Journal of Philosophy* (2008): 634–63.

———. "Alief in Action (and Reaction)." *Mind & Language* 23, no. 5 (2008): 552–85.

———. "On the Epistemic Costs of Implicit Racism." *Philosophical Studies* 156, no. 1 (2011): 33–63.

Gilens, Martin. *Why Americans Hate Welfare: Race, Media, and the Politics of Antipoverty Policy.* Chicago: University of Chicago Press, 1999.

Gilens, Martin, and Benjamin Page. "Testing Theories of American Politics: Elites, Interest Groups, and Average Citizens." *Perspectives on Politics* 12, no. 3 (2014): 564–81.

Goff, Phillip, Jennifer Eberhardt, Melissa Williams, and Matthew Christian Jackson. "Not Yet Human: Implicit Knowledge, Historical Dehumanization, and Contemporary Consequences." *Journal of Personality and Social Psychology* 94, no. 2 (2008): 292–306.

Graetz, Michael, and Ian Shapiro. *Death by a Thousand Cuts: The Fight over Taxing Inherited Wealth.* Princeton: Princeton University Press, 2005.

Gramsci, Antonio. *Prison Notebooks.* New York: Columbia University Press, 1992.

Gutmann, Amy, and Dennis Thompson. *Democracy and Disagreement.* Cambridge, Mass.: Belknap Press of Harvard University Press, 1996.

Habermas, Jürgen. "What Is Universal Pragmatics?" In *On the Pragmatics of Communication*, edited by Maeve Cooke, pp. 21–103 Cambridge, Mass.: MIT Press, 1998.

Hart, Carl. *High Price.* New York: HarperCollins, 2013.

Haslanger, Sally. "Ideology, Generics, and Common Ground." In *Resisting Reality*, pp. 446–75.

———. "Mom, but Crop Tops Are Cute! Social Knowledge, Social Structure, and Ideology Critique." In *Resisting Reality*, pp. 406–27.

———. "Oppressions." In *Resisting Reality*, pp. 311–37.

———. *Resisting Reality: Social Construction and Social Critique.* Oxford: Oxford University Press, 2012.

———. "Social Meaning and Philosophical Method." APA Presidential Address of 2013.

Hastorf, Albert H., and Hadley Cantril. "They Saw a Game: A Case Study." *Journal of Abnormal & Social Psychology* 129 (1954).

Hawthorne, John, and Jason Stanley. "Knowledge and Action." *Journal of Philosophy* 105, no. 10 (2008): 571–90.

Hayakawa, S. I. "General Semantics and Propaganda." *Public Opinion Quarterly* 3, no. 2 (1939): 197–208.

Hayek, Friedrich. "Individualism: True and False." In *Individualism and the Economic Order*, pp. 1–32. Chicago: Chicago University Press, 1948.

Heim, Irene. "The Semantics of Definite and Indefinite Noun Phrases." PhD diss., University of Massachusetts at Amherst, 1982.

Hoggan, James. *Climate Cover-Up*. Vancouver: Greystone, 2009.

Irwin, Terence. *Classical Thought*. Oxford: Oxford University Press, 1989.

James, C.L.R. "Every Cook Can Govern: A Study of Democracy in Ancient Greece." *Correspondence* 2, no. 12 (1956).

Jensen, Robert. "The Problem with Patriotism: Steps toward the Redemption of American Journalism and Democracy." In Artz and Kamalipour, *Bring 'Em On*, pp. 67–83.

Kahan, Dan. "Neutral Principles, Motivated Cognition, and Some Problems for Constitutional Law." *Harvard Law Review* (2011).

———. "Social Influence, Social Meaning, and Deterrence." *Virginia Law Review* 83, no. 2 (March 1997): 349–95.

Kahan, Dan, D. Hoffman, D. Braman, D. Evans, and J. Rachlinski. "They Saw a Protest: Cognitive Illiberalism and the Speech-Conduct Distinction." *Stanford Law Review* 64 (2012).

Kelly, Thomas. "Following the Argument Where It Leads." *Philosophical Studies* 154, no. 1 (2011): 105–24.

Kenyatta, Jomo. *Facing Mt. Kenya*. New York: Vintage, 1965.

King, Irving. *Education for Social Efficiency: A Study in the Social Relations of Education*. New York: D. Appleton, 1913.

Klemperer, Victor. *I Will Bear Witness: A Diary of the Nazi Years, 1933–1941*. New York: Random House, 1998.

———. *Language of the Third Reich: LTI, Linguii Tertii Imperii*. Translated by Martin Brady. London: Continuum, 2006. First published in German in 1947.

Kliebard, Herbert M. *Schooled to Work: Vocationalism and the American Curriculum*. New York: Teacher's College Press, 1999.

Krause, Sharon. *Civil Passions: Moral Sentiment and Democratic Deliberation*. Princeton: Princeton University Press, 1998.

Kripke, Saul. *Naming and Necessity*. Cambridge, Mass.: Harvard University Press, 1980.

Krug, Edward. *The Shaping of the American High School, 1880–1920*. 2nd ed. Madison: University of Wisconsin Press, 1969.

Kunda, Ziva. "The Case for Motivated Reasoning." *Psychological Bulletin* 108, no. 3 (1990): 480–98.

Labaree, David F. "How Dewey Lost: The Victory of David S. Snedden and the Social Efficiency in the Reform of American Education." In *Pragmatism and Modernities*, edited by D. Tröhler, T. Schlag, and F. Osterwalder, pp. 163–88. Rotterdam: Sense Publishers, 2010.

La Boétie, Etienne de. *Discourse on Voluntary Servitude*. Translated by James Atkinson and David Sices. Indianapolis: Hackett Publishing, 2012.

Landemore, Hélène. *Democratic Reason: Politics, Intelligence, and the Rule of the Many*. Princeton: Princeton University Press, 2012.

Langton, Rae. "The Authority of Hate Speech." Forthcoming.

———. *Sexual Solipsism*. Oxford: Oxford University Press, 2009.

———. "Speech Acts and Unspeakable Acts." *Philosophy and Public Affairs* 22, no. 4 (1993): 293–330.

Langton, Rae, and Caroline West. "Scorekeeping in a Pornographic Language Game." *Australasian Journal of Philosophy* 77 (1999): 303–19.

Lebron, Christopher. *The Color of Our Shame: Race and Justice in Our Time*. Oxford: Oxford University Press, 2013.

Leiter, Brian. "The Hermeneutics of Suspicion: Recovering Marx, Nietzsche, and Freud." In *The Future for Philosophy*, ed. Brian Leiter. Oxford: Clarendon Press, 2004.

Leslie, Sarah-Jane. "Carving Up the Social World with Generics." In *Oxford Studies in Experimental Philosophy*, vol. 1, edited by Joshua Knobe, Tania Lombrozo, and Shaun Nichols. Oxford: Oxford University Press, 2015.

———. "Generics: Cognition and Acquisition." *Philosophical Review* 117, no. 1 (2008).

———. "The Original Sin of Cognition: Fear, Prejudice, and Generalization." *Journal of Philosophy*. Forthcoming.

Lippmann, Walter. *The Phantom Public*. New Brunswick, N.J.: Transaction, 2009. First published in 1927.

———. *Public Opinion*. Sioux Falls: Greenbook, 2010. First published in 1922.

Locke, Alain. "Art or Propaganda?" (1928).

Madison, James. "Federalist 10." In *The Federalist Papers*.

Maitra, Ishani. "Subordinating Speech." In *Speech and Harm: Controversies over Free Speech*, edited by Ishani Maitra and Kate McGowan, pp. 94–120. Oxford: Oxford University Press, 2012.

Mannheim, Karl. "A Few Concrete Examples concerning the Sociological Nature of Human Valuations." In *Essays on Sociology and Social Psychology*, edited by Paul Keckemeti, pp. 231–42. London: Routledge and Kegan Paul, 1953.

Mansbridge, Jane, J. Bohman, S. Chambers, D. Estlund, A. Føllesdal, A. Fung, C. Lafont, B. Manin, and J. L. Martí. "The Place of Self-Interest and the Role of Power in Deliberative Democracy." *Journal of Political Philosophy* 18, no. 1 (2010): 64–100.

Marlin, Randal. *Propaganda and the Ethics of Persuasion*. Ontario: Broadview, 2002.

Mayseless, O., and A. W. Kruglanski. "What Makes You So Sure? Effects of Epistemic Motivations on Judgmental Confidence." *Organizational Behavior and Human Decision Processes* 39 (1987): 162–83.

McGowan, Mary Kate. "Conversational Exercitives: Something Else We Do with Our Words." *Linguistics and Philosophy* 27 (2004): 93–111.

———. "Oppressive Speech." *Australasian Journal of Philosophy* 87, no. 3 (2009): 389–407.

Medina, José. "Hermeneutical Injustice and Polyphonic Contextualism: Social Silences and Shared Hermeneutical Responsibilities." *Social Epistemology* 26, no. 2 (2012): 201–20.

Meiklejohn, Alexander. *Political Freedom*. New York: Harper and Row, 1960.

Mendelberg, Tali. *The Race Card*. Princeton: Princeton University Press, 2001.

Milgram, Stanley. "Some Conditions of Obedience and Disobedience to Authority." In *The Individual in a Social World*, pp. 102–23. Reading, Mass.: Addison-Wesley. Originally published in 1965.

Mills, Charles. "Ideal Theory as Ideology." *Hypatia* 20, no. 3 (2005): 165–84.

———. *The Racial Contract*. Ithaca: Cornell University Press, 1997.

Mills, Claudia. "Politics and Manipulation." *Social Theory and Practice* 21, no. 1 (1995): 97–112.

Mills, C. Wright. *The Power Elite*. Oxford: Oxford University Press, 1956.

Monson, Ingrid. *Saying Something: Jazz Improvisation and Interaction*. Chicago: University of Chicago Press, 1997.

Muhammad, Khalil. *The Condemnation of Blackness*. Cambridge, Mass.: Harvard University Press, 2010.

Murdoch, Iris. "The Idea of Perfection." In *The Sovereignty of Good*, pp. 1–44. New York: Routledge and Kegan Paul, 1970.

Murray, Sarah. "Varieties of Update." *Semantics and Pragmatics* 7, no. 2 (2014): 1–53.

Nagel, Jennifer. "Epistemic Anxiety and Adaptive Invariantism." *Philosophical Perspectives* 24 (2010): 407–35.

Page, Benjamin, Larry Bartels, and Jason Seawright. "Democracy and the Policy Preferences of Wealthy Americans." *Perspectives on Politics* 11, no. 1 (2013): 51–73.

Pareto, Vilfredo. *The Rise and Fall of the Elites: An Application of Theoretical Sociology*. Totowa, N.J.: Bedminster Press, 1901.

Paul, L. A. *Transformative Experience*. Oxford: Oxford University Press, 2015.

Payne, K. "Prejudice and Perception: The Role of Automatic and Controlled Processes in Misperceiving a Weapon." *Journal of Personality and Social Psychology* 81, no. 2 (2001): 181–92.

Pinillos, Ángel. "Knowledge, Experiments, and Practical Interests." In *New Essays on Knowledge Ascriptions*, edited by Jessica Brown and Mikkel Gerken. Oxford: Oxford University Press, 2014.

Pogin, Kathryn. "Conceptualizing the Atonement." Unpublished ms.

Potts, Christopher. *The Logic of Conventional Implicatures*. Oxford Studies in Theoretical Linguistics. Oxford: Oxford University Press, 2005.

Powdthavee, Nattavudh, and Andrew Oswald. "Does Money Make People Right-Wing and Inegalitarian?" University of Warwick Working Paper. February 2014.

Ravitch, Diane. "From History to Social Studies." In *The Schools We Deserve*, pp. 112–32. New York: Basic Books, 1985.

Rawls, John. *Political Liberalism*. Expanded ed. New York: Columbia University Press, 2005. The first edition was published in 1993.

Roberts, Craige. "Information Structure: Towards an Integrated Formal Theory of Pragmatics." *Semantics and Pragmatics* 12, no. 5 (2012): 1–69.

Rogers, Melvin. "David Walker and the Political Power of the Appeal." *Political Theory*. Forthcoming.

———. "The People, Rhetoric, and Affect: On the Political Force of Du Bois's *The Souls of Black Folk*." *American Political Science Review* 106, no. 1 (2012): 188–203.

Rosen, Michael. *On Voluntary Servitude*. Cambridge, Mass.: Harvard University Press, 1996.

Rosenberg, Shawn, ed. *Deliberation, Participation and Democracy: Can the People Decide?* London: Palgrave Macmillan, 2007.

Ross, Edward Alsworth. *Social Control.* New York: MacMillan, 1901.

Ross, Sheryl Tuttle. "Understanding Propaganda: The Epistemic Merit Model and Its Application to Art." *Journal of Aesthetic Education* 36, no. 1 (Spring, 2002): 16–30.

Rothschild, Emma. *Economic Sentiments: Adam Smith, Condorcet, and the Enlightenment.* Cambridge, Mass.: Harvard University Press, 2001.

Rousseau, Jean-Jacques. *The Social Contract.* South Bend, Ind.: Gateway, 1954.

Roy, S., and N. W. Park. "Dissociating the Memory Systems Mediating Complex Tool Knowledge and Skills." *Neuropsychologia* 48 (2010): 3026–36.

Rugg, Harold. *An Introduction to Problems of American Culture.* Boston: Ginn, 1931.

Russell, Gillian, and John Doris. "Knowledge by Indifference." *Australasian Journal of Philosophy* 86, no. 3 (2008): 429–37.

Saul, Jennifer. *Lying, Misleading, and What Is Said.* Oxford: Oxford University Press, 2012.

Scanlon, T. M. *The Difficulty of Tolerance: Essays in Political Philosophy.* Cambridge: Cambridge University Press, 2003.

———. "The Diversity of Objections to Inequality." In *The Difficulty of Tolerance*, pp. 202–18.

———. "Freedom of Expression and Categories of Expression." In *The Difficulty of Tolerance*, pp. 84–112.

Schmitt, Carl. *The Concept of the Political.* Chicago: University of Chicago Press, 1996.

———. *Political Theology: Four Chapters on the Concept of Sovereignty.* Chicago: University of Chicago Press, 2005.

Senghor, Léopold Sédar. *On African Socialism.* Translated by Mercer Cook. New York: Praeger, 1964.

Shelby, Tommie. "Ideology, Racism, and Critical Social Theory." *Philosophical Forum* 34, no. 2 (2003): 153–88.

———. "Justice, Deviance, and the Dark Ghetto." *Philosophy and Public Affairs* 35, no. 2 (2007): 126–55.

Sherman, David, and Geoffrey Cohen. "The Psychology of Self-Defense: Self-Affirmation Theory." *Advances in Experimental Social Psychology* 38 (2006): 183–242.

Siegel, Susanna. "Epistemic Evaluability and Perceptual Farce." Afterword to *Cognitive Effects on Perception: New Philosophical Perspectives,* edited by J. Zeimbekis and A. Raftopoulos. Oxford: Oxford University Press, 2014.

———. *The Rationality of Perception*. Forthcoming.

Smith, David Livingstone. *Less Than Human: Why We Demean, Enslave, and Exterminate Others*. New York: St. Martin's, 2011.

Sobieraj, Sarah. *Soundbitten: The Perils of Media-Centered Political Activism*. New York: New York University Press, 2011.

Sosa, Ernest. "How Must Knowledge Be Modally Related to What Is Known?" *Philosophical Topics* 26, nos. 1–2 (1999): 373–84.

———. "How to Defeat Opposition to Moore." *Philosophical Perspectives* 13 (1999): 141–54.

Spring, Joel. *Education and the Rise of the Corporate State*. Boston: Beacon, 1972.

Sripada, Chandra, and Jason Stanley. "Empirical Tests of Interest-Relative Invariantism." *Episteme* 9, no. 1 (2012): 3–26.

Stabler, Ernest. *The Schools of Kenya: Education since Uhuru*. Middletown: Wesleyan University Press, 1969.

Stalnaker, Robert. "On the Representation of Context." In *Context and Content*, pp. 96–113. Oxford: Oxford University Press, 1999.

Stanley, Jason. *Know How*. Oxford: Oxford University Press, 2011.

———. *Knowledge and Practical Interests*. Oxford: Oxford University Press, 2005.

Stanley, Jason, and John Krakauer. "Motor Skill Depends upon Knowledge of Facts." *Frontiers of Human Neuroscience* 29 (2013).

Stanley, Manfred. "The Mystery of the Commons: On the Indispensability of Civic Rhetoric." *Social Research* 50, no. 4 (1983): 851–83.

———. *The Technological Conscience: Survival and Dignity in an Age of Expertise*. Chicago: University of Chicago Press, 1978.

Stebbing, Susan. *Thinking to Some Purpose*. New York: Penguin, 1939.

Steele, Claude, and Joshua Aronson. "Stereotype Threat and the Intellectual Test Performance of African Americans." *Journal of Personality and Social Psychology* 69, no. 5 (1995): 797–811.

Streeck, Wolfgang. "The Crises of Democratic Capitalism." *New Left Review* (2011).

Tappenden, Jamie. "Extending Knowledge and 'Fruitful Concepts': Fregean Themes in the Philosophy of Mathematics." *Nous* 29, no. 4 (2005): 427–67.

Tarski, Alfred. "The Concept of Truth in Formalized Languages." In *Logic, Semantics, Metamathematics*, pp. 152–268. Indianapolis: Hackett, 1983.

Tedin, K. L. "Political Ideology and the Vote." *Research in Micro-Politics* 2 (1987): 63–94.

Tirrell, Lynne. "Genocidal Language Games." In *Speech and Harm: Controversies over Free Speech*, edited by Ishani Maitra and Mary Kate McGowan, pp. 174–221. Oxford: Oxford University Press, 2012.

Tonry, M., and M. Melewski. "The Malign Effects of Drug and Crime Control Policies on Black Americans." *Crime and Justice* 37, no. 1 (2008): 1–44.

Tucker, Robert, ed. *The Marx-Engels Reader*. 2nd ed. New York: Norton, 1978.

Veltman, Frank. "Defaults in Update Semantics." *Journal of Philosophical Logic* 25, no. 3 (1996): 221–61.

Walzer, Michael. *Spheres of Justice*. New York Basic Books, 1983.

Weatherson, Brian. "Can We Do without Pragmatic Encroachment?" *Philosophical Perspectives* 19 (2005): 417–43.

———. "David Lewis." *Stanford Encyclopedia of Philosophy*. Edited by Edward N. Zalta. Fall 2014 ed. http://plato.stanford.edu/archives/fall2014/entries/david-lewis/.

———. "Knowledge, Bets, and Interests." In *Knowledge Ascriptions*, edited by Jessica Brown and Mikkel Gerken, pp. 75–103. Oxford: Oxford University Press, 2012.

Weaver, Vesla. "Frontlash: Race and the Development of Punitive Crime Policies." *Studies in American Political Development* 21 (2007): 230–65.

Weber, Max. *On Law in Economy and Society*. New York: Clarion, 1967.

White, Roger. "You Just Believe That Because . . ." *Philosophical Perspectives* 24, no. 1 (2010): 573–615.

Williams, Bernard. "The Analogy of City and Soul in Plato's Republic." In *Plato*, edited by Gail Fine. Oxford: Oxford University Press, 1999.

———. "Deciding to Believe." In *Language, Belief, and Metaphysics*, edited by H. E. Kiefer and M. K. Muntiz. Albany, N.Y.: State University of New York Press, 1970.

Williams, Fannie Barrier. "The Woman's Part in a Man's Business." *Voice of the Negro* (November 1904): 543–47.

Williamson, Timothy. *Knowledge and Its Limits*. Oxford: Oxford University Press, 2000.

Wittgenstein, Ludwig. *On Certainty*. Edited by G.E.M. Anscombe and G. H. von Wright. New York: Harper and Row, 1969.

Wright, Richard. *Black Boy*. New York: Harper, 2006.

Wynter, Sylvia. "'No Humans Involved': An Open Letter to My Colleagues." *Knowledge on Trial* 1 (1994): 3–11.

INDEX